ROOTS OF OUR FAITH

The *Abstract of Principles* Explained and Applied

ROOTS OF OUR FAITH

The *Abstract of Principles* Explained and Applied

MORGAN BYRD

H&E
Publishing

hesedandemet.com

H&E Publishing, Peterborough, Ontario, Canada

Scripture quotations taken from the New American Standard Bible®, Copyright © 1960, 1971, 1977, 1995, 2020 by The Lockman Foundation. All rights reserved.

Design and editing by Janice Van Eck

ISBN 978-1-77484-042-9 (paperback)
ISBN 978-1-77484-043-6 (e-book)

For Mom and Dad, who have taught me with your words and with your lives that Jesus is the way, the truth and the life.

> Listen, my son, to your father's instruction,
> And do not ignore your mother's teaching;
> For they are a graceful wreath for your head
> And necklaces for your neck (Proverbs 1:8–9).

CONTENTS

CONTENTS

FOREWORD

Some years ago, I served on a discussion panel of five professors answering questions from prospective students who were considering attending our seminary in North Carolina. Among the guests was a gentleman who had journeyed all the way from west Africa to attend the preview day in hopes of enrolling at our school.

During the Q and A time, this African fellow informed us of serious strife in his hometown among the Christians. The issues ranged from theological differences to views on how to respond to persecution of Christians in his region of Africa. In light of this, he asked the panel of professors, "Don't you agree the best way forward is for me to start a new denomination?"

Immediately and in unison, all five of us exclaimed, "No!"

If someone had interviewed the panelists as to why we insisted this brother not start a new denomination, she would doubtless have received a dozen or more reasons. But as I've reflected on this event over the years, I believe it teaches us at least three lessons about the church and our role in it.

First, this story alerts us to the *importance of Tradition*. By tradition I mean at least two things. First is the capital "T" Tradition of the church, the tradition Paul speaks of in 2 Thessalonians 2:15 and 3:6. This is the "faith once for all delivered to the saints" of Jude 3, that gospel deposit entrusted to those who were discipled by the apostles then handed down to subsequent generations. Even in the wake of the Protestant Reformation, a period we may call the *denominational era*, it was of first priority for the Reformers and church leaders to connect their new traditions with the tradition of the apostles. This was accomplished especially by affirming not only Scripture, but the ancient creeds of the church such as the Nicene Creed, the Apostles' Creed and the Chalcedon Definition.

This points to the second meaning of *tradition*, a lower case "t" that we may think of as *denominational distinctiveness*. While differences abound concerning the mode of baptism, one's view on the nature of the Lord's Supper (Eucharist), proper ecclesiology and church authority, and much more, a little "t" tradition is only truly Christian if it is situated within the big "T" Tradition of the apostles.

A second lesson learned from the story above is the importance of *confession*. Within the first few centuries after the resurrection of Christ, the church was faced with difficult questions about precisely what she believed concerning, for example, the God who has revealed himself as Father, Son and Spirit. In the early centuries, the church addressed difficult doctrinal matters as the occasion demanded. But, by the sixth century, theology was becoming increasingly a systematic discipline, a subject-area of exploration about the nature of God and all things in relation to him. These theological developments continued with various twists and turns up to the sixteenth century. As new traditions (or denominations) emerged in light of the Reformation, it was necessary for each new group to develop a Confession of Faith to articulate their distinctive views, while also connecting their doctrinal commitments to the apostolic faith. Without a confession, a Christian community lacks identity and distinctiveness, not to mention a clear connection to the apostles. Confessions clarify and instruct on the ABCs of what Christians believe and how we are called to live for God in the world. Moreover, they anchor the church, protecting her against "every wind of doctrine"[1] that blows from one generation to the next.

A third lesson is the importance of communities, more specifically, *confessing communities*. Christian communities exist all over the world in various forms, but merely a gathering of Christians does not constitute a church. A church consists of a confessing community who gathers regularly to proclaim the gospel of God and celebrate the sacraments. Such a community of confessing Christians believes and

---

1   Ephesians 4:14.

proclaims a gospel the apostles would recognize. And in keeping with this gospel confession, these communities share an expectation of living consistent with their confession, what Eugene Peterson calls "congruent communities."

These communities share a common faith and confession, but they also share the conviction to walk worthy of their calling in Christ in all of life. This faith is not limited to the worship space but invades our living rooms, restaurants, smartphones, ball fields, work cubicles and grocery stores. This community confesses the faith and lives the faith.

Returning to our story, am I suggesting that by starting a new denomination our African friend couldn't cultivate a confessing and tradition-connected community? Certainly not. I am suggesting, however, what this brother seemed to be longing for—something I often hear Christians speak of—was a "true church." Meaning a church that believed the truth and lived the truth. And, to this I say both "Amen" and "Oh me."

"Amen" to the desire for a church that believes and lives rightly. "Oh me" to the fact that virtually every stripe of Christianity that ever emerged did so with the same goal in mind—right belief and right practice/living.

Longing for a pure church is virtuous but it is far from new. Such a goal is as old as the apostles, and I believe the Bible is clear we will not reach such a state of perfection this side of the return of Christ. Perhaps, then, we might turn our attention and align our desires toward the "one Lord, one faith, one baptism" spoken of in Ephesians 4:5; a longing for the unity of the body in continuity with the message of the apostles, indeed of Jesus himself?

Perhaps I'm overthinking and over-assuming our African brother's interest in a new denomination. But, even so, the Lord has used this experience to stir in me a new love for the *Traditional, confessional community*. In this vein, I'm honoured to recommend this new and creative work by my friend and former student, Morgan Byrd. I was proud to learn of Morgan's interest in drafting such a work and was even more excited when he decided to focus on the *Abstract of Principles* as his confessional framework.

This historic Baptist confession penned chiefly by Basil Manly Jr. in 1858 serves as the founding confessional document for The Southern Baptist Theological Seminary and is shared by other seminaries including my own, Southeastern Baptist Theological Seminary. It was inspired and informed by other well-known confessional statements including the London Baptist, Westminster, New Hampshire and Philadelphia Confessions. Each of these is linked to the apostolic faith, the Reformation and evangelical tradition, and to confessing communities, with the goal of instructing the church in the way of Christ, thinking and living rightly before God.

In Morgan's *Roots of Our Faith*, his aim is precisely the same. An explanation and application of orthodoxy and orthopraxy—right thinking and right living before God, for this is the Christian call. May this work challenge you and encourage you in your love for God, his church and his world.

Benjamin T. Quinn, Ph.D.
October 5, 2021
Wake Forest, North Carolina, USA

ACKNOWLEDGEMENTS

The list of those who deserve gratitude is much longer, but these people are especially to thank. Brandon Ayscue connected me with the right people to make this a reality after I told him what I was working on, and he consistently reached out to encourage me and prod me along. Daniel Lee may not even know this, but he first set me in the direction of the *Abstract of Principles* and our conversations have proven to be extremely influential on my theological thinking as a whole. I am very appreciative of my Dad (who I also serve alongside as a pastor) and Todd, who not only worked with me through this project, but encouraged me to set aside time to write. I love serving at Palmetto Shores Church where the Bible is preached and loved. A big thanks to Dr. Benjamin Quinn who was willing to give me helpful feedback and work with me on this project, and for writing the foreword. This book would not have come together if it weren't for a few evening groups of folks at our church who came out to seminars that we called, "What we believe." Their input and curiosity pushed this work forward. I am very thankful to one of my closest friends, Grant Clayton, who has helped me, by the power of the Holy Spirit, to work some of my own theology down into my heart and out into my life. I am very grateful for the consistent willingness of the people at H&E Publishing to communicate and help me along the way, and for Janice Van Eck who was willing to take on my project. A big thanks to my family and especially my mom, who read some of the earlier chapters and provided invaluable feedback. Finally, and most importantly, I must say thank you to my wife, Alli, who graciously allowed me to give quality time to writing, even while we were navigating life with a baby boy and some health and family difficulties that were very challenging to process. May the Lord bless this work to the extent that it is true, praiseworthy and honours Christ, and may whatever is not in accordance with his Word pass away into obscurity.

PREFACE & INTRODUCTION

This work is first and foremost for my church. It was written with them in mind, and it was written with them on my heart. This material has been ironed out over two years of teaching, with helpful interaction and thoughtful questions. In some ways, this book was a happy accident. We decided as a church to adopt the *Abstract of Principles* (1858). After joining with other leaders in our church to teach through the material on Sunday nights, I realized my teaching notes began to shape into chapters. Some who attended the teachings were eager to think, study and chew on these articles and the Scriptures which grounded them. And so there were inquiries for notes to be passed out. There is a real place for live and in-person teaching—the opportunity to experience the passion and engage in question and answer is invaluable. But there is also a real place for written text. There is a precision, an ability to pick up and put down and the ability to slow down and think. And that is what I believe made this project worth the time and effort. Theology is worth the effort. Truth is worth the effort. Gospel clarity is worth the effort. The beauty of the church is worth the effort. The glory of God is worth the effort.

So that is how this work came about, but what about the *Abstract of Principles*? I have found the *Abstract* is a relatively obscure document. It has played a vital role in Southern Baptist life in the United States from the very beginning, and it is still in active use both at The Southern Baptist Theological Seminary and at Southeastern Baptist Theological Seminary. However, after graduating from Southeastern, I believe it would have been possible for me to skate through without ever knowing the *Abstract* existed. I may have been to blame for that, owing to my drowsy class participation or some other excuse, but it wasn't until after I graduated that I even knew the document existed or that it was an authoritative confession at the Seminary I had just graduated from. And, to be honest, that is one of the reasons I wanted to write this book. The *Abstract* is a hidden gem. It deserves more press. And, as Baptist confessionalism continues to experience somewhat of a resurgence, I pray the *Abstract of Principles* will become more widely known and enjoyed.

Here are a few things that caught my attention and initially attracted me to the *Abstract*, and eventually why our church adopted it.

1. Brevity

I fell in love with how brief the *Abstract* was. The first copy I remember seeing was a download from Southern Seminary's website, which easily fit all twenty articles on two pieces of paper.[1] When I was thinking about my own church and what kind of confession would resonate, I couldn't help but be drawn to how brief the *Abstract* was.

2. Diversity

While the *Abstract* is brief, it is simultaneously extremely diverse. It covers a massive amount of doctrine in less than two pages. It starts with a clear statement on the Scriptures and then takes you from God and his governance of the world, all the way to the resurrection and the final judgment—with a whole lot of almost everything that is important in between. All the while, it highlights the centrality of redemption accomplished by the Son, redemption applied by the Spirit and redemption displayed in the church. It covers a ton of ground, without making you flip a bunch of pages.

3. Clarity

I loved how clear it was. I want to be careful here because I love the truth contained in the *Baptist Faith and Message*, but I don't think it would win any awards for being clean and tidy.[2] The *Abstract of Principles*

---

1   You can still find that download here: https://sbts-wordpress-uploads.s3.amazonaws.com/sbts/uploads/2009/01/abstract2.0.pdf.

2   See https://bfm.sbc.net/bfm2000.

has a clarity about it that is refreshing—especially for those who are new to this kind of a confessional document like many folks in my church.

4. Rich

While the *Abstract* is brief and clear, it is extremely rich. It is a deep document. The statements plunge quickly, getting right down to the bottom of some of the most precise and articulate details of theology. I will admit, the combination of brevity and depth makes the sentence structure a little difficult to follow at times. However, knowing what it covers, how it covers it and the depth at which it is covered, I will take a few clunky, run-on sentences!

5. Rooted

Finally, what I found refreshing over and over again was the *Abstract* was seriously rooted in Southern Baptist history. These statements weren't written yesterday. They bring forward the best of Reformation heritage, which is at the core of Southern Baptist theology, with brevity, clarity and depth. When it comes to being Southern Baptist, there is nothing more rooted than these statements. Certainly, there are other confessions which outdate the *Abstract of Principles* in Baptist life—London, Philadelphia, New Hampshire, Charleston—but the *Abstract* was the foundation which shaped pastors and churches in the newly formed Southern Baptist Convention. After all, *abstract*, as it is used here, is like a summary. These aren't the full and complete picture, but they summarize the essentials. And that is what a good confession ought to do. It is a synthesis and a summary of what the Bible teaches. This is an absolutely vital aspect for a healthy church—for it's members to have a grasp on the summary of Christian doctrine. That they can tell the story. That they see how the pieces fit into the whole. It helps us make sense of our lives, our churches, our Bibles and our mission. If we want to be rooted to the history of the church, and particularly to historic Southern Baptist theology, there is no better place to go than to the *Abstract*.

Limitations

When anyone sets out to write a book like this, it is good to acknowledge its limitations and potential pitfalls. So, from the outset, I want to admit one danger of the book you hold in your hands. It is easy to think of these articles as isolated frames, but this is a mistake. All of what is separated below for clarity is, in reality, enmeshed and intertwined. The best way to keep all of these distinctions together is to remember this is all part of a grand story. And so I want to briefly tell the story and give a slight shade on the story from the angle of all twenty articles, so you can have that story in mind as you approach each article. This may keep us from making the mistake of isolating an individual article, without connecting it to the others or to the larger story to which it belongs.

The grand narrative

There is a book called the Bible, and the Bible tells the best, most beautiful and only true story in the world. This book was given as a gift of God. It is perfect because it was given by a perfect God, and this God has given it to us so we might find our place in his story. Far and away, the most important thing the story is about is God himself. He is the beginning of the story and the end of the story because it is his story. All things make sense because of his perfections, and all things exist for him. God's story is a story about community. Community is not something God created, it is something God is, so when God in all of his infinite love overflowed with the joy to create, he did so to reflect his own internal and eternal relationship within himself—Father, Son and Holy Spirit. God, inviting others into communion with himself, by communicating himself, is what we might call the *purpose* of the story. God would not—he could not—leave the unfolding of this story up to chance. It is not a story about warring equals. It is not a story about being the master of your fate. It is not a story about a distant puppet-master. It is a story about a loving and caring God who governs and guides history along from himself and for himself, so this God will come to demonstrate how utterly loving he is. He intentionally highlights from the beginning his grace and his glory. God had an eye to our future failure. In his goodness, he set man as the defining motif of his masterpiece. God made a choice to redeem, and it was this choice which set his story apart from all the other stories that would be told, and set him apart from all other gods that would be worshipped. God had made human beings out of the overflow of his love, and he loved them so much he made them like him. They were his image.

Sadly, the human beings God made and loved, rebelled against him. They turned their backs on God and turned their hearts toward themselves. As a representative and as the fountainhead of all humanity, the first man Adam plunged the whole creation into the depths of depravity. But before man had even rebelled, God had made a choice. And so, out of a further and deeper love, God the Father sent God the Son—as a man—to die for sinners. He put grace on display. Jesus Christ, God's Son, came down into history to redeem rebels. In other words, God literally wrote himself into the story. In Jesus Christ, God was now the central player in the human story from the human perspective. But there was still a great tension in the story. The life, death and resurrection of God's Son must come to affect sinners, so God the Father and God the Son sent the Spirit to awaken sinners. The Spirit began to recreate sinners from the inside of their hearts, out into their minds and lives. He worked a real trust back into man's heart, and he worked the turning away from God into a turning back to God. The Spirit was on a mission to administer the new creation the Son had established by rising from the dead. And the problem right at the heart of what it would take to transfer rebels into this new creation was what their sin meant to God. It meant death, it meant guilt and it meant condemnation. And that is exactly what fell upon Jesus. The Spirit of God came on a mission to transfer God's people from death to life, from guilty to righteous, from cursed to blessed, by virtue of being found in Jesus. Those who came to him by faith were set apart, devoted to God and launched on a new lifelong course of being formed into his image. The image of God in man was being restored. They were also promised that while life would feel like death, Jesus was strong enough to hold them fast until the end.

This promise and the presence of the Spirit of God, launched all who would believe in the name of Jesus into a body called the church, and into a mission to tell the whole world about the good news of Jesus. Those brought into the church entered the drama of God's story by reenacting the life, death and resurrection of Jesus in their one time initiation (baptism) into the believing community. And all those who entered this drama, were invited to a meal which retells the story of Jesus over and over and over until he returns (the Lord's Supper). While they have been called by God to go and tell, they also gather every week to celebrate the truth that God's Son came into the world, conquered the world and promised to come back and remake the world again. These members of God's community now have a dual reality—they are citizens of this earth and they are simultaneously citizens of the kingdom of heaven. The Spirit of God is with them always, to guide them in wisdom and to embolden them toward valiant obedience to Jesus and radical love toward one another. The great hope that fuels the mission, comforts the oppressed and infuses life with meaning, is a future appointed day when God will raise the dead. And when the dead are raised comes a final reckoning, when God will make all things right. And his original design to have his people, in his place, for his glory and in his community, will be the eternal joy of people from every tribe and tongue and nation forever—all to the praise of the one true God, Father, Son and Holy Spirit.

All the articles in the *Abstract of Principles* fit into this grand story. It is the story of the world. It is God's story. And it is worth studying the details because it shapes and stabilizes our very existence.

Setup of the book

I want to just give a brief word on the setup of this book. Each chapter has the same basic components. Every chapter begins with an "Intro + overview" of the article being examined. Sometimes this will connect to church history, examine contrasting ideas or simply provide helpful definitions and clarity on the article. Next, every chapter will consider the "Scriptural foundations" undergirding the truth of the article. There will be short expositions of texts to frame the biblical evidence for the doctrines. Similarly, every chapter will briefly unpack the actual statement from the *Abstract* in an "Explanation" section. Line by line, there will be a brief clarification on the wording of the *Abstract* in light of what was examined in the introduction and brought out from the Scriptures. Then, common "Misconceptions" will be considered. These misconceptions will range from historical heresies and cultural mis-understandings, to unhelpful church traditions and mindsets. And finally, every chapter will end with "Application." This is not merely an intellectual exercise. Theology is practical. And every single article has important implications for our lives and our churches.

A concluding thing to note before we dig in is these articles have been lightly amended for this work. I wrote this book for our church, and our pastors felt some slight updating of the wording would benefit our people. You will find the greatest changes to the original *Abstract of Principles* come in the articles on The Lord's Day (Article XVII) and on Liberty of conscience (Article XVIII). Beyond that, any changes were only intended to modernize a few words here and there. We aren't afraid of teaching our church family new concepts and words, but we are afraid of being unnecessarily confusing. I think you will find that whether you want to go back and consult the 1858 edition, or you engage with the updated edition, the theology is consistent and similarly brief, diverse, clear, rich and rooted.

For the sake of the gospel,
Morgan Byrd, 2021
Palmetto Shores Church
Myrtle Beach, South Carolina, USA

I

The Scriptures

The Scriptures of the Old and New Testaments were
given by inspiration of God, and are the only
sufficient, certain and authoritative rule of all saving
knowledge, faith and obedience.

The Scriptures

INTRO + OVERVIEW

The most important question of the twentieth century may have been, "What is the Bible?"[1] And while this does not seem to be the most pressing question we face in the twenty-first century, it is certainly not a question we can afford to leave behind. If for no other reason than that this question has been asked in almost every generation of the church, we must take it seriously. Does the Bible *contain* God's words? Does the Bible *reflect* God's words? Is *every word* of the Bible God's very Word? How do we think through the human authorship of the Bible? What was the Holy Spirit's role in producing the Bible? Can we trust the reliability of the Bible? Can and should we translate the Bible into new languages? There may be more *pressing* questions, but there certainly are not more *important* questions.

When it comes to the Bible, there are three major levels at which we must consider the discussion. One level is that of *authority*. Who or what gets to tell us what to do? From what source do we look to be commanded? What body of information will we ultimately be accountable to? The next level is that of *certainty*. Where do we find the answers to life's major questions? What provides for us a solid foundation upon which to build our lives and our churches? What, in this world, can we trust to lead us to truth? The third level is that of *sufficiency*. What do we look to as essential? What can we look to and say, "That is all we need." Is there one central location where we find everything we need for life, godliness and salvation? By examining these three levels of inquiry with regard to the Bible, we have the ability to embrace clear commands, assured truths and real answers to life's biggest questions.

---

1   See, Owen Strachan's comment in The Pastor Theologian podcast, episode 17: https://www.pastortheologians.com/podcast.

Authority

There are at least three different historical situations that display for us the need to be clear about the Bible with regard to these three levels. They present for us illustrations of why it is important to have a fully orbed approach to the Scriptures. The first deals with the level of authority. Reformation theology[2] distinguishes between the *formal principle*[3] and the *material principle*.[4] While the material principle absolutely presents distinguishing factors between the Roman Catholic position and the Protestant position, it is the formal principle that was at the root of the division. The formal principle deals with authority: What carries the weight of ultimate authority? The clergy? Tradition? The Scriptures? A mixture?

Reformation theology is based on the belief that it is God's Word alone (*sola Scriptura*) that has authority with regard to the doctrine and life of the church. This formal principle, that the Scriptures of the Old and New Testaments are the only ultimate source of authority for the church, was at the heart of the division that led to the Protestant Reformation. *Sola Scriptura* does not mean the church ignores other helpful books, traditions and leadership, but it does mean that all of those things are evaluated and judged by the Scriptures. Whatever else we look to (for example, the book you are holding) must come underneath the Scripture, to be tested and governed by it. Nothing stands equal to the Scriptures with regard to authority, and anything that claims hold of our eyes, ears, mouths and thoughts must find its source in the Scriptures.

Certainty

The next historical illustration deals with the level of certainty. In the nineteenth and twentieth centuries, the reliability of the Bible came under attack like never before. In many Protestant denominations and

---

2 "Reformation theology" refers to beliefs about God, his world and his salvation, which flow from the thoughts and influence of the leaders and churches who broke away from (or were asked to leave) the Roman Catholic Church during the sixteenth century Protestant Reformation.

3 Think of this principle as the *trunk* of the tree.

4 Think of this principle as the *branches* of the tree.

churches, the certainty of the Bible was eroded by higher criticism,[5] scientific progress[6] and naturalism.[7] This erosion led to widespread division over confidence in the Bible and its doctrines. The traditional authorship of the Bible was discredited, the miracles and supernatural events in the Bible were doubted and the textual unity of the Bible was mocked.

In the twentieth century, many of these denominations split, many of their leaders fought and many of their institutions of higher education adopted new identities and theologies that presented more "progressive" and "modern" bodies of thought. One such cooperating group of churches that went through a battle over the certainty of the Bible was the Southern Baptist Convention in the United States. In what has now come to be known as the "Conservative Resurgence," the Southern Baptist Convention became one of the few Protestant groups that was able to hold firm to the certainty of the Bible as a majority position.

The Southern Baptist Convention affirmed the doctrine of inerrancy in 2000, as a response to the erosion of confidence in the Bible's reliability. They defined their position on the Scriptures with regard to its certainty by asserting, "It has God for its author, salvation for its end, and truth, without any mixture of error, for its matter. Therefore, all Scripture is totally true and trustworthy."[8] In other words, because God is the author of the Bible, it must be a certain document because God does not produce error.[9] The Bible is as reliable as its author, which means we can trust it with complete certainty.

---

5   The attempt to uncover the "original meaning" of a body of text by endeavouring to peel back its "layers" and understand its literary "development."

6   Notions and theories about the objective study of the world which seem to compete with the biblical narrative and worldview.

7   The belief that all that exists is what is possible to observe.

8   See the most recent statement on the Scriptures in the *Baptist Faith & Message 2000*: http://www.sbc.net/bfm2000/bfm2000.asp.

9   For a very helpful and nuanced discussion of the doctrine of inerrancy, see *The Chicago Statements on Biblical Inerrancy and Hermeneutics*: http://www.danielakin.com/wp-content/uploads/old/Resource_545/Book%202,%20Sec%2023.pdf.

Sufficiency

The final historical situation that illustrates for us the need to examine the Bible's sufficiency, is really a series of moments. In the seventh century with Islam, in the eighteenth, nineteenth and twentieth centuries with Mormonism, Unitarian Universalism, Rastafarianism, etc., groups have looked to the Bible as an important but incomplete book. Many groups like these claim the Bible has been distorted or only presents part of the truth. In subsequent "revelations" or "prophecies" the Bible has been given interpretive boundaries and corrections through other works like the Qur'an, The Book of Mormon, etc. These groups see the Bible as helpful, but insufficient. In other words, from some of the earliest days of Christianity until today, the sufficiency of the Bible has been under attack. The reason this matters is that the addition of new sacred texts like these leads to a wide range of doctrinal differences. Everything from our conception of God, the account of creation, the view of the world and humanity, the person and work of Jesus, the necessary aspects of salvation, entry into the church or group and eschatological or end-time beliefs, become vastly different with the introduction of further "revelation" or "prophecy."

One cannot help but think about the words of the apostle Paul in his letter to the Galatians, "But even if we, or an angel from heaven, should preach to you a gospel contrary to what we have preached to you, he is to be accursed!"[10] Paul must have foreseen these kinds of supposed "angelic appearances" because this is exactly what these groups have done. They say "angels from heaven" have come preaching a different gospel, and instead of refusing it as accursed, it has been welcomed and embraced by many. We must not lose our conviction of the sufficiency of the Bible or the gospel it proclaims because our eternal state hangs in the balance.

---

10 Galatians 1:8.

SCRIPTURAL FOUNDATIONS

Genesis 1:1-3

> In the beginning God created the heavens and the earth. And the
> earth was a formless and desolate emptiness, and darkness was over
> the surface of the deep, and the Spirit of God was hovering over the
> surface of the waters. Then God said, "Let there be light"; and there
> was light.

While Genesis 1 does not teach about the Scriptures themselves, what
we see from the very outset of the Scriptures is that the speech of God
is powerful. Look how God's speech is the active agent in verse 3,
"Then God said…." It was as God spoke that he brought together the
form of creation. His words carried life in them. From the very first
page of the Bible, the speech of God is held in highest esteem.

Psalm 19:7-11

> The Law of the LORD is perfect, restoring the soul;
> The testimony of the LORD is sure, making wise the simple.
> The precepts of the LORD are right, rejoicing the heart;
> The commandment of the LORD is pure, enlightening the eyes.
> The fear of the LORD is clean, enduring forever;
> The judgments of the LORD are true; they are righteous altogether.
> They are more desirable than gold, yes, than much pure gold;
> Sweeter also than honey and drippings of the honeycomb.
> Moreover, Your servant is warned by them;
> In keeping them there is great reward.

In all the beauty of poetry, Psalm 19 gives witness to a body of speech
from God that gives life to our life. It is called Law, testimony, precepts,
commandment and judgments. This body of God's speech restores the
soul, makes wise the simple, rejoices the heart, enlightens the eyes,
warns the servant of God and offers great reward. God's Word is treated

as a very necessity for life. It is through the revelation of himself that we can understand, believe and obey him.[11]

Matthew 5:17-18

"Do not presume that I came to abolish the Law or the Prophets; I did not come to abolish, but to fulfill. For truly I say to you, until heaven and earth pass away, not the smallest letter or stroke of a letter shall pass from the Law, until all is accomplished!"

This Law, which Psalm 19 spoke so highly about, while giving commands and judgments, also carried with it prophecies. The New Testament in no way supplanted the Old, but rather displayed the fulfilment of it in Jesus Christ. These testaments work together as a unified witness, each reflecting light on the other. Jesus Christ is the organic connection between these two testaments through the lens of promise and fulfilment.

2 Timothy 3:14-4:2

You, however, continue in the things you have learned and become convinced of, knowing from whom you have learned them, and that from childhood you have known the sacred writings which are able to give you the wisdom that leads to salvation through faith which is in Christ Jesus. All Scripture is inspired by God and beneficial for teaching, for rebuke, for correction, for training in righteousness; so that the man or woman of God may be fully capable, equipped for every good work.

I solemnly exhort you in the presence of God and of Christ Jesus, who is to judge the living and the dead, and by His appearing and His kingdom: preach the word; be ready in season and out of season; correct, rebuke, and exhort, with great patience and instruction.

Here we see, in no uncertain terms, that Scripture is inspired by God.

---

11 Psalm 19 also addresses the reality that creation speaks of God. However, sinful men and women suppress the truth of God, even though it is clearly seen. See note 13 for further comments.

This is the foundation for the authority, certainty and sufficiency of the Bible. The fact that it comes from God gives it a weight and a power we cannot live without. These Scriptures lead to salvation, these Scriptures are profitable in many ways and it is these Scriptures which should be the content of the proclamation of God's church. Even when the times and seasons change, God's Word never changes. Whether it is popular or not, what better word could we preach than the very Word of God? If it is inspired then it is indispensable.

1 Peter 1:22–2:3

Since you have purified your souls in obedience to the truth for a sincere love of the brothers *and* sisters, fervently love one another from the heart, for you have been born again not of seed which is perishable, but imperishable, *that is*, through the living and enduring word of God. For,

"ALL FLESH IS LIKE GRASS,
AND ALL ITS GLORY IS LIKE THE FLOWER OF GRASS.
THE GRASS WITHERS,
AND THE FLOWER FALLS OFF,
BUT THE WORD OF THE LORD ENDURES FOREVER."

And this is the word which was preached to you.
Therefore, rid *yourselves* of all malice and all deceit and hypocrisy and envy and all slander, and like newborn babies, long for the pure milk of the word, so that by it you may grow in respect to salvation, if you have tasted the kindness of the Lord.

Look how Peter connects the new birth to the Word. The Word of God has the power to bring about a second birth in human beings. The Word of God is an imperishable thing that never grows stale or old. The Word of God is not like men and women with their fading glory; rather, it shines forever. The Word of God should be longed for, because it is what gives growth to the church and to the individuals who make up the church. This is one craving that we don't have to try and stuff down or pacify. We *must* pursue it with our whole lives.

2 Peter 1:16–21

> For we did not follow cleverly devised tales when we made known to you the power and coming of our Lord Jesus Christ, but we were eyewitnesses of His majesty. For when He received honor and glory from God the Father, such a declaration as this was made to Him by the Majestic Glory: "This is My beloved Son with whom I am well pleased"—and we ourselves heard this declaration made from heaven when we were with Him on the holy mountain.
>
> And so we have the prophetic word *made* more sure, to which you do well to pay attention as to a lamp shining in a dark place, until the day dawns and the morning star arises in your hearts. *But* know this first *of all*, that no prophecy of Scripture becomes *a matter* of *someone's* own interpretation, for no prophecy was ever made by an act of human will, but men moved by the Holy Spirit spoke from God.

According to Peter, the witness of the Scriptures is not one of cleverly devised tales. Instead, it is one that is attested by eyewitnesses of the glory and majesty of Jesus. These Scriptures are actually *more certain* than if we had been there to witness the events which they present because the Scriptures give us certain interpretation.[12] The Bible was written by men, through their own words and personalities, but they were moved by the Holy Spirit. In other words, while each author wrote in a different genre and style, the Holy Spirit was ultimately responsible for maintaining the accuracy and meaning of what these authors recorded. Because the Spirit did this, we can be sure of both the transmission of the Word and the meaning of the Word.

Revelation 22:18–19

> I testify to everyone who hears the words of the prophecy of this book: if anyone adds to them, God will add to him the plagues that are written in this book; and if anyone takes away from the words of

---

12 See Mark 9:1–13. When Peter had this eyewitness experience of Jesus in glory, he and the other disciples were clearly bewildered by what they had seen. Seeing was not believing. But in the Scriptures we have *interpreted glory*, which is why it is a "word made more sure."

the book of this prophecy, God will take away his part from the tree of life and from the holy city, which are written in this book.

On the very last page of the Bible we learn there are serious consequences for tampering with God's Word. These Scriptures are not to be added to and they are not to be subtracted from. The Scriptures are God's self revelation, so to tamper with them is to tamper with God himself. God has so connected himself to his Word, that to reject his Word is to reject him.

EXPLANATION

"The Scriptures of the Old and New Testaments..."

These two testaments present the same God, the same theology, the same truth, the same teaching and the same sure foundation for understanding life in this world. While they do emphasize different things, and at times relate to one another as shadow and substance, neither testament is more accurate or less accurate, neither testament is more Christian or less Christian, and neither testament is more necessary or less necessary. Both testaments together, in their totality, present the authoritative revelation of God. These testaments are so inextricably linked, that any system that attempts to interpret one of the testaments without regard to the other will, in fact, miss the mark. The New Testament gives us the interpretive framework for the Old, and the Old Testament gives us the foundation necessary for understanding the New.

"were given by inspiration of God..."

Some of our modern translations give us a helpful rendering of 2 Timothy 3:16: "All Scripture is *breathed out* by God" (ESV). The very words of Scripture are what they are because *God* spoke them. This in no way denies human authorship. In a mysterious and miraculous way, the Holy Spirit used the words and personalities of men to reveal himself in his written Word. The grounds for the authority, certainty and sufficiency of the Bible is the fact that it comes from God himself.

"and are the only sufficient..."

The Bible contains everything necessary. Whatever the Bible speaks to, it speaks to in a satisfactory way. Whatever the Bible does not speak to, is not necessary. While other books may be helpful, only the Bible is indispensable. There is no other sacred text, there is no other place to hear from God[13] and there is no other truth that we need for life and godliness other than the inspired Word of God.

"certain..."

The Scriptures, in their original manuscripts,[14] are inerrant. In other words, they do not contradict and they do not present any mixture of error. They are fully trustworthy in all that they say. The theology[15] that the Bible contains is consistent. No other body of truth in the world can be trusted fully. Only the Bible gives us a sure foundation on which to build our lives and our churches.

"and authoritative rule..."

The Bible shares its place of authority with no other agent. No person, no church, no office and no document stands alongside the Bible in its rule. It, and nothing else, stands over us, commanding us, leading us, controlling our faith and our practice.

"of all saving knowledge..."

What the Bible presents is the knowledge of God. It presents the knowledge of sin. It presents the knowledge of redemption in Christ. All of the truth needed for salvation is contained here and nowhere else. All truth regarding salvation is derived from the Bible.

---

13 While God has revealed himself in nature, all men and women suppress this truth because of sin. Therefore it is only through the Scriptures that people come to see how God has revealed himself in nature. Even what God has revealed in nature (while it is enough to make all people everywhere accountable to God) is not enough to lead them to saving knowledge, faith and obedience.

14 This is a short and helpful interaction regarding the original Bible manuscripts: https://www.thegospelcoalition.org/blogs/kevin-deyoung/what-good-is-innerancy-if-we-dont-have-the-original-manuscripts.

15 *Theology*, in simple terms, means *speech about God*.

"faith..."

The Bible alone leads to faith. It leads to faith in God and to repentance of sin. It leads to faith in Christ and to rejection of idols. The Bible shows us the righteousness of God and the righteousness given as a gift of God in Christ. Only through the Scriptures are we led to true faith.

"and obedience."

The Bible teaches us what God demands of us. It leads us to life-giving guidelines that stabilize and harmonize life. There is no other place where we find what God wants from our lives. There is no other place where we find out how life works best. Through the Bible, we are led to follow God and to find the joy of saying, "Yes," to his perfect way.

MISCONCEPTIONS

There are two major misconceptions about the Bible. On one hand, there is a misconception called *dictation theory*. This theory removes the human authorship of the Bible. It portrays the writing of the Bible as if God is grabbing the hand of the human authors, more or less against their will, and writing the Scriptures without regard to their personalities or language styles. On the other hand, there is a misconception that portrays the writing of the Bible as a purely *human invention*.

It is helpful for us to understand that the group of writings which have been written and gathered together by the Holy Spirit, which together form the Bible, were not arbitrarily or randomly chosen. These Scriptures were given through authoritative prophets who were empowered by God to reveal him to us.[16] For example, as the apostle Paul opens his letter to the Galatians, "Paul, an apostle (not sent from men nor through human agency, but through Jesus Christ and God the Father, who raised Him from the dead), and all the brothers who are

---

16 For a brief and helpful discussion on the formation of the biblical canon, see "Four Myths Related to the Bible's Origins," by John Meade: https://ca.thegospelcoalition.org/article/four-myths-related-bibles-origins/

with me. To the churches of Galatia" (Galatians 1:1–2). Paul makes it clear that he did not receive his message from men, but from God.

If we move toward dictation theory, then we lose the real and vibrant texture of the Bible. The Bible clearly comes to us through different voices and different genres. The very personalities of these men are embedded in the text. However, if we move toward a view that removes God's inspiration, then we cannot look to the Bible as authoritative, certain or sufficient. When we take both the human authorship and the divine authorship seriously, then we take the Bible's own witness to itself seriously.[17]

A final misconception, on a more popular level, is revealed in how we view the general and overall *purpose* of the Bible. It is true that the Bible contains the rule of all saving knowledge, faith and obedience. In other words, the Bible does in fact speak to humanity, calling us and commanding us in what it reveals. However, it is a misconception to think the Bible is mainly *about us*. The Scriptures teach us unequivocally that its main subject is Jesus Christ. Jesus, on the road with two of his disciples after his resurrection, says,

> O foolish men and slow of heart to believe in all that the prophets have spoken! Was it not necessary for the Christ to suffer these things and to enter into His glory?' Then beginning with Moses and with all the prophets, He explained to them the things concerning Himself in all the Scriptures (Luke 24:25-27).

The main purpose of the Bible is not about us—it is the revelation of Jesus Christ!

---

17 The Bible's own witness to itself includes both the things it says about itself, and its unity, clarity and beauty, which together make a strong argument for its veracity.

APPLICATION

Article I: The Scriptures

The Scriptures of the Old and New Testaments were given by inspiration of God, and are the only sufficient, certain and authoritative rule of all saving knowledge, faith and obedience.

---

1. ***We should humbly receive the Christian Scriptures with faith and obedience.***
We should look to them for our standards. We should bow before God—the God who has revealed himself to us in his Word—as we read and listen to the Bible. By faith, we engage in relationship with its saving knowledge and with the God who saves. In obedience, we submit our lives to God's perfect way, both out of love for him and out of a desire to enjoy life as it was meant to be lived.

   All that is true with regard to faith and obedience personally, is true with regard to the church as well. The doctrine of the church should flow from the Scriptures, and the practices of the church should be governed by the Scriptures. The Bible takes ultimate authority both in the teaching and in the governing of the church.

2. ***The Bible should establish our preaching and philosophy of ministry.***
Simply put, sermons should be soundly anchored to the Bible. They should be locally and culturally appropriate extensions of the Scriptures themselves. The main point of the Scripture should be the main point of the sermon. The tone of the Scripture should be the tone of the sermon. The applications found in the Scripture should be the applications of the sermon. These same principles can and should apply in whatever setting the Bible is being taught or preached, no matter the age or type of gathering.

3. *We should learn to trust the Bible's use in evangelism and discipleship.*

While personal wisdom and personal testimony have their place, the main mode of calling people into the faith, and helping people grow in the faith, should be the proclamation of the gospel of Jesus Christ revealed in the Scriptures. After all, if the Scriptures are the only sufficient, certain and authoritative body of saving knowledge, faith and obedience, then their contents should be our primary message both for believers and for those who have yet to believe. And this is not just the job of the preacher—every Christian should seek out opportunities to deliver the Word of God to a lost and dying world and to other members of the body who need to be discipled. We must withstand the temptation to trust other methods and sources above Scripture, and we should honour God's self-revelation by fully employing his Word in all our ministry strategies.

The reason we should trust the Bible as our great method is because it tells the true story of the universe. It situates us in God's reality, answering the questions our souls are asking. God's Word places our everyday lives within a grand sweeping narrative that explains our longings and satisfies our desires. Only the Bible is appropriately realistic about the situation we find ourselves in and seriously hopeful about God's plan for the world through the life, death and resurrection of Jesus. Only God's authoritative, sufficient and certain Word reaches with clarity into our daily existence and paints a picture of the future that is big and bright enough for us to hang all our expectations upon.

II

God

There is but one God, the Maker, Preserver and Ruler of all things, having in and of himself, all perfections, and being infinite in them all; and to him all creatures owe the highest love, reverence and obedience.

God

INTRO + OVERVIEW

▬▬▬▬

There is only one true God, the triune God—Father, Son and Holy Spirit. Getting "God" right (or wrong) may seem like a fun and harmless intellectual exercise. But when we realize that, whether consciously or unconsciously, what we believe about God affects how we look at everything else in life, the stakes are raised. C.S. Lewis wrote,

> I read in a periodical the other day that the fundamental thing is how we think of God.
> By God Himself, it is not! How God thinks of us is not only more important, but infinitely more important. Indeed, how we think of Him is of no importance except in so far as it is related to how He thinks of us.[1]

This is a sobering thought from Lewis! It is not we who will stand in judgment of God, it is God who will stand in judgment of us.

But, even with this thought in mind, Lewis is assuming God is a judge. Lewis is assuming one day we will appear before this God to be inspected by him. So, while *ultimately* it will be more important what God thinks of us, we cannot neglect to see the importance of what we think of him. After all, Lewis's view of God is what leads him to his sobering conclusion!

So, how should we think of God?

---

1   Cited in Justin Taylor, "Tozer vs. Lewis: What's the Most Important Thing about Us?, *The Gospel Coalition Blog* (June 4, 2016); https://www.thegospelcoalition.org/blogs/justin-taylor/tozer-vs-lewis-whats-the-most-important-thing-about-us.

Atheism: There is no God

The first option we have is that there is no God. Some people call this *atheism*.[2] In this view, the world has no creator, no governor and no preserver. The world is natural, and anything beyond or outside of the natural does not exist.

The main problem with this view, is that the Bible, from its opening line, points us to a world where there is a God. Beyond this, a no-god perspective leads to a world that is aimless, meaningless and hopeless.

Without God, the world would be aimless because it would mean we are headed nowhere in particular. Without God, the world would be meaningless because the reason why things carry meaning is because they either do or do not support the overall aim. Without God, the world would be hopeless because the pain and brokenness we feel over our aimlessness and meaninglessness would have no resolution. These things—aim, meaning and hope—are integral to the human experience.

As humans, we find purpose in going places. It is why we ask people: *What do you want to be when you grow up? What goals do you have for the next five years?* All of us know that we haven't hit every target we have aimed for, and we haven't found the purpose that we crave deep down. So, we must ask, is there any hope for a better future? This question drives our lives more than we realize. In fact, it is where things like the "American Dream" come from. The desire to evaluate our current circumstances and strive for a better future demonstrates that we need hope in this life. Without aim (some place to go), meaning (a reason to care about the details of the trip) or hope (the idea of a better future), there would be no point in living.

Agnosticism: There is a God but this God cannot be known

A second option is there is a God, but this God cannot be known. Some people call this *agnosticism*.[3] There is something endearing about this view. While it is flawed at one major point, it at least gets this right: God is so "other" that there is no way that we could find him or fully comprehend him. With that being said, the very existence of the Bible makes the unknowable God perspective unviable. While God cannot

---

2   A meaning *no*, and *theism* meaning *god*.

3   A meaning *no*, and *gnosticism* meaning *knowledge*.

be found in our own strength, and he cannot be fully comprehended by our own intuition, he has revealed himself in his Word. The unknowable God, has made himself known.

So, there is a genuine humility that looks to God and thinks, "Wow, You are more than I can comprehend," and, "Wow, if You hadn't revealed Yourself I would have never found You." But there is also a false humility that uses the truth that God cannot be known unless he reveals himself as an excuse not to accept God's self revelation. This is a false humility because it doesn't show a desire to submit to this vast and uncomprehendible God, but instead, hides behind this "truth" as an excuse not to give up control. Yes, it is true that God cannot be found and that he cannot be fully known, however it is also true that God has revealed himself and that he can be truly known through what he has revealed.

Polytheism: There are many gods

A third option is that there are many gods. This one is a little tricky with regard to the biblical data. The Bible is not a book that only talks about one god. There are many gods that are discussed throughout the Bible. However, the Bible clearly and consistently teaches that there is only *one true God*. All the other gods that are mentioned are *false* gods.

The closest thing that the Bible gives us to a view of many gods, or what some might call *polytheism*,[4] is the existence of rational and responsible beings that are spiritual in nature. These beings are referred to as angels, demons, spirits, powers, etc. While they are different from human beings and animals, in that they are spirit, they are also different from God, in that they are creatures.

The Serpent, or Satan, who seems to be the most powerful of all of these beings is in no way presented as another god or in any way equal to God. Whatever dominion he has, has been given to him by permission of God, and whatever power he has has been derived from God for God's purposes. God alone is God, and whatever else exists has been made by him.

---

4   *Poly* meaning *many*, and *theism* meaning *god*.

Pantheism: God is everything

A fourth option is that god is simply everything, or at least everything that is physical. He is all that is, and he is made up of the same stuff that we are. Whatever is visible, whatever is invisible, whatever is physical, and whatever is spiritual—all of it and all of us are collectively "god." Some people call this *pantheism*.[5]

This is not the same as the notion the Bible puts forth when God says, "I AM." That fact that "God is," does not mean that "God is everything." "I AM" signifies that God has no beginning and no end, he is not bound by body or space, and he is the ultimate reality in all the universe. If "I AM" were synonymous with pantheism, then it would also be true that every human being is, "I AM," and every plant, animal and... everything. This clearly does not represent the Creator/creature divide the Bible holds forth.

On a more theoretical level, the main problem with this is that it fails to acknowledge God's *transcendence*.[6] The Bible paints God ultimately as an object of worship who stands in contrast to us—as a Creator with creatures and as a Being without a body. If everything is god, then nothing is god. If we are god, then god is us.

And on a more practical level, when we view god this way, we are tempted to create a god who is simply a little bit bigger and better version of ourselves. This god must like what we like, think like we think and act like we act, because this god is no different from us. It is the inability to worship God in his transcendence that leads us to see him and treat him in ways that are offensive and paltry.

Deism: God is distant

The final option we will explore before turning to the God of the Bible, is the distant god. This is a conception of god that sees him as creator and sees him as transcendent, but that views him as stepping away from creation rather than being involved in creation. Some people call this *deism*.[7]

While the Bible does present God as having created all things, towering over and separate from what he has made, it also demonstrates

---

5 *Pan* meaning *all*, and *theism* meaning *god*.

6 Think *separate, matchless, over all* and *timeless*.

7 *Deism* meaning *god. Deism* unlike *theism* comes from the Latin instead of the Greek.

his continued care and preservation for his creation. God is both transcendent and *immanent*.[8] In one sense, this care is not by necessity, at least on God's part, but creation would not survive without God's continued upholding of it. Therefore, it is impossible to conceive of God completely separating himself from the affairs of the universe, because without his power and preservation it would dissolve into nothing.

Beyond this, the Bible presents God as a loving God. This God graciously gives life to creation. The God of the Bible is not less than Maker, but he is so much more in relation to what he has made.

One final note before we look at what the Scriptures say about God: it is highly intentional in the *Abstract of Principles* that the article on the Scriptures precedes the one on God himself. The reason for this is because all of the views cited above have come from men—their imaginations and scientific enterprises. This search toward getting God "right" is impossible. The only way that we can know who God is, is through his self revelation.

Therefore, it is not that the Bible is more important or more central than God himself, but by putting the Scriptures first, we are making a statement about who this God is. He is not a God who we can "study" scientifically and come to conclusions about—he is a God who we must receive and worship. So, we acknowledge from the outset that the God we are seeking to know and love is the one, true and living God found in the Christian Scriptures.

SCRIPTURAL FOUNDATIONS

Genesis 1:1–3

In the beginning God created the heavens and the earth. And the earth was a formless and desolate emptiness, and darkness was over the surface of the deep, and the Spirit of God was hovering over the surface of the waters. Then God said, "Let there be light"; and there was light.

---

8   Think *close, alongside* and *in the midst of.*

Genesis 1 is where we began in Article 1 on the Scriptures—seeing that God's speech has power. It is also where we begin with reference to God, because we learn from the outset that God simply "is" in the beginning. The only thing before creation is God himself. There he is, pre-beginning, self-sustaining and self-fulfilling.

Exodus 34:5-8

> And the LORD descended in the cloud and stood there with him as he called upon the name of the LORD. Then the LORD passed by in front of him and proclaimed, "The LORD, the LORD God, compassionate and merciful, slow to anger, and abounding in faithfulness and truth; who keeps faithfulness for thousands, who forgives wrongdoing, violation of *His Law*, and sin; yet He will by no means leave *the guilty* unpunished, inflicting the punishment of fathers on the children and on the grandchildren to the third and fourth generations." And Moses hurried to bow low toward the ground and worship.

A man named Moses had the opportunity to have a conversation with God on multiple occasions. The first time they talked, God told Moses his name is, "I AM." Here, in Exodus 34, during a different conversation, God expounds on the name he had first revealed to Moses. This time, as God revealed his name, it came out in the form of characteristics and actions. We sense both the transcendence and the immanence of God in his own self-revealed name. He is judge. He is over us. He punishes us. And yet at the same time, he is gracious. He is compassionate. "I AM" is loving and forgiving.

Deuteronomy 6:4-9

> "Hear, Israel! The LORD is our God, the *Lord* is one! And you shall love the LORD your God with all your heart and with all your soul and with all your strength. These words, which I am commanding you today, shall be on your heart. And you shall repeat them diligently to your sons and speak of them when you sit in your house, when you walk on the road, when you lie down, and when you get up. You shall also tie them as a sign to your hand, and they shall be as frontlets on your

forehead. You shall also write them on the doorposts of your house and on your gates."

There are two things that rise to the top from this passage. The first is that there is only one God—there is no competition in or for God. No matter what we say about the plurality of persons in the next article on the Trinity, we cannot mean by what we say about the triune God that there is more than one God. "I AM" is one! A second thing is that this one God deserves to be loved and worshipped. If he is God, then we owe him our reverence. If he is God, then being commanded to love him is actually the best thing for us.

Isaiah 40:9–31
This passage from Isaiah is so rich and so long that we are going to break it into sections.

> Go up on a high mountain,
> Zion, messenger of good news,
> Raise your voice forcefully,
> Jerusalem, messenger of good news;
> Raise *it* up, do not fear.
> Say to the cities of Judah,
> "Here is your God!"
> Behold, the Lord GOD will come with might,
> With His arm ruling for Him.
> Behold, His compensation is with Him,
> And His reward before Him.

What amazing truth! First we learn that God is someone we simply behold. We gaze at him; we step back in awe of him. We are not first to study him, we are simply to look at him and gasp.

> Like a shepherd He will tend His flock,
> In His arm He will gather the lambs
> And carry *them* in the fold of His robe;
> He will gently lead the nursing *ewes*.

Next, we learn that this same God, whom we are called to behold, is also a shepherd. The transition back and forth between transcendence and immanence in this passage is staggering. Here is this great God, who will gather the people he has made and bring them close to himself. There, in his bosom, he protects, nurtures and guides them.

> Who has measured the waters in the hollow of His hand,
> And measured the heavens with a span,
> And calculated the dust of the earth with a measure,
> And weighed the mountains in a balance
> And the hills in a pair of scales?

Lest we think too little of this shepherd, we find him measuring the universe and holding it in his hands. He may choose to come close to us, but it is not because he is down where we are by nature. This God is so outside of our universe, he can walk around it, hold it and measure it.

> Who has directed the Spirit of the LORD,
> Or as His counselor has informed Him?
> With whom did He consult and *who* gave Him understanding?
> And *who* taught Him in the path of justice and taught Him knowledge,
> And informed Him of the way of understanding?
> Behold, the nations are like a drop from a bucket,
> And are regarded as a speck of dust on the scales;
> Behold, He lifts up the islands like fine dust.
> Even Lebanon is not enough to burn,
> Nor its animals enough for a burnt offering.
> All the nations are as nothing before Him,
> They are regarded by Him as less than nothing and meaningless.
> To whom then will you liken God?
> Or what likeness will you compare with Him?
> *As for* the idol, a craftsman casts it,
> A goldsmith plates it with gold,
> And a silversmith *fashions* chains of silver.
> He who is too impoverished for *such* an offering
> Selects a tree that does not rot;
> He seeks out for himself a skillful craftsman
> To prepare an idol that will not totter.

This is in contrast to all other false gods. There is no God like this, so there is none to liken to him. All other gods get their "life" from human beings. They are carved and crafted carefully to meet specific needs people desire. But "I AM" has no origin. No one gives him counsel. He fits in no one's hands.

> Do you not know? Have you not heard?
> Has it not been declared to you from the beginning?
> Have you not understood from the foundations of the earth?
> It is He who sits above the circle of the earth,
> And its inhabitants are like grasshoppers,
> Who stretches out the heavens like a curtain
> And spreads them out like a tent to live in.
> *It is* He who reduces rulers to nothing,
> Who makes the judges of the earth meaningless.
> Scarcely have they been planted,
> Scarcely have they been sown,
> Scarcely has their stock taken root in the earth,
> But He merely blows on them, and they wither,
> And the storm carries them away like stubble.
> "To whom then will you compare Me
> That I would be *his* equal?" says the Holy One.
> Raise your eyes on high
> And see who has created these stars,
> The One who brings out their multitude by number,
> He calls them all by name;
> Because of the greatness of His might and the strength of *His* power,
> Not one *of them* is missing.

In fact, we find it is just the opposite. Everything that exists holds together in his mighty hands. All the stars, all the planets and all the galaxies remain intact through his great power. When we look up and not one of them is missing, it is because he is holding them in place.

> Why do you say, Jacob, and you assert, Israel,
> "My way is hidden from the LORD,
> And the justice due me escapes the notice of my God"?
> Do you not know? Have you not heard?

The Everlasting God, the LORD, the Creator of the ends of the earth
Does not become weary or tired.
His understanding is unsearchable.

This God, He does not grow weary, though he gives away so much strength to others. He is the everlasting God, the Lord, the Creator, which means that he can give and give and give, and there will always be more to give. He does not grow old, he does not change and he does not diminish.

He gives strength to the weary,
And to *the one who* lacks might He increases power.
Though youths grow weary and tired,
And vigorous young men stumble badly,
Yet those who wait for the LORD
Will gain new strength;
They will mount up *with* wings like eagles,
They will run and not get tired,
They will walk and not become weary.

Finally, lest we grow in despair that this great God would be too far from us and would want to remove himself from our existence, we are told he gives strength to the weary. Yes, this God of *all* strength, comes to those robbed of strength, and empowers them to go on. He is over, above and beyond us. And yet, he is right here with us. He is both transcendent and immanent.

John 4:21–24

Jesus said to her, "Believe Me, woman, that a time is coming when you will worship the Father neither on this mountain nor in Jerusalem. You *Samaritans* worship what you do not know; we worship what we do know, because salvation is from the Jews. But a time is coming, and even now has arrived, when the true worshipers will worship the Father in spirit and truth; for such people the Father seeks *to be* His worshipers. God is spirit, and those who worship Him must worship in spirit and truth."

There are many reasons why it matters that we get God "right." For example, if we misunderstand who he is, then we will misunderstand how we are to worship him. Here, in John 4, Jesus explains to a woman why our worship is not about geographical location. We ought to be more concerned with worshipping in spirit and truth, than we are with what building we are in or what mountain we are on. And the reason Jesus gives is that *God is spirit*. In this sense, Jesus is not speaking of one of the persons of God, the Holy Spirit. He is saying God does not have a body and God is not material—he is spirit. Therefore, to be a true worshipper, we must worship God in spirit and in truth.

1 John 1:5

This is the message we have heard from Him and announce to you, that God is Light, and in Him there is no darkness at all.

While we have in John's gospel the statement that God is spirit, we find at the beginning of John's first letter that *God is light*. There are many different ways we could take this, but to look at the opposite of this helps us understand what John means. In negative terms, for God to be light means "in Him there is no darkness at all." In other words, God cannot be evil, he cannot be impure and he cannot be out of the loop. God is light—whatever is darkness cannot be in him.

1 John 4:7-14

Beloved, let's love one another; for love is from God, and everyone who loves has been born of God and knows God. The one who does not love does not know God, because God is love. By this the love of God was revealed in us, that God has sent His only Son into the world so that we may live through Him. In this is love, not that we loved God, but that He loved us and sent His Son *to be* the propitiation for our sins. Beloved, if God so loved us, we also ought to love one another. No one has ever seen God; if we love one another, God remains in us, and His love is perfected in us. By this we know that we remain in Him and He in us, because He has given to us of His Spirit. We have seen and testify that the Father has sent the Son *to be* the Savior of the world.

Finally, John shows us that while God is spirit and God is light, it is also true that *God is love*. It is not that God is loving. It is not that God is able to love, or that he has a propensity to love—it is that his very makeup *is love*. Here we learn something very striking from John: God is the sum of all of his attributes. In other words, *whatever God does* (for example, love this world) comes from *whatever God is* (in this example, God is love). So, the reason God is loving is because God *is* love. This is always true of God—his attributes and his actions are inseparably linked.

EXPLANATION

"There is but one God..."
God cannot be divided. There are no competing visions of the purpose and makeup of the universe. God has no rivals. He is all alone in the category of "God." As we move toward thinking through the next article on the Trinity, this article guards us from thinking that because there is God the Father, God the Son and God the Holy Spirit, who are distinct persons in the Godhead, there are then three gods. No. There is *one* God. So whatever we say of this one God, we say of the Father, we say of the Son and we say of the Spirit. They together are spirit, light and love.

"the Maker..."
Here, the article uses the word *Maker* whereas the word *Creator* could have been used. It is not that God in any way is less than Creator, but it is that he is much more. He is the transcendent Creator and he is also the immanent Maker.[9]

"Preserver..."
As the Creator and Maker, God is the sufficient cause of all that exists. Therefore, for all that exists to continue, he must also preserve. He sustains, protects and upholds the integrity of all things. If God left

---

9 Genesis 1 establishes God as both Creator and Maker. If you read through this first chapter of the Bible, you will find both terms in use.

the scene, the whole creation would fall apart. His preserving power is what keeps all of creation from rotting away and dissolving into nothing.

"and Ruler of all things..."

He didn't just create and he doesn't just preserve, he also governs. He is over creation. His rule goes. He is the King. He decides how things work and how things are governed. Life was meant to be lived under his reign. And in the end, he will judge us for who we are before him.

"having in and of himself all perfections..."

This Creator God needs no help. He is abundantly full. Creation was not a necessity. Creation does not diminish God in any way. And this is so because he has all perfections.

Perfections is a really helpful and beautiful way of saying *attributes*. The reason this word is so helpful is because it reminds us that even as we say God is love, his love is a higher and more perfect love than human love. Or when we say God is holy, his holiness is a higher and more perfect holiness than human holiness. Whatever God is, he fully is—he is perfect in whatever he is.

These perfections or attributes divide into two categories, communicable and non-communicable. The first are those which are true of God and can also be true of God's creatures—like love and righteousness. The second are those which can only be true of God—like being all-powerful and all-knowing. But we must keep in mind that even the communicable attributes of God are still only found in men and women at a lesser degree.

"and being infinite in them all..."

To keep this simple, God's perfections don't compete with one another. It is not like there is love on one side of him and wrath on the other, and we are always sort of wondering, "Okay, is love going to outweigh wrath?" God doesn't have mood swings, and he is not riding a roller-coaster of emotions. Whatever he is, he is perfect in. That means, all he is remains in perfect harmony at all times.

"and to him all creatures owe"

If this is who God really is, then we owe him some things. It is right to think this way because he made us. If he makes us, preserves us and rules us, then all we are is from him and for him.

"the highest love, reverence and obedience."

What we owe God, first and foremost, is love. He deserves to be first, and not just in our love but also in our reverence. We bow before him. We ought to respect him more than any other thing or person, and not just with love and reverence, but with full obedience. Whatever he says, it would be treason not to submit. Simply by the fact that he made us, it stands to reason we owe him these things. This is both reasonable and biblical, "Worthy are You, our Lord and our God, to receive glory and honor and power; for You created all things, and because of Your will they existed, and were created."[10]

MISCONCEPTIONS

There are two categories of misconceptions that we need to tackle. The first is how we understand God's *makeup*. The other is how we understand God's *purpose*. But, these two categories actually flow from the same root: being man-centred in our approach to God.

First, with regard to how we conceive of God's makeup, we tend to think God is physical and emotional like we are. We misunderstand the Bible's accommodating language to think God has body parts or God rides the same rollercoaster of emotions we do.[11] This is unhelpful. If God is spirit, then it means he does not have parts or a body. He is not made of flesh and therefore does not have eyes, ears, hands, etc. It is also true that if God is infinite in his perfections, then he does not have emotions like we do. He is steady, constant and unsurprised by anything. As creatures, our loves ebb and flow, our tempers rise and fall and our joys swell and shrink, but it is not so with God. He is made

---

10 Revelation 4:11.

11 With regard to physicality, this is generally called *anthropomorphism*, which is when the Bible describes God with human characteristics to help us understand him. With regard to the emotions, this is generally called *anthropopathism*, which is when the Bible describes God with human emotions to help us understand him.

up of perfections, and those perfections are infinite. There is no ebb and flow to God, there is no rise and fall with him and there is no swell or shrink. Whatever God is, he perfectly and infinitely is. The accommodating language of the Bible does help us to grasp and understand God by revealing him in ways we are able to comprehend.

Second, with regard to how we conceive of God's purpose, we can treat God as if he exists for us. We see ourselves at the centre of the universe. We think we are owed certain things. This, probably more than any other thing, displays our man-centred approach to God. The Bible wholly and clearly reminds us again and again that if we are to find our purpose in this life, we must gladly acknowledge that we exist for God. It is true that God is *for us*, but we must cherish this grace in balance lest we begin to believe he exists for us.

APPLICATION

Article II: God

> There is but one God, the Maker, Preserver and Ruler of all
> things, having in and of himself, all perfections, and being
> infinite in them all; and to him all creatures owe the highest
> love, reverence and obedience.

Just like the article on the Scriptures, we get application embedded in the article itself. We discover we owe God some things just because he created us. If this is truly who God is, then three things rise to the top.

1. God deserves to be first.

In a world full of things trying to grab our attention, God must take first priority. This means we reject all the false gods we create, the things that serve us and fit in our hands. In some sense, that is what it means for us to love God—for us to naturally and repeatedly find him at the top and the bottom of our affections.

2. God deserves to be feared.

He ought to inspire awe in us. We ought to step back and simply behold him. Reverence is a matter of honour and solemnity. When we fear God, we give him the gravity in our lives. His reality weighs us down. Not in a way that is debilitating, rather in a way that grounds us in the things that matter. The beginning of seeing life correctly and living life meaningfully is fearing God—the Christian God, "I AM."[12]

---

12 When the Bible tells us how important fearing God is, for example in Proverbs 1:7, "The fear of the LORD is the beginning of knowledge," it isn't asking us to fear *a* god, as if fearing *any* god will do. The reason LORD is in all caps is because that is how our English Bibles present the proper name for our God, "I AM." So, the beginning of knowledge isn't just fearing a god, it is expressing reverential awe for the "I AM" in particular.

3. *God deserves to be followed.*

Whatever God says is right and helpful. Whatever he does is good and loving. Wherever he leads is wise and best. Whatever area in our life we can conceive of—vocational, familial, recreational—we ought to be following his commands. Obeying him is both right and wise, just as disobeying him is both evil and foolish.

Let us marvel that what we owe God and what brings about the best life for us coincide, as we love, revere and obey him. What he demands of us is the best thing for us. To God be the glory, forever!

The Trinity

God is revealed to us as Father, Son and Holy Spirit, each with distinct personal attributes, but without division of nature, essence or being.

The Trinity

INTRO + OVERVIEW

I n A.D. 325, something unprecedented happened, something that up until that time could not have happened. Leaders from the global church were able, under the supervision of Emperor Constantine, to gather at Nicaea to settle some disputes regarding Jesus Christ and his relationship to God. For almost 300 years, the global church had honoured and worshipped Jesus in relative obscurity. Many Christians had been persecuted and ostracized, but most were just set aside as atheistic fools.[1] But Christianity was gaining traction, and it was about to explode.

The main dispute had to do with the teachings of a pastor in Alexandria named Arius. Arius was not the first person to believe or teach what he did, but he was the first to have his ideas brought before an ecumenical council.[2] The whole Christian world was seeking to clarify how the faith could maintain its monotheism, while at the same time worshipping God as God and Jesus as God. For example, the last article we looked at on God says, "There is but one God, the Maker, Preserver and Ruler of all things." How can this be true, while at the same time Christians worship God, Jesus and the Holy Spirit?

The answer Arius gave was essentially that Jesus was *like* God, but he was not the same as God. He believed Jesus was to be reverenced since he was the first creature, but only God could be truly God. The dispute centred over the question of whether or not Jesus was eternal.

There is some helpful terminology that came from Nicaea which helps gets to the heart of the debate. Arius taught that Jesus was of similar *substance* to the Father God. The word in Greek that Arius put

---

1   Yes, many early Christians were labelled *atheists* because they did not worship "the gods."

2   A *council* is the name given to an official meeting of church leaders from the global church.

forward to describe this relationship was, *homoiousious*. We can see by the language of the Nicene Creed, the document put together by the ecumenical council, that the global church did not side with Arius. They tell us that Jesus is *homoousious* with the Father, meaning that he is the exact same substance. These words are extremely close to one another! Just a few minor changes make the difference. But, when we are talking about God, it matters that we speak about him and believe in him with precision. The global church declared that Jesus was in fact eternally co-equal with God. And they did it using the language of the Bible.

While the dispute at Nicaea mainly revolved around the relationship between Jesus and the Father, a few years later the Cappadocian Fathers[3] began arguing for the necessity to clarify the divinity of the Holy Spirit along with the Father and the Son. In A.D. 381, the second ecumenical council met in Constantinople. After this council, the Nicene Creed was further clarified and this is how it reads:

> We believe in one God, the Father,
> the Almighty, maker of heaven and earth,
> of all that is, seen and unseen.

> We believe in one Lord, Jesus Christ, the only Son of God,
> eternally begotten of the Father,
> God from God, Light from Light, true God from true God,
> begotten, not made, of one substance with the Father.
> Through him all things were made.
> For us men and for our salvation he came down from heaven;
> by the power of the Holy Spirit
> he became incarnate of the virgin Mary,
> and was made man.
> For our sake he was crucified under Pontius Pilate;
> he suffered death and was buried.
> On the third day he rose again in accordance with the Scriptures;
> he ascended into heaven and is seated
> at the right hand of the Father.

---

3   Basil the Great, Gregory of Nyssa and Gregory of Nazianzus.

He will come again in glory to judge the living and the dead,
and his kingdom will have no end.

We believe in the Holy Spirit, the Lord, the giver of life,
who proceeds from the Father and the Son.
With the Father and the Son he is worshiped and glorified.
He has spoken through the prophets.
We believe in one holy catholic and apostolic Church.
We acknowledge one baptism for the forgiveness of sins.
We look for the resurrection of the dead,
and the life of the world to come.
Amen.

A few things stand out about this creed.[4] First, is the way each person of the Godhead receives his own section. Second, is how much of the language is biblical language. Third, is how (like other early statements of Christianity) it is both a mixture of history ("incarnate of the virgin Mary," "crucified under Pontius Pilate," etc.) and doctrine ("God from God, Light from Light, true God from true God, begotten, not made, of one substance with the Father"). And finally and most importantly, it emphatically and clearly teaches that God is One, and yet he is Three.

It is in the last section that things are made clear—the Holy Spirit, "with the Father and the Son he is worshiped and glorified." There is no subordination in God. There is no "tiering." There is simply one God who exists in three persons.

The reason the language of Nicaea is so important is it explains to us how God is *triune*. We worship and glorify each of these three persons as the one God because they all, and they alone, share *the same substance*. All we said about God in Article II is true of each of these persons and makes them together one God. If there is a person who has all perfections in and of himself, and that being is infinite in all of those perfections, then that person is God—there are three persons of whom this is true, which means they together are one God. This means whatever is true in nature, being and essence of the Father is also true of the Son and is true of the Spirit. This one God has one will, one mind and one work.

---

4 *Creed* is from the Latin *credo*, meaning *I believe*.

The best way for us to understand how God relates within himself, is to consider how each person relates to the other. For example, the Father is the Father because he has a Son. He has always had a Son and this Son has eternally enjoyed his life with and from his Father. The Son is a Son because he has a Father. He has always proceeded forth from the Father, and has always been enjoying life in the Father. The Spirit, like the Son also proceeds out of the Father, but he comes out of the Father and the Son. He is both the Spirit of the Father and the Spirit of the Son. He is the bond of unity between the Father and the Son. Ultimately, this means *God is love.* It means God, the one God, is a community within himself. There is no God without each person as they together make up the one God, since they, and they alone, possess the divine nature.[5]

While some of this technical language may seem a little mind numbing (or mind blowing!), we should remember that this God is only known *by revelation*—no one could have made this up! Also, because God is God, there will always be divine mystery. If we could fully comprehend him, would he really be God? We must remember, we can know God *truly,* even if we cannot understand him *fully.*

SCRIPTURAL FOUNDATIONS

Genesis 1:26-27

Then God said, "Let Us make mankind in Our image, according to Our likeness; and let them rule over the fish of the sea and over the birds of the sky and over the livestock and over all the earth, and over every crawling thing that crawls on the earth." So God created man in His own image, in the image of God He created him; male and female He created them.

---

5 For a very accessible and helpful resource on the doctrine of the Trinity and its doctrinal formulation, see Justin S. Holcomb, *Know the Creeds and Councils* (Grand Rapids: Zondervan Academic, 2014).

While this is no slam dunk proof for the doctrine of the Trinity, it does however point us to the fact that from the very first chapter of the Bible God is revealing himself in some type of multiplicity. He calls himself an, "Us." It makes no sense why God would be speaking of himself in this way unless there is some type of community within himself.

Isaiah 9:6-7

> For a Child will be born to us, a Son will be given to us;
> And the government will rest on His shoulders;
> And His name will be called Wonderful Counselor, Mighty God,
> Eternal Father, Prince of Peace.
> There will be no end to the increase of *His* government or of peace
> On the throne of David and over his kingdom,
> To establish it and to uphold it with justice and righteousness
> From then on and forevermore.
> The zeal of the LORD of armies will accomplish this.

This text is a prophecy. It speaks of a child, someone who will come into the world. The names of this child are staggering. And none more staggering than, "Mighty God." We know from other Scriptures that God is very jealous for his name. We also know at this point that there is only one God. And yet, here is a Son being given to us who is God. Again, this is not a formula of the triune God by any means. But, at the least, it shows the Trinity is not a New Testament invention.

Matthew 3:13-17

> Then Jesus arrived from Galilee at the Jordan, *coming* to John to be baptized by him. But John tried to prevent Him, saying, "I have *the* need to be baptized by You, and *yet* You are coming to me?" But Jesus, answering, said to him, "Allow *it* at this time; for in this way it is fitting for us to fulfill all righteousness." Then he allowed Him. After He was baptized, Jesus came up immediately from the water; and behold, the heavens were opened, and he saw the Spirit of God descending as a dove *and* settling on Him, and behold, a voice from the heavens said, "This is My beloved Son, with whom I am well pleased."

Here, at the beginning of the New Testament, we witness a holy scene. It is the baptism of Jesus. As Jesus comes up from the water, the Spirit of God descends and the voice of God speaks from heaven. And this voice is the voice of a Father. In this moment, we see Father, Son and Spirit in one location, each partaking of the divine nature, yet existing as three distinct persons. There is no division of will, mind or activity, but there is community within God himself.

Matthew 28:16–20

> But the eleven disciples proceeded to Galilee, to the mountain which Jesus had designated to them. And when they saw Him, they worshiped *Him*; but some were doubtful. And Jesus came up and spoke to them, saying, "All authority in heaven and on earth has been given to Me. Go, therefore, and make disciples of all the nations, baptizing them in the name of the Father and the Son and the Holy Spirit, teaching them to follow all that I commanded you; and behold, I am with you always, to the end of the age."

Here, at the end of the same book, we get another glimpse of the importance of the Trinity. The resurrected Jesus is about to ascend and return to the Father as the triumphant Lord of history. Before he leaves his disciples, he gives them some last instructions and encouragement. As they go to make more disciples of Jesus, they are to follow specific commands. One is that when a person is made a disciple of Jesus, they should be baptized, just like Jesus was. They are to identify with him and with his people in this way. But, Jesus is clear—this baptism is not just a Jesus baptism, this is a *triune* baptism. When a person becomes a disciple of Jesus, they become a worshipper of the one triune God. That is why a new Christian is baptized, "in the name of the Father and the Son and the Holy Spirit."

We should notice two important things about this command. Jesus does not say to baptize in, "the *names* Father, Son and Spirit." That might indicate that God is simply one person with three names, like Wonderful Counselor, Mighty God, Eternal Father, Prince of Peace. But, Jesus also does not tell them to baptize in, "the name of the Father, and in the name of the Son, and in the name of the Holy Spirit." That might indicate that these three different people are separated out with no singular essence. What Jesus is actually teaching us is there is a God who's name is "I AM," and his name belongs to three different people. When we baptize people, "in the name of the Father and the Son and the Holy Spirit," we are baptizing them into life with the *one* God, "I AM," who shares his name with three persons—the Father, the Son and the Holy Spirit.

Romans 8:9–11

> However, you are not in the flesh but in the Spirit, if indeed the Spirit of God dwells in you. But if anyone does not have the Spirit of Christ, he does not belong to Him. If Christ is in you, though the body is dead because of sin, yet the spirit is alive because of righteousness. But if the Spirit of Him who raised Jesus from the dead dwells in you, He who raised Christ Jesus from the dead will also give life to your mortal bodies through His Spirit who dwells in you.

At first glance, it may not appear why this Scripture would be chosen as a proof for the tri-unity of God. However, many of the Scriptures that have traditionally been chosen follow the same script as the first ecumenical council at Nicaea—they major mostly on the biblical witness to the fact that Jesus and the Father are one.[6] This is why there was a need to follow up Nicaea with the second council at Constantinople to affirm the full divinity and personhood of the Holy Spirit.

In this passage, we see three important things about the Holy Spirit. First, we see that he is the Spirit of God. It is the Spirit of God—God's Spirit—who removes us from being in the flesh, and puts us in the Spirit. Second, we see that this same Spirit of God is also the Spirit of Christ. God's Spirit is Christ's Spirit. In fact, if the Spirit of God resides in a person, then *Christ* is in that person. Now, maybe we think this only shows us that the Father is God and Christ is God, but the Spirit is no person at all. However, here and in many other passages, the Spirit of God is referred to with the personal pronoun, "he." It is, "He who raised Christ Jesus," who "will give life to [the] mortal bodies" of those who are in Christ Jesus. The Spirit is not an impersonal power

---

6   See the overwhelming way in which the Gospel of John argues for this, especially in chapters 1,5,10 and 14.

or force flowing from God. The Spirit is a person who is co-equal and co-substantial with the Father and the Son.

Ephesians 1:3–6, 13–14

> Blessed be the God and Father of our Lord Jesus Christ, who has blessed us with every spiritual blessing in the heavenly *places* in Christ, just as He chose us in Him before the foundation of the world, that we would be holy and blameless before Him. In love He predestined us to adoption as sons *and daughters* through Jesus Christ to Himself, according to the good pleasure of His will, to the praise of the glory of His grace, with which He favored us in the Beloved.... In Him, you also, after listening to the message of truth, the gospel of your salvation—having also believed, you were sealed in Him with the Holy Spirit of the promise, who is a first installment of our inheritance, in regard to the redemption of *God's own* possession, to the praise of His glory.

From beginning to end, it is God who works together for our salvation. The Father, the Son and the Spirit are fully involved in redemption. God the Father chooses us for salvation before the foundation of the world, and his choice is in Christ. It is through the life and work of Jesus that we are adopted by the Father. The Spirit applies the work of Christ to us in accordance with the choice of the Father. This is God, in the fullness of his tri-unity working together to redeem fallen humanity. Hallelujah!

EXPLANATION

"God is revealed to us..."

Who we know God to be has *only* come to us by way of revelation. God is "other" in substance, and there is no way we would know him in his tri-unity other than by revelation. We should relate to and enjoy God in the way he has revealed himself to us because any other conception of God is founded on the imaginations of men and women.

"as Father..."

This God has revealed himself to us in the person of the Father. We know the Father as one who has a Son. We know the Father as the source of all life. We know the Father as the giver of all good gifts. He is Father, first in relation to the Son, but he is also Father to us, since we all find our origin in him.

"Son..."

This God has revealed himself to us in the person of the Son. We know the Son as one who has a Father. We look to him especially as Saviour, knowing that for us and for our salvation he took on flesh. Only the Son was made man. Only the Son was crucified and raised to redeem us. As the Son of the Father, Jesus is who we look to as our brother. He has the rights of the firstborn, and through faith in him, we are adopted by the Father and share in the inheritance of the Son.

"and Holy Spirit, ..."

This God has revealed himself to us in the person of the Spirit. We know the Spirit as the Spirit of the Father and the Son. He is the bond of unity between the Father and the Son. We recognize him as the one who unites us to Christ so that we receive all Christ has done for us in redemption. So while Jesus accomplished salvation objectively, the Spirit applies his accomplishment subjectively.

"each with distinct personal attributes..."

There is real distinction between these three persons. They are not synonymous with one another, and yet, each is the same one God—not three gods, but one. So we must be careful about how we talk about what distinguishes the persons and what unites the persons. Since there is no analogy for the triune God, it is better to speak of him as he has revealed himself, instead of trying to use illustrations or parallels. The Christian God has no valid parallel.

"but without division of nature, essence or being."

Whatever we say about the distinct persons, we must guard any division in God. God is one, which includes *what* he is, *how* he is and *who* he is. His substance, his mode of existence and his total life is indivisible. It is not possible for the Son to be cut away from God. It is not possible for the Father to possess different perfections than the Son. It is not possible for the Spirit to execute plans contrary to the Father's heart. We worship one God in three persons, not because it is easy or obvious, but because that is who God has revealed himself to be.

MISCONCEPTIONS

To get at the misconceptions related to the Trinity, we will look at a number of "isms." There are, in fact, endless ways to believe in a false god. But specifically with regard to the Christian God, there have been a few misconceptions, whether on a popular level or a more academic level, that have been very prevalent.

The first comes in different degrees and with different names, but we will call it *dualism*. This idea is that the God of the Old Testament and the God of the New Testament are two *different* gods. We might say, "The 'I AM' God seems so mean, but Jesus seems so nice." Or we might say, "The Old Testament seems so harsh and the New Testament seems so pleasant."

The main problem with this view is that the Old Testament has very wonderful expressions of God's love, and the New Testament has very striking expressions of God's judgment. It almost seems if we decide to take this approach to the Bible then we show we haven't really read it at all. After all, it is in the New Testament where we see God's Son put to death in such gruesome detail—and that according to God's predestined plan. And yet, no one took his life from him. Rather, Jesus *offered it up* as a sacrifice for sinners.[7] The *unity* of the Bible is one of the things that makes it so compelling, as we behold God the Father, God the Son and God the Holy Spirit working together to save men and women from their sins and reconcile them to himself.

The second misconception we will call *modalism*. Modalism is the idea that there is one God who is the Father, and the Son and the Spirit, but not as three *individual persons*. This God is *uni*-personal. He does not exist as three *distinct* persons, but as three *modes* of operation.

---

7   John 10:18.

The Bible, especially the Gospels, show this perspective is impossible. We see Jesus praying to the Father. We see the Spirit descending upon Jesus. We experience the "he" and "him" and "we" in the text, which pushes beyond mere modes of operation, to persons of relation. It is God as he reveals himself at work in history that forces us to acknowledge his tri-unity.

The third misconception we need to be aware of is *subordinationism*. This is any view which places the persons of God in some kind of ascending or descending order with regard to glory, power or reverence. It is true that the Son and the Spirit are proceeding. However this procession is eternal. So, while the Son is begotten of the Father, He is *eternally* begotten. In other words, there is no sense in which the Son is less than the Father in glory, power or reverence. If, for example, the Son was not of the Father, then the Father would cease to be. We should be careful when we say things like, "Jesus is the second member of the Trinity." By "second," we in no way mean inferior. There is no greater or lesser in an eternal Being, even if one member finds its life source in the other, since there was never a time when this life was not present.

The fourth misconception is *adoptionism*. This idea is that Jesus only became God's Son by virtue of his life on earth. It does not view Jesus as the *eternal* Son. This view would see a moment like the baptism of Jesus or the resurrection of Jesus as the beginning of the sonship of Christ. The reason this is confusing is, in some sense, Jesus did become God's Son in a new way in the incarnation. He became God's Son according to the flesh. Just as Adam was God's first son according to the flesh, Jesus is the second Adam—God's Son according to the flesh. This however, does not account for the clear witness that God brought his Son into the world. The pre-existent Son, came into the world, not to *become* the Son, but because he *was* the Son.

The final misconception we should address is *spiritualism*. This view treats the Holy Spirit as a *force* and not a person. This, especially on a popular level, is extremely prevalent. The Holy Spirit is a "he" not an "it." The Holy Spirit is a person to whom we can relate, not a power we can tap into. Certainly, all spiritual power comes from him to the believer, but it is because of his presence and at his will.

APPLICATION

Article III: The Trinity

God is revealed to us as Father, Son and Holy Spirit, each with distinct personal attributes, but without division of nature, essence or being.

---

1. ### *We should enjoy God in the fulness of his persons.*
   Today and every day we should enjoy God in the fulness of his persons. We relate to the Father as our Father. We relate to Jesus as our Brother. We relate to the Spirit as our Helper. We receive the gifts that come from each of them to us, and we respond to those gifts in appropriate ways to each of them. This is how we worship the one God—how we have communion/communication with the one God.

   For example, we enjoy being adopted by the Father. This adoption means we are his sons and daughters. As his children, we can respond to him in obedience, thanksgiving and love.

   We also enjoy being redeemed by the Son. Redemption means we have been bought with Jesus' own blood. We respond to him by trusting in his salvation work on our behalf and by living lives worthy of his sacrifice.

   We also enjoy being empowered by the communion of the Spirit. The communion of the Spirit means God has gifted us to serve and renewed us to live. We respond to the Spirit by faithfully witnessing to the gospel in his power, living holy lives and using the gifts he has given us to serve his church.

   This is what it means to have a relationship with God. We know the one true God by receiving from each person what they communicate to us, and by responding in ways that communicate our love, obedience and delight in return. Our Christian life and our relationship with God must be a tri-personal relationship.

2. ### *Life is meant to be lived in community.*
   Christianity, with its emphasis of one God in three persons, gives us

a framework for understanding life. Life is meant to be lived in relationship. The eternal God is an eternal community. Therefore, we cannot take lightly our own calling to live in relationship with this God and in relationship with one another. And we cannot take lightly our calling to be "diligent to preserve the unity of the Spirit in the bond of peace"[8] within the church.

---

8   Ephesians 4:3.

IV

—

Providence

God from eternity, decrees or permits all things that come to pass, and perpetually upholds, directs and governs all creatures and all events; yet so as not in any way to be the author or approver of sin nor to destroy the free will and responsibility of intelligent creatures.

Providence

INTRO + OVERVIEW

One of the most interesting books of the Bible is the book of Esther. The most intriguing aspect of the book is that God is not mentioned by name. And yet, Esther is in no way a godless book. The story presents for us real life—life governed by an invisible God, life upheld and carried along by a God we must receive by faith. Looking at some of the major plot points in Esther leads us to the conclusion that God is intimately involved in the everyday affairs of life, guiding all things according to his purposes and his decreed ends.

One of the exciting things about the book of Esther is that while God is not mentioned, we see that a robust view of providence actually *leads to* courageous action—and not the other way around. The Christian view of providence is not fate or fatalism. Rather, since God decrees or permits all things that come to pass, we can actually have certainty about the outcome of history. And this can propel us to join in on what God is doing in the world.

In Esther 4, we see this play out. Up to this point in the story, we have learned Esther is one of the women chosen to be a wife to King Ahasuerus. Her uncle Mordecai has realized that unless Esther steps in, all the Jews are going to be wiped out. Esther is afraid because no one is allowed to go into the king's presence unless they are invited. And this is where we dive in:

> Then Mordecai told *them* to reply to Esther, "Do not imagine that you in the king's palace can escape any more than all the *other* Jews. For if you keep silent at this time, liberation and rescue will arise for the Jews from another place, and you and your father's house will perish. And who knows whether you have not attained royalty for such a time as this?" (Esther 4:13-14).

Now, much has been written about those famous words, "for such a time as this," but what I want us to focus on is the way Mordecai is processing life. He is telling Esther that if she doesn't do this, then she is going to die. But because he knows God's plan, Mordecai doesn't believe the salvation of the Jews is totally dependent on Esther. He knows that if Esther isn't the person for the job, then deliverance will arise in some other way. He is sure of it! He knows where history is headed and he knows God is sovereign over it all. It is from this settled certainty about the future that Mordecai and Esther are emboldened to make a courageous move on behalf of God's people.

And look at the way Esther responds:

> Go, gather all the Jews who are found in Susa, and fast for me; do not eat or drink for three days, night or day. I and my attendants also will fast in the same way. And then I will go in to the king, which is not in accordance with the law; and if I perish, I perish (Esther 4:15–16)

The providence of God, the truth that God is moving history forward by his own governance and direction, ignites in Esther a new courage. But, this does not exclude real human responses like risk, persuasion, fasting and praying. This is a story about the way providence feels. It feels a lot like real life, just more daring, more courageous and more certain about the ultimate outcome of life. God was absolutely at work, but in an interesting way, he was giving his people the courage to work through ordinary means to accomplish what would be an impossible result without him.

Notice neither Mordecai nor Esther actually mention God. God is, in some sense, taken for granted. But not in the negative sense of taking for granted. If the entire Bible was this way, then we would be in trouble. But in this one biblical narrative, God being taken for granted means they process life through God-coloured glasses. And this is how we interact with providence. While to us things seem to be hanging in the balance, and life feels like a string of decisions that change the course of history, providence reminds us that God's plan is being worked out in the world. Knowing God is, most of the time very quietly, working through the events of human history and carrying forward *his* plan, has the ability to give us deep certainty and courage.

It is important to come at providence from an "on the streets" perspective, but it is also important to ground the *feeling* of providence in the *theory* of providence. Providence is happening whether we know it or not, but if we know it, then we can feel it.

We turn now to ask, how does the Christian doctrine of providence situate itself among many of the other common theories?[1]

Natural view

One option for a view of the movement of the history of the world is the *natural view*. Many of the proponents of this view would hold to the theory of scientific evolution. A hard evolutionistic perspective[2] leads to a view of history with no origin and no final goal. What we experience simply is, and there is nothing beyond it. There is no end and there is no beginning. Everything is by chance and yet nothing is by chance. In this view, human beings are soul-less, and life is transcendent-less.

The Christian Scriptures completely contradict this view. The Bible, even in its very literary form, presents both an origin in its first book, Genesis, and a goal in its last book, Revelation. The Bible says *God* simply is, and that everything else has been made by him. God clearly sets forth a world where human beings have souls, where both body and soul will last forever, and where the world is full of meaning, purpose and value.

Destiny

A second option for a view of the movement of history is that of *destiny*. People who hold to this view may believe there is some sort of higher

---

1   It becomes clear that where someone lands with regard to Article II on God, will inevitably dictate their answer to the big questions of life like we are discussing here in Article IV. We should notice a connection between the options we have for how to conceive of God and the options we have for how to conceive of the movement of history.

2   The reason why I qualify evolution in this way is there have been some attempts to reconcile scientific evolution with the biblical data. This view has been called *theistic evolution*. Theistic evolution teaches that what science has discovered through its searching, observing, categorizing and evaluating of reality, is compatible with the Bible and God was involved in carrying along the evolutionary process. Some prominent evangelical theologians hold this view, while others stand firm against it.

power or supernatural force, but they certainly do not believe in a personal God. Some of the concepts that relate to this view are *fate* and *karma*. While each of these terms has its own religious origins and nuances, they essentially represent a similar perspective. Life is given meaning, but there is no personal God to whom we attribute this meaning.

There are some sympathetic aspects in these perspectives. For example, the Bible does teach the principle that we reap what we sow. In other words, there is a certain measure of truth to the fact that what goes around comes around. But the Bible never presents this as some kind of impersonal formula. Rather, the Bible puts this in the context of both the role of wisdom[3] and the fact of God's justice—God will not be mocked.

Another sympathetic aspect of this view is the reality that there is a pre-determined plan for all of life. Again, the only problem is that when we remove the loving care and wisdom of a personal God, we miss the fact it is *God* who is planning and working. Without God in the picture, we run the risk of being brought to despair when we see that wrongs may not be made right and the pain and suffering we experience is purposeless.

A final aspect of this view that we might be sympathetic toward is the desire for purpose and meaning. This view, at least over against a natural perspective, acknowledges some sort of goal or purpose to our existence. However, dislodged from the God of the Bible, purpose becomes some sort of vague personal fulfilment with no real anchor. Only the Bible offers real meaning and purpose—anchored in God himself.

Reactive view/open theism

A third option for how a person might think of the movement of history is the *reactive view*. While this view does not conceive of life

---

3 Wisdom could be seen as knowing what to do in the grey areas of life. That is why it is a false step to think the Bible teaches fate or karma. Wisdom says, you will probably get out of life what you put into it. But, it is wisdom talking because it is not a black and white formula. Many people get more out of life than what they put in and many others get far less. God wants us to use wisdom, but we can't use his wisdom against him when life doesn't go the way we thought it might. Again, that is why it is called wisdom and not certainty.

as natural, it also does not offer an end or purpose toward which history is moving. Some call this view *open theism*. In this conception, God is involved in the world, but only as an actor—just like all the other free agents whom he has created. God is not moving history toward a specific goal, and he has not planned or decreed anything that will happen. He is simply sitting back, watching and responding to what he sees.

The main problem with this view, is that it sets God and creation on the same level. God is too much like us. The Bible emphasizes that we are like God, but not that God is like us. In an attempt to give the created order freedom, God's own governing freedom is stripped from him. In this view, everyone is free except for God—he is bound to our decisions and our innovations.

Now, as we move toward our fourth and fifth option, we must recognize that these two are close to the biblical position. However, each of these options overemphasizes itself to the exclusion of the biblical data which reflects its opposite.

Forward looking view

The fourth option for how history is moving forward is the *forward looking view*. This perspective highlights the foreknowledge of God. Foreknowledge becomes the explanation for how God can speak in the Bible about a plan and a goal of history without impeding on the freedom of creation. So, it is not that God is sitting back and waiting to see what will happen in time, rather, he has created his plan based on what will happen in the future.

While the Bible clearly teaches God knows everything that will happen before it happens, this view does not recognize God as the decisive sovereign, rather than the forward-looking executive. Many passages teach that God's plan and his will in the world is not based on any outside counsel. God's plan is *effective*, not reactive.

Puppet master view

A fifth option is the *puppet master view*. This view of history emphasizes God's sovereignty to the extreme. People who hold this view would be outraged by the idea that God's sovereignty can even be conceived of in "extreme" measures, since they believe nothing happens for which God is not responsible. Human choice is a myth, and God is simply pulling levers and strings, like a puppet show where his will is the only cause at work.

Now, as we will see below, the Christian view of providence does in fact teach that God upholds, directs and governs all creatures and events. But, the main problem with the puppet master view is that it removes God's sovereignty out of its relational context of foreknowledge. Foreknowledge, after all, is not so much about God's ability to see the future as it is about God's desire to know and love his people. This view sees life and the movement of history as unbiblically rigid, all the while portraying God as cold and detached rather than warm and fatherly.

It is important to note, just like the word *Trinity*, the word *providence* is not used in the Bible. However, this does not mean the *concept* is not biblical. In theology, we try to find the best way to synthesize and summarize what the Bible teaches and the word *providence* is an excellent term to describe the way God is moving history forward.

SCRIPTURAL FOUNDATIONS

Genesis 50:15-21

When Joseph's brothers had seen that their father was dead, they said, "What if Joseph holds a grudge against us and pays us back in full for all the wrong which we did to him!" So they sent instructions to Joseph, saying, "Your father commanded *us* before he died, saying, 'This is what you shall say to Joseph: "Please forgive, I beg you, the offense of your brothers and their sin, for they did you wrong."' And now, please forgive the offense of the servants of the God of your father." And Joseph wept when they spoke to him. Then his brothers also came and fell down before him and said, "Behold, we are your servants." But Joseph said to them, "Do not be afraid, for am I in God's place? As for you, you meant evil against me, *but* God meant it for good in order to bring about this present result, to keep many people alive. So therefore, do not be afraid; I will provide for you and your little ones." So he comforted them and spoke kindly to them.

The book of Genesis is jam-packed with wonderful stories that give us categories for understanding life in God's world. One of the longest of these stories—the narrative revolving around the life of Joseph—spans roughly fifteen chapters. The condensed version of the story is that Joseph had dreams in which he would one day rule over his family. When Joseph relayed his dreams to his brothers, they hated him. They hated him enough to sell him off into slavery. At this point, it seems Joseph's life is a great tragedy. However, later in the narrative we realize Joseph was actually being sent ahead of his brothers into Egypt so he could be instrumental in saving them from a famine.

The story is wild and winding. Joseph is up, and then he is down. He is shown favour and then he is forgotten. The story climaxes when Joseph is given the opportunity to serve Pharaoh by doing for him something only God could do: interpret Pharaoh's weird dream about fat and skinny cows and the coming famine. In the end, Joseph is placed in just the right position to save both Egypt and his own family, those who had betrayed him and sold him into slavery in the first place.

Like Esther, but in some ways more explicitly, Genesis portrays God's providence as *all encompassing*. Even the terrible things that happened to Joseph were part of God's direction and governance. If Joseph had not been sent to Egypt, his family would have died and the Messianic line[4] would have died off with them. God was working out his purposes in a way that no one could have ever known, and that is the most exciting thing about providence. That is why the mature and godly Joseph is able to see that man's responsibility and God's sovereignty are not mutually exclusive. Surely, his brothers meant what they did for evil, but just as surely, God meant what his brothers did for good. None of the alternative views identified in the last section would do justice to the wonder and wisdom displayed by God throughout these chapters at the end of Genesis.

Psalm 139:1–6,13–16

LORD, You have searched me and known *me*.
You know when I sit down and when I get up;

---

4   The promised Saviour, Jesus, is a descendant of Joseph's brother Judah.

You understand my thought from far away.
You scrutinize my path and my lying down,
And are acquainted with all my ways.
Even before there is a word on my tongue,
Behold, LORD, You know it all.
You have encircled me behind and in front,
And placed Your hand upon me.
Such knowledge is too wonderful for me;
It is *too* high, I cannot comprehend it....

For You created my innermost parts;
You wove me in my mother's womb.
I will give thanks to You, because I am awesomely and wonderfully *made*;
Wonderful are Your works,
And my soul knows it very well.
My frame was not hidden from You
When I was made in secret,
And skillfully formed in the depths of the earth;
Your eyes have seen my formless substance;
And in Your book were written
All the days that were ordained *for me*,
When as yet there was not one of them.

No Scripture weaves together the importance of foreknowledge and sovereignty within the context of relationship better than Psalm 139. On the one hand, David is known intimately by God, and that from his mother's womb, intimating foreknowledge (knowing relationally, before). On the other hand, all of David's words are known by God before he ever speaks them, which displays the more popular view of foreknowledge (knowing historically, before). But lest we think this supports a mere forward looking approach, we learn that God has a book, and in that book he had ordained or decreed all the days of David's life. God cannot be a puppet master because he cares too much about knowing and being known, and at the same time he cannot merely be forward looking because he orders, numbers and decrees our days.

Proverbs 16:9,33

> The mind of a person plans his way,
> But the LORD directs his steps....
>
> The lot is cast into the lap,
> But its every decision is from the LORD.

In Proverbs 16, we get two pithy statements about how life really works. These two verses reveal how God is ultimately the only free and decisive actor in the universe. He must be so, because he alone is God. He alone is independent and everything else depends on him. The key word here is *ultimately*. We are in control of the plans of our mind, and we are in control of casting the lot, but God is ultimately and decisively upholding, directing and governing all things. While my choices matter, God's choices matter *more*—while my will is real, God's will is *effective*. Much like the doctrine of the Trinity, there is mystery as to how all of this works out on a philosophical level. But we should never allow *mystery* to keep us from affirming what the Bible clearly says.

Matthew 6:25-34

> "For this reason I say to you, do not be worried about your life, as to what you will eat or what you will drink; nor for your body, *as to* what you will put on. Is life not more than food, and the body more than clothing? Look at the birds of the sky, that they do not sow, nor reap, nor gather *crops* into barns, and *yet* your heavenly Father feeds them. Are you not much more important than they? And which of you by worrying can add a single day to his life's span? And why are you worried about clothing? Notice how the lilies of the field grow; they do not labor nor do they spin *thread for cloth*, yet I say to you that not even Solomon in all his glory clothed himself like one of these. But if God so clothes the grass of the field, which is *alive* today and tomorrow is thrown into the furnace, *will He* not much more *clothe* you? You of little faith! Do not worry then, saying, 'What are we to eat?' or 'What are we to drink?' or 'What are we to wear for clothing?' For the Gentiles eagerly seek all these things; for your heavenly

Father knows that you need all these things. But seek first His kingdom
and His righteousness, and all these things will be provided to you.

"So do not worry about tomorrow; for tomorrow will worry about
itself. Each day has enough trouble of its own."

Jesus explains here how God is intimately involved in the very details
of our lives. He is involved in the lives of birds and lilies, and he keeps
an eye on his people. This passage reveals the importance of believing
in the providence of God. It is the loving and attentive care of God that
sends our anxieties away. People who do not have this view of the
movement of history (called *Gentiles*[5] in this Scripture) are left on their
own to try to provide for themselves. The Christian, however, can
bank their lives on this promise: since God upholds, directs and
governs all things, we can wholeheartedly seek God's kingdom and
his righteousness and trust in his provision for all our needs.

Acts 4:27-28

For truly in this city there were gathered together against Your holy
servant Jesus, whom You anointed, both Herod and Pontius Pilate,
along with the Gentiles and the peoples of Israel, to do whatever Your
hand and purpose predestined to occur.

One tough but precious truth is that God's providence extends even
over suffering. Again, there is mystery about how this practically and
philosophically works out, but biblically we can and should affirm
that God is over all things. We have already looked at the story of
Joseph, how his brothers meant something for evil, while simultaneously God meant the same thing for good. But, if we need more
biblical help for coming to terms with life in this way, we can turn to
the cross of Jesus Christ.

The cross of Jesus Christ is at the same time the worst event in the
history of the universe *and* the most wonderful event in the history of
the universe. In Acts 4, the apostles begin praying to God, and they
attribute God as the ultimate cause behind the events of the cross. The

---

5 *Gentiles* technically means any person who is not of Jewish decent. During the
time of the writing of Matthew's Gospel, *Gentile* was synonymous to a non-believer
or a lost person.

Jews, Herod and Pilate are all culpable in the death of Jesus, but at the same time, according to the providence of God, it was God's hand and his purpose that had predetermined the cross to come about. This is both difficult to hear *and* comforting to hear. God is intimately and relationally involved in the details of our lives, and not just the good details. We can be comforted in knowing God is carrying out his wonderful and wise plan, even in and through our greatest suffering.

Romans 8:28-30

> And we know that God causes all things to work together for good to those who love God, to those who are called according to *His* purpose. For those whom He foreknew, He also predestined *to become* conformed to the image of His Son, so that He would be the firstborn among many brothers *and sisters*; and these whom He predestined, He also called; and these whom He called, He also justified; and these whom He justified, He also glorified.

This is probably the most famous text on the Christian doctrine of providence. It is all encompassing, it is relationally driven, it is hope filling and it is purpose explaining. It is places like this in the Bible, where God takes the general doctrine of providence and aims it at our hearts. We are not ignorant of God's ultimate purposes. We may not know the details, and we cannot predict exactly how God will choose to uphold, govern and direct the events of our lives, but we can know God's heart is for us. God's heart is to have a people who are found in Christ Jesus, who are conformed to the image of Christ Jesus and who participate in the glory of Christ Jesus. And God doesn't leave this up to chance. He is causing and working and willing his heart into reality; in fact, it is as good as done.

EXPLANATION

"God from eternity..."
The doctrine of providence is rooted in the doctrine of God. All of the other options we previously looked at stem from a misconception

about who God is. A world with no god is a world where history is natural and moves forward by chance. A world with many gods is a world where history is wide open. A world with an impersonal god is a world where history is slave to harsh fate, rigid karma or a cold dictator. A world with a god who is just like us, is a world where the weight of history is on our shoulders, a world where freedom is actually slavery. The Christian view of providence starts with the Christian view of God—transcendent and immanent, personal and eternal.

"decrees or permits all things that come to pass, …"

This personal and eternal God is never caught off guard by anything whatsoever that happens in our world. Everything comes from his mind and passes through his hand. He is totally sovereign. There is no possibility for history to get away from him, or for his goals and purposes to be thwarted. We can be sure that nothing in life is an accident.

"and perpetually upholds, directs and governs…"

The decree and permission of God does not make him distant or cold. It is not that he spoke once, back in eternity, and then walked away. God could not walk away from our universe without it ceasing to exist. In that sense, God is ever and always upholding it. It is *his* power, *his* decision and *his* grace that keeps things from falling apart and deteriorating. God has *purpose*. In that sense, he is ever and always directing. He is a gentle but firm conductor pressing forward all of life toward his wise and wonderful desires. God is seated on his throne. In that sense, he is calmly and totally in control. He is not worried and he is not scurried. He is just and he is gracious, which means his governance is always and only good.

"all creatures and all events; …"

There is nothing outside his upholding, directing and governing care. All people, animals, insects and plants, and all government elections, job interviews and hospital rooms belong to his decree and permission. What seems to be chaos is under control. What appears to be deformity is in his care.

"yet so as not in any way to be the author or approver of sin…"

One very important thing we must note about providence is the mystery of it means while God is over sin and he uses sin (i.e. Joseph, Jesus, etc.), he is neither responsible for sin nor excited about sin. In other words, human beings are responsible for their own sin and, even if sin in some way is used by God to further his plan (i.e., the cross of Jesus Christ), that in no way deems the sin itself as agreeable to God. Sin is naturally repulsive and contradictory to God; therefore, it would be impossible for sin to have originated *from* him or to find delight in him.

"nor to destroy the free will and responsibility of intelligent creatures."

We must always seek to be biblical. We must take the Bible at its word up to the boundaries of its conclusions and then be willing to shut our mouths beyond those boundaries. So, while the Bible does not give the practical or philosophical explanation for *how* God can be over sin but not responsible for sin, it clearly teaches that God is sovereign over all things *and* that men and women are morally responsible for their own choices. Although God decrees or permits all things, it does not mean human beings do not make choices or have free will.[6] God is moving history toward *his* purposes and pleasure, but he is using all sorts of means, including the choices of people, to accomplish his wise and wonderful plan.

MISCONCEPTIONS

One of the most practical misconceptions related to how God governs the world is that he doesn't care about the details of our lives. Sure, God cares about major stuff like who I marry and what career path I choose, but he can't care about what I eat and drink, how I spend my Saturday or whether my favourite football team wins the game. The

---

6 Free will is being used here differently than it is used in other places. This is not talking about free will in the sense that people are born neutral and have the opportunity to choose good or bad, life or death. We must understand free will in light of Article VI on the Fall of Man. In view of the Fall, men and women are free to choose, but they are slaves to sin. Therefore, their fallen freedom always leads them toward sin, so their only hope to choose the good requires a radical intervention of grace.

doctrine of Christian providence teaches that God does in fact know and care about *all* of the details of our lives. If not one sparrow falls to the ground apart from the Father, and all the hairs on our head are numbered (Matthew 10:29–30), then we should assume God does in fact care about every single detail of our lives. We may not know how God is weaving together what I eat for lunch, my trip to the garbage dump on Saturday and the football game happening down the road, but we can know this: the immortal, invisible and eternal God is weaving all things together for his purposes.

Another similar but slightly different misconception is that if God is sovereign then my choices and prayers don't matter. If everything is predetermined, then why even live my life? This misconception fails to take two things into account. First, it fails to take the *relational* aspect of God's providence into account. As we have already seen, what makes the Christian view of providence unique is the Christian God is unique. He is a personal God, who wants to know and be known. His upholding, directing and controlling are to be understood through the lens of a loving Father. Second, this misconception does not take into account the fact that God upholds, directs and governs through *ordinary means*. It is not just the *ends* God has predetermined, he has also predetermined the *means*. In other words, God doesn't work independently from our desires, prayers and decisions, he works through them. He accomplishes his divine purposes through ordinary means, which are themselves prepared beforehand so that we would walk in them.[7] That is the wonder of a story like Esther. In a book where God is not even mentioned, it is obvious he is at work through the ordinary and everyday experiences of people like us.

A third, and very important misconception that needs to be addressed is the idea that prosperity is always a blessing and suffering is always curse. It is all too natural for us to ask, "Why did God allow this to happen to me?" when something bad comes our way. On the other hand, it is just as natural to say, "God has really blessed me this year," when everything seems to be going our way. The doctrine of Christian providence gives us a more thoughtful and wise approach to life. Sometimes suffering is the way God is trying to teach us or grow us. So, while suffering itself is not a good thing, we can rejoice in it

---

7 Ephesians 2:10.

because we know God will use it for our good. And many times, prosperity is a sign of a cursed life, displaying that we have embraced the ways of the world and Satan actually has a foothold in our life. The point is made in the "sometimes" and in the "many times." When we immediately jump to conclusions about blessings and curses, we trivialize the fact God has planned and is working through billions of people and situations. Also, we fail to remember that the most blessed human being who has ever lived, Jesus Christ, experienced the greatest suffering imaginable. This must broaden our category for how God treats people through blessings and curses, beyond simply earthy prosperity and earthly trouble.

A final thought is not necessarily a misconception, but is a sad truth. Most people—even Christians—live their lives without realizing that God has revealed so much about the direction, movement and end goal of history. We are constantly asking, "What is God's will for my life?" when we haven't stopped to simply ask, "What is God's will?" *period.* If we knew what God was up to in the world, we would have a better idea of what he is up to in our own lives. To get a general understanding of where the world is headed, one does not need to do an indepth study on the book of Revelation. Scriptures like Hebrews 11–12 show us that God's people have always had their eyes on a future kingdom, and this has shaped the way they lived and the choices they made. Scriptures like Ephesians 1 show us how God's plan for the world centres around Jesus Christ, and the goal of all things can be understood most fully when God opens our eyes by his Spirit to see the glory and beauty of the gospel. And Scriptures like Psalm 7 show us that one day we will all stand before God's judgment throne to give an account for our lives—and, on that day, God will make all things right. These are just a few examples of the truths we can bank our lives on because when we know what God is up to in the world we have the opportunity to see our lives through his eyes, rather than being taken captive by any other human philosophy.

APPLICATION

Article IV: Providence

> God from eternity, decrees or permits all things that come to pass, and perpetually upholds, directs and governs all creatures and all events; yet so as not in any way to be the author or approver of sin nor to destroy the free will and responsibility of intelligent creatures.

---

1. *We can trust God with our whole lives.*

We trust can God is good. We can trust he has us where he wants us. We no longer need to scheme or scurry to try and help ourselves or prop ourselves up. I think these things apply both on a personal level and on a local church level. God will take care of his people. He is involved in our lives and ministries. He sees, knows and cares about us, and he promises to work on our behalf.

2. *We can be comforted in our suffering, knowing nothing is wasted.*

Suffering is real, and suffering is hard. God never tells us to simply get over it and suck it up. However, the Bible does teach us to view our suffering so radically different from what is natural that we can learn to take joy in our suffering, even as we mourn. Only the Christian doctrine of providence can lead people to be sorrowful yet always rejoicing (2 Corinthians 6:10).

3. *We can have confidence God is at work in the world.*

A huge lesson we learn about providence from the book of Esther is that we can have a new and unusual kind of confidence when we know God is at work in the world. Remember, Mordecai was certain deliverance would come for God's people, even if it didn't come through Esther. But, he thought, "Why not come through Esther?" This certainty about what God was doing in the world gave Mordecai and Esther explosive confidence. God worked through the ordinary means of self-sacrifice and dignified courage to deliver his people, just as Mordecai thought. When we know where history is heading, then the edge is taken off of taking risks. When we take risks for the gospel, God is liable to bless those risks, since we are moving in the same direction he is.

4. *We can be content.*

Another thing providence compels us toward is *contentment*. If we know all things come from God's mind or pass through his hand, we can trust that we have what God wants us to have and we are where God wants us to be. If God has wrapped his people up into his grand plan for the world, then we can keep our hearts humble before him as he works out all the details. This means we accentuate gratitude and refrain from complaining and grumbling. When providence truly hits our hearts, we can't help but overflow with thanksgiving to God, since his upholding, directing and governing hand is so gracious and good.

5. *We don't need to be anxious or worry about the future.*

Finally, what we saw from Matthew 6 is that God's providence evacuates worry. We can fully pursue God's kingdom and his righteousness, instead of pursuing other things, even our basic needs. People who don't know this God or understand his workings in the world will be a slave to their selfish pursuits. But, in light of God's plan for the world, Christians don't have to be enslaved to the same kinds of worries and anxieties as people who don't know God. We should be prepared to give people a defense for the hope we have, because we know our future is gloriously bright (1 Peter 3:15).

V

—

Election

Election is God's eternal choice of some persons unto everlasting life—not because of foreseen merit in them, but of his mere mercy in Christ—in consequence of which choice they are called, justified and glorified.

Election

INTRO + OVERVIEW

Throughout the history of the church there has been much discussion about how God deals with people, and more specifically how God saves people. In what sense should we call God *Saviour*? Does God save with our help or without it? Does he save through the church or outside of it? Does God save exclusively in Christ or does he save outside of him? Does God save the world in *general*, or does he save individual people in *particular*?

In his work, *The Plan of Salvation*,[1] B.B. Warfield discusses three couplets of ideas that work like a funnel. Each couplet asks a different question about how God deals with people. Each couplet presents two differing opinions. The couplets are *Naturalists v. Supernaturalists*, *Sacerdotalists v. Evangelicals* and *Universalists v. Particularists*. These couplets help us think carefully about what our options are, and why we should join the Bible to affirm, "Salvation belongs to the LORD; May Your blessing be upon Your people!"[2]

Naturalists v. Supernaturalists

With the image of a funnel in mind where the mouth at the top is very wide and the straw at the bottom is very small, we come to our first couplet which is like the big wide mouth. In the conversation between Naturalists v. Supernaturalists,[3] we are trying to decide whether God is a God of miracles or not. When God deals with people, does he simply let nature take its course or does he get involved in ways that are over, under and beyond nature?

---

1   Benjamin B. Warfield, *The Plan of Salvation* (1915), can be accessed here: https://www.monergism.com/thethreshold/articles/onsite/WarfieldPlan01.html.

2   Psalm 3:8.

3   Salvation is possible for people in their own strength v. salvation is only possible with God's strength.

This couplet really is the difference between a person or a church being able to call themselves Christian or not. Warfield put it this way, "Does man save himself or does God save him?" If we take a naturalist perspective then we are saying man can in fact bring himself to worship God, man can in fact present himself holy before God and man in fact can, by his own initiative, find his way into the family of God. This man-centred approach to life is futile. If man was so noble and agile as to save himself, then humanity would not be the wreck that it is as we know it.

The supernaturalist perspective says that we are doomed if God does not intervene. God must come to man with grace if we are to know and enjoy him. If we were left to what was natural, we would never find God. We depend upon him for life and for our very life with him.

Sacerdotalists v. Evangelicals

The next and more narrow section of the funnel is our second couplet. In the conversation between Sacerdotalists v. Evangelicals,[4] we are trying to decide how God supernaturally engages a person. Has God placed his supernatural intervention inside of the church like a bank, to be dispensed and withdrawn through mediation, or does God work *directly* in the hearts of men and women with his supernatural activity?

This couplet is one of the fractures that caused the Reformation in the sixteenth century. We have already seen in Article I on the Scriptures how the *foundation* for the Reformation dealt with authority, but we see the *substance* of the Reformation dealt with salvation. Warfield puts the question this way, "Does God save men by immediate operations of his grace upon their souls, or does he act upon them only through the medium of instrumentalities established for that purpose?" Those *instrumentalities* were what exploded the church. It was the idea that God placed salvation or grace inside of certain rituals, people or relics. Rather than seeing grace as personalized in Jesus Christ, grace was seen as a *commodity*. The Roman Catholic Church claimed to give away salvation through rites, priests, indulgences and sacraments. In doing so, it put itself *between* God and individual

---

4   The church gives out salvation v. the church receives salvation.

people. The abuse that was evident during that time was simply a by-product of human beings standing in the place of God. There is only one human who is worthy of and who can handle that role: the only Mediator between God and man, the man Christ Jesus.

The evangelical perspective sees grace as intimately tied to God himself. Salvation is not a thing to be dispensed or withdrawn, rather salvation is a person named Jesus. We are saved by grace alone, through faith alone, in Christ alone, to the glory of God alone. This, the substance of the Reformation, broke the church apart because it presented a radically different and more biblical picture of how God saves. The church doesn't exist to give out salvation, the church is made up of people who have received salvation.

Universalists v. Particularists

Finally, if we move down the funnel toward an evangelical perspective, we are met with the straw and our final couplet. In the conversation between Universalists v. Particularists,[5] we are trying to decide if God's saving power is a *potential* power or a *certain* power. When a person is saved, is it because God decided to rescue that person, or was a rescue simply made available so that whoever could find their way would benefit from it?

Both universalists and particularists believe that God saves by grace, through faith in Christ and for his glory, but they differ in how they conceive of this happening. Really, the difference is how much *grace* is stressed in salvation. Warfield puts the question this way,

> The point of division here is whether God is conceived to have planned actually himself to save men by his almighty and certainly efficacious grace, or only so to pour out his grace upon men as to enable them to be saved, without actually securing, however, in any particular cases that they shall be saved.... Does the presence [of the saving grace of God] mean salvation, or may it be present, and yet salvation fail?[6]

---

5   Salvation is a potential for everyone but certain for no one v. salvation is offered to everyone and certain for many.

6   Warfield, *The Plan of Salvation*: https://www.monergism.com/thethreshold/articles/onsite/WarfieldPlan01.html.

The goal in moving down through the funnel is to be biblical, thoughtful and humble. So, we must humbly and thoughtfully ask, which of these two most faithfully represents the Bible?

If one decides to go the route of a universalistic perspective, it does not mean they necessarily believe *everyone* will be saved. Here, we mean that what God has done for one, he has done for all. This means the final and decisive burden of salvation lies on the shoulders of the individual. God's salvation in Christ Jesus is merely *potential*. The implication of this is that we could very easily live in a world where there no Christians at all. When Jesus came to save, he had no one in particular in mind, and there was no certainty his mission would end in success. This view, while it does justice to the universality of God,[7] does not do justice to the biblical evidence of the *particular* nature of Christ's mission in the gospel. When God saves his people, it is hard to imagine his family as a nebulous potential, rather than a concrete reality.

Particularism, then, is the reality that God does in fact actually save people, in himself, by himself and for himself. That is why the Bible uses words like *chosen* and *elect* because they ground salvation in God's grace and nothing else. When a person becomes a Christian, by grace alone, through faith alone, in Christ alone, for the glory of God alone, they come because *God has chosen them* before the foundation of the world. God is not surprised when a person gets saved because he himself is the one rescuing them out of sin and hell. Particularism places the ultimate emphasis on grace in salvation, leading to the ultimate amount of glory to God, to the praise of his glorious grace.

Now that we have worked down through Warfield's funnel, a final note before we turn to Scripture. Chapter 3, Paragraph 7 of *The 1689 Baptist Confession of Faith* reads,

> The doctrine of the high mystery of predestination is to be handled with special prudence and care, that men attending the will of God revealed in His Word, and yielding obedience thereunto, may, from

---

7   In other words, seeing the universality of God in the Bible (i.e., that he is the only God, and therefore, he demands repentance and worship from all people) is an appropriate thing to see. Because God is the only God, he is the God of the whole world. But just because God loves the whole world, and places demands upon the whole world, does not mean he has redeemed every single person in the world. It is a false step to make this assumption.

the certainty of their effectual vocation, be assured of their eternal election; so shall this doctrine afford matter of praise, reverence, and admiration of God, and of humility, diligence, and abundant consolation to all that sincerely obey the gospel.[8]

These seventeenth-century believers understood they were speaking of things that bordered the lines of mystery. However, they believed the church should not be ashamed to teach and love the very truths which had been given to the church to establish, ground and ignite their worship in and through the gospel. Predestination and election are not topics for debate. They are necessary matters of discipleship, which lance our pride and awaken our affections. Bitter argument and unnecessary infatuation can take these beautiful graces of the gospel and turn them into wedges of disunity. As we thoughtfully, humbly and biblically wade forward, let us join our seventeenth-century brothers and seek to pursue the knowledge of these wonders, "with special prudence and care" in order that the doctrine of election would be a "matter of praise, reverence, and admiration of God, and of humility, diligence, and abundant consolation to all that sincerely obey the gospel."[9]

SCRIPTURAL FOUNDATIONS

Genesis 12:1–3

Now the LORD said to Abram,

"Go from your country,
And from your relatives
And from your father's house,
To the land which I will show you;
And I will make you into a great nation,

---

8   *The 1689 Baptist Confession of Faith*; see https://www.the1689confession.com/1689/chapter-3.

9   *The 1689 Baptist Confession of Faith.*

And I will bless you,
And make your name great;
And *you shall* be a blessing;
And I will bless those who bless you,
And the one who curses you I will curse.
And in you all the families of the earth will be blessed."

There was no backstory, no reason and no explanation for why God chose Abram.[10] After a long list of relatives and generations, God speaks, and he chooses to speak to Abram. This kind of thing in the Old Testament by no means confirms the doctrine of election, but it shows how God deals with people. God comes to people on *his* terms, and he chooses people based on *his* purposes.

Deuteronomy 7:6–8

"For you are a holy people to the LORD your God; the LORD your God has chosen you to be a people for His personal possession out of all the peoples who are on the face of the earth."

"The LORD did not make you His beloved nor choose you because you were greater in number than any of the peoples, since you were the fewest of all peoples, but because the LORD loved you and kept the oath which He swore to your forefathers, the LORD brought you out by a mighty hand and redeemed you from the house of slavery, from the hand of Pharaoh king of Egypt."

This is a staggering announcement from Moses to God's people. This is not the kind of flowery love letter we might expect from God. Surely, even if it wasn't true, God would want to flatter his people by telling them he had chosen them because they were the most worthy, powerful or beautiful. But we hear just the opposite. We can imagine God standing back and observing all the nations. He says to himself, "Who will I choose?.. Hmm, too big, too strong, too sophisticated, too advanced. Aha, small, insignificant and stubborn. That's more like it!" And then he sets *his love* on little Israel for the very reason they have absolutely nothing to boast about.

---

10 Abram's name was eventually changed by God to Abraham.

John 6:60-65

So then many of His disciples, when they heard *this*, said, "This statement is *very* unpleasant; who can listen to it?" But Jesus, aware that His disciples were complaining about this, said to them, "Is this offensive to you? *What* then if you see the Son of Man ascending to where He was before? It is the Spirit who gives life; the flesh provides no benefit; the words that I have spoken to you are spirit, and are life. But there are some of you who do not believe." For Jesus knew from the beginning who they were who did not believe, and who it was who would betray Him. And He was saying, "For this reason I have told you that no one can come to Me unless it has been granted him from the Father."

The *1689 Baptist Confession of Faith* instructs us on how we should handle the doctrine of election with care, since we are prone to take the most precious things and squander them. But Jesus, the ultimate Prophet, can say things sinners should be cautious about emulating. Can you imagine being there? Can you imagine what it would have been like for Jesus to publicly, boldly and loudly proclaim the doctrine of election in the negative sense[11]—that no one can come to Jesus unless it is granted by the Father? If Jesus wasn't afraid of election, then we shouldn't be either. But, we should also remember Jesus had a unique mission,[12] he possessed unique offices[13] and he was full and filled with the Holy Spirit.[14] In other words, Jesus means to offend us by what he says, but he has the right to do so! We should be cautious about meaning to offend others in this same kind of way.

---

11 *Negative* here does not mean *bad*. Negative means the opposite of positive. In other words, positively stated, election means God chooses people to come to Jesus. Negatively stated, election means no one can come to Jesus unless God chooses them.

12 Only Jesus was sent into the world by God to save sinners. No one else shares that mission.

13 As the chief Prophet, Priest and King, Jesus stood *by himself* as our representative.

14 What I mean by full and filled is although Jesus is just as much human as we are, he possessed *all* of the gifts and graces of the Spirit. The *fruit* of the Spirit was perfectly *embodied* in Jesus, and the *gifts* of the Spirit were perfectly *exercised* by Jesus.

Acts 13:44-48

The next Sabbath nearly all the city assembled to hear the word of the Lord. But when the Jews saw the crowds, they were filled with jealousy and *began* contradicting the things spoken by Paul, and were blaspheming. Paul and Barnabas spoke out boldly and said, "It was necessary that the word of God be spoken to you first. Since you repudiate it and consider yourselves unworthy of eternal life, behold, we are turning to the Gentiles. For so the Lord has commanded us,

'I HAVE APPOINTED YOU AS A LIGHT TO THE GENTILES,
THAT YOU MAY BRING SALVATION TO THE END OF THE EARTH.'"

When the Gentiles heard this, they *began* rejoicing and glorifying the word of the Lord; and all who had been appointed to eternal life believed.

If salvation is not particularistic, it makes no sense that the Bible would use language like this to describe the conversion of individuals. The universalistic viewpoint does not do justice to Scriptures like this. But that is not all that this passage offers us with regard to this doctrine. We also see in Acts 13 that while God has chosen people for eternal life, he also uses the *ordinary means* of faithful service, prayer and gospel proclamation to call his people from death to life. In this sense, election and providence work together. If you have believed, it is because you have been appointed to eternal life; if you have believed, it means God is upholding, directing and governing all the details of your life—including the prayers, people and truths that have worked together to awaken your heart to faith in Christ.

Romans 8:28-34

And we know that God causes all things to work together for good to those who love God, to those who are called according to *His* purpose. For those whom He foreknew, He also predestined *to become* conformed to the image of His Son, so that He would be the firstborn among many brothers *and sisters*; and these whom He predestined,

He also called; and these whom He called, He also justified; and these whom He justified, He also glorified.

What then shall we say to these things? If God *is* for us, who *is* against us? He who did not spare His own Son, but delivered Him over for us all, how will He not also with Him freely give us all things? Who will bring charges against God's elect? God is the one who justifies; who is the one who condemns? Christ Jesus is He who died, but rather, was raised, who is at the right hand of God, who also intercedes for us.

We have seen the importance of understanding God's sovereignty and foreknowledge in the context of relationship. The basis of this context is election. God's work in the world, through his wisdom and for his glory, has been wonderfully connected to the people he has chosen to be holy and blameless before him forever. Election gives a believer grounds for confidence because what the ever faithful God began in eternity, he will bring to completion.[15] This chain of foreknowledge, predestination, calling, justification and glorification is delivered to us in the *past* tense. It is as if it is already done. And this is the kind of confidence election is supposed to stir in the heart and life of a believer. That is why the very next sentence reads, "If God is for us, who is against us?" That kind of resolve is ours for the taking if we embrace from our sovereign God the wonder of predestination. When we realize salvation is all of God, we understand our salvation is built on a rock solid foundation that can't be shaken by *anything*—not hell, Satan, sin or even death itself.

Romans 9:6–24

But *it is* not as though the word of God has failed. For they are not all Israel who are descended from Israel; nor are they all children because they are Abraham's descendants, but: "through Isaac your descendants shall be named." That is, it is not the children of the flesh who are children of God, but the children of the promise are regarded as descendants. For this is the word of promise: "AT THIS TIME I WILL COME, AND SARAH WILL HAVE A SON." And not only *that*,

---

15 See Philippians 1:6.

but there was also Rebekah, when she had conceived *twins* by one man, our father Isaac; for though *the twins* were not yet born and had not done anything good or bad, so that God's purpose according to *His* choice would stand, not because of works but because of Him who calls, it was said to her, "THE OLDER WILL SERVE THE YOUNGER." Just as it is written: "JACOB I HAVE LOVED, BUT ESAU I HAVE HATED."

What shall we say then? There is no injustice with God, is there? Far from it! For He says to Moses, "I WILL HAVE MERCY ON WHOMEVER I HAVE MERCY, AND I WILL SHOW COMPASSION TO WHOMEVER I SHOW COMPASSION." So then, *it does* not *depend* on the *person* who wants *it* nor the one who runs, but on God who has mercy. For the Scripture says to Pharaoh, "FOR THIS VERY REASON I RAISED YOU UP, IN ORDER TO DEMONSTRATE MY POWER IN YOU, AND THAT MY NAME MIGHT BE PROCLAIMED THROUGHOUT THE EARTH." So then He has mercy on whom He desires, and He hardens whom He desires.

You will say to me then, "Why does He still find fault? For who has resisted His will?" On the contrary, who are you, you *foolish* person, who answers back to God? The thing molded will not say to the molder, "Why did you make me like this," will it? Or does the potter not have a right over the clay, to make from the same lump one object for honorable use, and another for common use? What if God, although willing to demonstrate His wrath and to make His power known, endured with great patience objects of wrath prepared for destruction? And *He did so* to make known the riches of His glory upon objects of mercy, which He prepared beforehand for glory, *namely* us, whom He also called, not only from among Jews, but also from among Gentiles

This is probably the most important text in the Bible on the doctrine of election. Unfortunately, this passage has been argued and fought over rather than meditated and worshiped over. If the truth of this Scripture hit us correctly, we would be more humble, more quiet and more patient people. Again, election is not a debate topic, it is a discipleship necessity. And the main discipleship emphasis is found right in the heart of this text, "So then, it does not depend on the person who wants it nor the one who runs, but on God who has mercy." This lands a deadly blow in two directions. It puts pride to death because it teaches us how totally dependent we are on God. We may not need to think of ourselves less to be humble people, but we do need to think of our contribution as less—in fact as nothing—so that we can rightly appreciate the honour and glory that God is due. Election also puts despair to death because it teaches us that it doesn't matter how slow we run or how bad the choices of our will have been, God's mercy is not dependent on those things. How depressing it would be to people who sin and struggle if their salvation was a potential, dependent upon their running and willing!

The problem most of us have with election is that we assume free will means we have the ability to choose God. Free will does mean we have real and free choices, but people who are slaves to sin *always and only* choose what is opposed to God. Election drops from the level of argumentative debate down to the heart level of discipleship when we come to delight in *God's* free will instead of our own free will—when we come to delight in God's ability to choose wisely, instead of our ability to choose wisely.

Ephesians 1:3–6

> Blessed *be* the God and Father of our Lord Jesus Christ, who has blessed us with every spiritual blessing in the heavenly *places* in Christ, just as He chose us in Him before the foundation of the world, that we would be holy and blameless before Him. In love He predestined us to adoption as sons *and daughters* through Jesus Christ to Himself, according to the good pleasure of His will, to the praise of the glory of His grace, with which He favored us in the Beloved

Ephesians 1 reveals two major things about the doctrine of election. First, election is a precious aspect of our union with Christ, and we should enjoy and praise God for it. A believer should be moved to scream from the top of their lungs, "Praise God! He loved me and chose me when I was unlovable and unworthy!" Second, election, God's choosing, is in Christ Jesus. God's choice is grounded in, and the fruit of, the eternal merit of Christ. If it weren't for Jesus, no one could be chosen. It was within the scope of redemption that God made his choice. It was in view of the Lamb that was slain before the foundation of the world[16] that God was moved to predestine many sinners to adoption so that they might be part of his family. Election—along with all the other wonderful promises of the gospel—comes to us only through our union with Jesus Christ.

EXPLANATION

"Election is God's eternal choice..."

God makes the choice, and he makes that choice before he created the world. God sets his love on a people before time is invented. The all wise, all good, all loving, all glorious God, who is captive only to his own pleasures and purposes, makes a decisive move that shapes all of history forever.

"of some persons unto everlasting life..."

This choice is a choice of *individuals*. And the choice is to give them everlasting life. These individuals are chosen out of death into life. They are to receive the most undeserved and unbelievable gift imaginable: unashamed and unburdened life with God forever.

"—not because of foreseen merit in them..."

This is the negative[17] statement behind election. It has nothing to do with anything God saw beforehand which would lead him to choose one person over another person. If we describe God's choosing as based on anything he saw in the future, then it isn't actually choosing. There would be no meaning to the word *choice* or *elect*, if God weren't free in his decision. The Bible would be extremely misleading in using this terminology if by "gracious choice" the Scriptures actually meant "merited reaction."

"but of his mere mercy in Christ—"

If there is anything to base his choosing upon, what would that be? What could a person possibly even plead as the reason God would

---

16 See Revelation 13:8.

17 See footnote 11.

choose them over any other person? The only thing to plead is the mercy of Christ. If we were to ask God, "Why did you do this?", he would say, "To display my mercy and show off my infinite love in the most benevolent and gracious way possible."

"in consequence of which choice..."

At this point, we might think the doctrine has been explained thoroughly enough. God chooses particular people to save, and not because of anything in them. That is clear enough, but is that all? No, this choice is an *effective* choice. This election causes other things to happen. It is a powerful choice; it is a pregnant choice. Is this important? It is important to see that every aspect and benefit of life in Christ was as good as ours before we were even born because God foreknew us with his predestinating and electing grace. And if this is true, then our only boast in life is Jesus Christ, his gospel and his glory.

"they are called..."

One of the inevitable causes or consequences of God's eternal choice of some individuals is that all of those individuals are *called effectively* into the family of God. The Bible talks about the calling of the Christian in this way,

> For consider your calling, brothers *and sisters*, that there were not many wise according to the flesh, not many mighty, not many noble; but God has chosen the foolish things of the world to shame the wise, and God has chosen the weak things of the world to shame the things which are strong, and the insignificant things of the world and the despised God has chosen, the things that are not, so that He may nullify the things that are, so that no human may boast before God. But *it is* due to Him *that* you are in Christ Jesus, who became to us wisdom from God, and righteousness and sanctification, and redemption, so that, just as it is written: "LET THE ONE WHO BOASTS, BOAST IN THE LORD."[18]

We cannot afford to neglect the weight of a Scripture like this in our discipleship. We need to know that when we got into this thing called

---

18 1 Corinthians 1:26–31.

Christianity, it was all of God's doing. He planned it, he caused it, he provided what was necessary and he did all of it so that we would step back, be amazed and never stop declaring how great he is.

"justified..."

Another certain cause or consequence of God's eternal choice of some individuals is all of those individuals are justified freely in Jesus Christ. If God chose people before the foundation of the world to be holy and blameless before him, then something would have to be done to set them in the right in his judgment. Justification is a consequence of election. These individuals whom God has chosen are just that, they are chosen beforehand, but they are not justified beforehand. The Bible talks about the justification of the Christian in this way,

> But now apart from the Law *the* righteousness of God has been revealed, being witnessed by the Law and the Prophets, but *it is* the righteousness of God through faith in Jesus Christ for all those who believe; for there is no distinction, for all have sinned and fall short of the glory of God, being justified as a gift by His grace through the redemption which is in Christ Jesus, whom God displayed publicly as a propitiation in His blood through faith. *This was* to demonstrate His righteousness, because in God's *merciful* restraint He let the sins previously committed go unpunished; for the demonstration, *that is,* of His righteousness at the present time, so that He would be just and the justifier of the one who has faith in Jesus.
>
> Where then is boasting? It has been excluded. By what kind of law? Of works? No, but by a law of faith. For we maintain that a person is justified by faith apart from works of the Law.[19]

When we get to Article XI on justification we will unpack the doctrine with more precision and clarity, but for now we can see that there is at least a similar motivation for why God has justified his people by grace, through faith and in Christ. It is the same reason he called us into the faith in the first place, so no one would boast in themselves, but instead boast in Christ alone.

---

19 Romans 3:21–28.

"and glorified."

A final, definite consequence of God's eternal choice of some individuals unto everlasting life is that all of those individuals are glorified eternally with Jesus Christ. Part of being chosen in Christ, means that wherever he is, we will be also, whatever kind of body he has, we will receive also, and whatever inheritance he deserves, we deserve also. This is the glory of union with Christ—we share in *his* glory. The Bible talks about the glorification of the Christian in this way,

> But we should always give thanks to God for you, brothers *and sisters* beloved by the Lord, because God has chosen you from the beginning for salvation through sanctification by the Spirit and faith in the truth. It was for this He called you through our gospel, that you may obtain the glory of our Lord Jesus Christ.[20]

If we have died with Christ, and if we have been raised with Christ, then we are *one* with Christ. And the end goal of the gospel call in our lives, and the union we receive by faith in Christ, is that we might gain his very glory. But can we boast in this gain? Can we take credit for this glory? Not one of us can, because the cause of it—the gaining of glory—was his choice. All we can do is give thanks, forever!

MISCONCEPTIONS

We don't have to try very hard to think of potential misconceptions related to this article because the doctrine of election is so offensive to us all that no one receives it without difficulty. Election is so naturally against our sinful perspectives, desires and tendencies that we immediately come up with all sorts of objections to the free will of God.

A first natural gut reaction is this misconception: *If this is true, then did God create some people for hell?* No. God did not create anyone for hell, or hell for anyone. Hell was created for Satan and the angels who

---

20 2 Thessalonians 2:13–14.

followed him instead of remaining in the service of God alongside those faithful angels the Bible calls elect or holy angels.[21]

What we have to remember is when God made his choice of individuals, all he had before him were fallen and sinful individuals. In Romans 9, when it says the Potter has the right to make vessels for honourable use and vessels for dishonourable use from the same lump of clay, then we must conceive of the lump of clay as *sinful* clay. It is a tragedy, that when one day God condemns sinful people found outside of Christ to hell, the final cause will be their *own choice* and not God's. The only thing that will send human beings to hell is free will uninterrupted by divine will. God's gracious choice of many people to everlasting life was just that, from *death* to life.

Another natural reflex to the doctrine of election is this: *If this is true then why do we pray, share the gospel and send missionaries all over the world?* The quick and easy answer is, "Because God says so." But the answer is deeper than this. This wonderful truth of predestination handled with special prudence and care should not lead us to see life as more rigid and robotic, but rather to see life as more exciting and enchanted. We can know our prayers will be a part of bringing people from death to life, our evangelism will call our long lost family members into the household of God and our missions efforts will not be for nothing—people from every tribe, tongue and nation will one day stand before the throne of God and praise the Lamb. And these people are not wishful potentials but definite realities. This kind of certainty keeps us praying, proclaiming and sending.

A final and serious concern regarding the doctrine of election is *there are biblical references which at first reading seem to contradict it.* Remember, we saw what universalists get right: the universality of God. There are times when the Bible emphasizes this universality of God in a way closely related to salvation. After all, God *did* send his only begotten Son into the world as a demonstration of his love *for the world.* Perceptively, people ask, "If unconditional election is true, does that mean God really doesn't desire that all men come to a saving knowledge of the truth?" Two problematic passages typically pop into our minds:

---

21 Mark 8:38.

First of all, then, I urge that requests, prayers, intercession, *and* thanksgiving be made in behalf of all people, for kings and all who are in authority, so that we may lead a tranquil and quiet life in all godliness and dignity. This is good and acceptable in the sight of God our Savior, who wants all people to be saved and to come to the knowledge of the truth (1 Timothy 2:1-4).

But do not let this one *fact* escape your notice, beloved, that with the Lord one day is like a thousand years, and a thousand years like one day. The Lord is not slow about His promise, as some count slowness, but is patient toward you, not willing for any to perish, but for all to come to repentance (2 Peter 3:8-9).

I think there are two ways to approach these passages. One deals more with careful reading, and the other deals with attentive thinking. When we carefully read these two passages we must slowly ask what do these Scriptures actually say? The first says God "wants all people to be saved." This in no way contradicts the doctrine of election. God has all sorts of desires, many we know and understand, and many we do not. All Christians have to account for the fact that unless we are willing to say all people will actually eventually be saved, this text teaches us God has a desire he chooses not to act upon. Surely this is a mystery, but it in no way contradicts election.

The other passage says the Lord "is patient toward you, not willing for any to perish." From a purely grammatical standpoint, the "any" in this statement is qualified by "you" before it. So it essentially reads, God is patient toward you, not willing for any (of you Christians) to perish. When we slow our reading down, we realize we sometimes import what we already think is true into a passage, without letting it speak for itself.

When we think attentively about these two passages we need to ask this question, "What are Paul and Peter, respectively, trying to accomplish by using the phrases 'all people' and 'any'? In other words, what are they wanting us to hear when we read this language? They are trying to persuade us God is extremely gracious and he is a universal God. For example, in 1 Timothy 2, the same phrase "all people" is used in verse 1. There it is immediately qualified, "for kings and all who are in authority." So in this passage, "all people" is more about all *types* of people (universal God), than it is about every single person (universal salvation)—whether it is with regard to prayer (v. 1) or with regard to God's desire for all people to be saved (v. 4). God is wonderfully universal—salvation is offered to, and repentance is demanded of all people, but his universality does not mean his election is universal. God *deserves* the repentance of all people, and in that sense he *desires* it from them. But God *grants* the repentance of his chosen people; in that sense, he *completes* what he desires for all people, for his elect alone.

APPLICATION

___

Article V: Election

Election is God's eternal choice of some persons unto everlasting life—not because of foreseen merit in them, but of his mere mercy in Christ—in consequence of which choice they are called, justified and glorified.

___

1. The truth of election should empower us with certainty in our evangelism and missions.

We can have confidence in the fact that God has already effectualized the mission. Those who proclaim the gospel of Jesus Christ cannot fail, because there are those all over the world who are currently dead in their sins, but because of election, they are as good as glorified. And God is excited to use us to call them into the family!

2. The truth of election should make us humble.

We do absolutely nothing and God does absolutely everything in our salvation. It is not that election teaches us to think less of ourselves, but it does teach us to think less of what we bring to the table. We have no boast, except Christ alone.

3. The truth of election grounds our assurance of salvation in God himself.

So much of our struggle with assurance comes because we can't be certain if God loves us or not. Election teaches God loves sinners and he chooses those who are messed up. Our salvation is grounded in God's love and not in our performance, which means our assurance is weighed down by eternity itself—God is not going to change his mind after all this time.

4. The truth of election should move us to worship.

When we understand all God has done for us in salvation, and how it is all by his redeeming grace, we should be moved to worship. Over and over again, when the Bible brings up election it connects it to worship—that is why this is such a crucial discipleship issue. We ought to want to praise God for all he is and all he has done, and God wants us to be motivated by all he is and all he has done for us— including his gracious choice of us—to worship him with our everything.

If for nothing else, this final reason should encourage us to work through the truths of the doctrine of election. If we choose to be silent about one of the glories of the gospel, then we might just be shorting God for worship he is due. With God's help, we can thoughtfully, humbly and biblically enjoy the doctrine of election as a, "matter of praise, reverence, and admiration of God, and of humility, diligence, and abundant consolation to all that sincerely obey the gospel."[22]

---

22 *The 1689 Baptist Confession of Faith*; see https://www.the1689confession.com/1689/chapter-3.

VI

The Fall of Man

God originally created man in his own image, and free from sin; but, through the temptation of Satan, he transgressed the command of God, and fell from his original holiness and righteousness; whereby his posterity inherit a nature corrupt and wholly opposed to God and his law, are under condemnation, and as soon as they are capable of moral action, become actual transgressors.

The Fall of Man

INTRO + OVERVIEW

I f we remember back to Article III on the Trinity, we learned about the Nicene Creed. That creed was forged between A.D. 325 and 381. With that creed, the trinitarian controversy was settled. Just a few short years later, at the age of thirty-two, the man now known as Augustine of Hippo was converted to Christianity. Many church historians look at Augustine as one the most important figures who has ever lived outside of the Bible. Augustine was a prolific thinker, writer and preacher. His own life and ministry leads us to consider the next big controversy in the church: the controversy over sin.

We might not think sin is controversial. Doesn't it seem obvious something is wrong with us? Isn't it common knowledge the world is not the way it is supposed to be? And yet, the reason sin has created controversy, and always will, is that sin goes right to the heart of who we are as human beings. Sin makes a claim on our lives. What we believe about sin is impossible to disentangle from who we believe God to be and what we believe Christ to have accomplished.

Augustine and Pelagius

A major controversy over sin arose between Augustine and a man named Pelagius. Pelagius may have had the best of intentions, even though he was in error. He saw a certain moral decay among the Christians of his day, and deeply desired to see reform and a pursuit of holiness. He believed this moral decay may have been partly due to certain people believing that since they were sinners, they were inevitably going to sin. These people, he believed, acted as though they were helpless in fighting sin, since sin was unavoidable. (Pelagius is a good example of someone who recognized a real problem, but made an incorrect assessment of the cause of the problem.)

An easy way for us to understand how Pelagius viewed the world is to think of Adam and Eve. Pelagius believed all human beings, when they are born into the world, basically have the same innocence, the same opportunity and the same experience Adam and Eve had in the Garden of Eden. Pelagius believed human beings are *posse non peccare* or "able *not* to sin." His view had major implications for how he viewed human nature, God's commands and Christ's salvation.

On the other hand, Augustine argued all humanity had been plunged into depravity by Adam's first sin in the garden. This meant, while there was hope for humanity because of Jesus, outside of Jesus there was no hope. Augustine taught that humans are *non posse non peccare* or "*not* able *not* to sin."

Augustine believed the Bible teaches that sin is both an *act* and a *state*. It is easy for us to grasp sin is an act—it is the bad things we do and the good things we fail to do. But Augustine also taught sin was a state. The first sin, he believed, had corrupted Adam and Eve, so that all of their children—all humans who have ever lived—received a corrupt human *nature*. This meant sin was not just an act, it was a state of being. We are born into sin and are by nature children of God's wrath.[1] Sin isn't just something we *do*, sin is who we *are*.

Pelagius believed the nature of man was pure and Augustine believed the nature of man was corrupt. Pelagius believed all the commands of God were attainable by human beings, Augustine believed all of the commands of God had been broken by human beings. Pelagius believed salvation was on the basis of good works, Augustine believed salvation was on the basis of grace.

On a more simplified level, this is the question that we must ask ourselves: Do we believe human beings are born neutral, with a choice between good and evil? Or, do we believe human beings are born sinful with evil inside of them from the very beginning? Augustine and the Bible teach the latter. We aren't hanging in the balance, we are dead in the water. A helpful phrase for understanding this is *total depravity*.

Total depravity sounds terrible, and it should. Sin is terrible. But, it actually might not be as terrible as we first realize. Total depravity does not mean every single human being is as bad as they possibly could be. Total depravity does mean every single *aspect* of our humanity has been affected by sin. Our minds are depraved, our wills are depraved, our affections are depraved, and that is why our actions are depraved. The

---

1   See Ephesians 2:1–3.

doctrine of the Fall of man means the reason we sin is because we are sinners. When we *act* in sin, it only proves we live in the *state* of sin.

In what sense is our mind depraved?

In the state of sin, we do not understand life, we do not know God and we do not interpret reality correctly. To put it bluntly, sin makes us ignorant. We think the wrong things, we think about the wrong things and we think wrongly about things.

In what sense is our will depraved?

In the state of sin, we do not make good choices. As we have already seen, we are free as human beings, but with a depraved will our freedom leads us in the wrong direction. Our free will, in the state of sin, always chooses the way of the world instead of God's ways.

In what sense are our affections depraved?

In the state of sin, we do not desire or enjoy the right things. We find delight in things that should disgust us, and we are disgusted by what brings God delight.[2] We were made to love God and to enjoy him as our highest good, but sin sets our love on God's creation instead of God himself.

With a depraved mind, a depraved will and with depraved affections, it is no wonder the state of sin produces acts of sin. We can't help but do the wrong things when we think, choose and love the wrong things. Jesus frames this idea around a tree and its fruit. A good tree will produce good fruit while a bad tree will produce bad fruit.[3] When bad fruit keeps coming and keeps coming, we are left with only one conclusion: the tree itself is bad. Indeed we are *non posse non peccare* —not able not to sin.

---

2   Romans 12:9.
3   Matthew 7:15–23.

SCRIPTURAL FOUNDATIONS

Genesis 1:26-27

Then God said, "Let Us make mankind in Our image, according to Our likeness; and let them rule over the fish of the sea and over the birds of the sky and over the livestock and over all the earth, and over every crawling thing that crawls on the earth." So God created man in His own image, in the image of God He created him; male and female He created them.

There is a good reason that with almost all of our articles so far, we have found ourselves in Genesis 1. It is extremely important for us to see how God originally made Adam and Eve. They were made in God's very image. God did not make people sinful, he made them good. God did not make people corrupt, he made them to reflect his image. While the image of God gives us the context for the Fall of man, it has much wider implications than that. It means God bestowed upon humanity a unique importance, value and dignity. Everything God made was good, but only the man and the woman together were made according to God's likeness.

Genesis 3:1-15

Now the serpent was more cunning than any animal of the field which the LORD God had made. And he said to the woman, "Has God really said, 'You shall not eat from any tree of the garden'?" The woman said to the serpent, "From the fruit of the trees of the garden we may eat; but from the fruit of the tree which is in the middle of the garden, God has said, 'You shall not eat from it or touch it, or you will die.'" The serpent said to the woman, "You certainly will not die! For God knows that on the day you eat from it your eyes will be opened, and you will become like God, knowing good and evil." When the woman saw that the tree was good for food, and that it was a delight to the eyes, and that the tree was desirable to make one wise, she took some of its fruit and ate; and she also gave some to her husband with her, and he ate. Then the eyes of both of them were opened, and they knew that they were naked; and they sewed fig leaves together and made themselves waist coverings.

Now they heard the sound of the Lord God walking in the garden in the cool of the day, and the man and his wife hid themselves from the presence of the Lord God among the trees of the garden. Then the Lord God called to the man, and said to him, "Where are you?" He said, "I heard the sound of You in the garden, and I was afraid because I was naked; so I hid myself." And He said, "Who told you that you were naked? Have you eaten from the tree from which I commanded you not to eat?" The man said, "The woman whom You gave *to be* with me, she gave me some of *the fruit of* the tree, and I ate." Then the Lord God said to the woman, "What is this *that* you have done?" And the woman said, "The serpent deceived me, and I ate." Then the Lord God said to the serpent,

> "Because you have done this,
> Cursed are you more than all the livestock,
> And more than any animal of the field;
> On your belly you shall go,
> And dust you shall eat
> All the days of your life;
> And I will make enemies
> Of you and the woman,
> And of your offspring and her Descendant;
> He shall bruise you on the head,
> And you shall bruise Him on the heel."

This is a long passage, but it is worth deep consideration and long reflection. Here, we see humankind plunged into depravity. This serpent character, who we later find out is Satan, comes to Adam and Eve and questions God's goodness and love. He makes it seem like God is holding out on them. In the most sad tragedies ever witnessed, we watch the innocence, purity and delight of humanity unravel before our eyes. This is not uncommon to us, it is all too familiar. We know what it is like to question God. We know what it is like to be deceived. We know what it is like to immediately regret our decisions. We know the feeling of shame and embarrassment that accompany our fallen condition. And most fundamentally, all of us know that our sin has wrecked our relationship to God and every other person. There is hostility, confusion, blame-shifting and insecurity that now comes between ourselves and everyone else, especially God.

Psalm 51:1–15

Be gracious to me, God, according to Your faithfulness;
According to the greatness of Your compassion, wipe out my
    wrongdoings.
Wash me thoroughly from my guilt
And cleanse me from my sin.
For I know my wrongdoings,
And my sin is constantly before me.
Against You, You only, I have sinned
And done what is evil in Your sight,
So that You are justified when You speak
And blameless when You judge.

Behold, I was brought forth in guilt,
And in sin my mother conceived me.
Behold, You desire truth in the innermost being,
And in secret You will make wisdom known to me.
Purify me with hyssop, and I will be clean;
Cleanse me, and I will be whiter than snow.
Let me hear joy and gladness,
Let the bones You have broken rejoice.
Hide Your face from my sins
And wipe out all my guilty deeds.

Create in me a clean heart, God,
And renew a steadfast spirit within me.
Do not cast me away from Your presence,
And do not take Your Holy Spirit from me.
Restore to me the joy of Your salvation,
And sustain me with a willing spirit.
Then I will teach wrongdoers Your ways,
And sinners will be converted to You.

Save me from the guilt of bloodshed, God, the God of my salvation;
Then my tongue will joyfully sing of Your righteousness.
Lord, open my lips,
So that my mouth may declare Your praise.

Psalm 51 has much more to say than what it says about sin, but the statements made about sin are extremely important. First, we learn sin is to be understood as a crime against God. When we sin, we transgress God's law and therefore make ourselves liable to condemnation. Next, we learn sin is to be understood as immorality. It is socially unacceptable, not because our culture says so, but because God's culture says so. Then, we learn sin, even sin against other people, is actually sin against *God*. We are accountable to God for the way we treat other people. So whether we judge someone in our heart, or murder someone, it is *God* whom we have offended. Finally, what else could this psalm mean when it says, "in sin my mother conceived me," other than that all human beings are born into sin? David acknowledges the reason he sins is because he is a *sinner*.

Mark 7:14-23

After He called the crowd to Him again, He *began* saying to them, "Listen to Me, all of you, and understand: there is nothing outside the person which can defile him if it goes into him; but the things which come out of the person are what defile the person."

And when He *later* entered a house, away from the crowd, His disciples asked Him about the parable. And He said to them, "Are you so lacking in understanding as well? Do you not understand that whatever goes into the person from outside cannot defile him, because it does not go into his heart, but into his stomach, and is eliminated?" (*Thereby* He declared all foods clean.) And He was saying, "That which comes out of the person, that *is what* defiles the person. For from within, out of the hearts of people, come the evil thoughts, *acts of* sexual immorality, thefts, murders, *acts of* adultery, deeds of greed, wickedness, deceit, indecent behavior, envy, slander, pride, *and* foolishness. All these evil things come from within and defile the person."

Here, maybe more clearly than in any other Scripture, we learn where sin comes from. Sin shouldn't surprise us. We know sinful *actions*—like theft, murder, envy, etc.—come from sinful *hearts*. Jesus says that all these evil things come out of evil hearts. Sin is not something that goes *into* us, sin is something that comes *out* of us—the root of sin is already in us, and under the right circumstances and pressures, it spews out in many disgusting ways.

Romans 1:18-25

> For the wrath of God is revealed from heaven against all ungodliness and unrighteousness of people who suppress the truth in unrighteousness, because that which is known about God is evident within them; for God made it evident to them. For since the creation of the world His invisible *attributes, that is,* His eternal power and divine nature, have been clearly perceived, being understood by what has been made, so that they are without excuse. For even though they knew God, they did not honor Him as God or give thanks, but they became futile in their reasonings, and their senseless hearts were darkened. Claiming to be wise, they became fools, and they exchanged the glory of the incorruptible God for an image in the form of corruptible mankind, of birds, four-footed animals, and crawling creatures.
>
> Therefore God gave them up to vile impurity in the lusts of their hearts, so that their bodies would be dishonored among them. For they exchanged the truth of God for falsehood, and worshiped and served the creature rather than the Creator, who is blessed forever. Amen.

In Psalm 51, we learned that all sin is against God, and here in Romans 1 we learn why. Sin is an exchange. That is what happened to Adam and Eve in the Garden of Eden and it is what happens in all of us. We *choose* unrighteousness instead of God's righteousness, we *choose* lies instead of God's truth and we *choose* the glory of the creation instead of the glory of the Creator. Sin is foolish, sin is offensive and sin is futile.

Romans 5:12-19

> Therefore, just as through one man sin entered into the world, and death through sin, and so death spread to all mankind, because all

sinned—for until the Law sin was in the world, but sin is not counted against *anyone* when there is no law. Nevertheless death reigned from Adam until Moses, even over those who had not sinned in the likeness of the violation *committed* by Adam, who is a type of Him who was to come.

But the gracious gift is not like the offense. For if by the offense of the one the many died, much more did the grace of God and the gift by the grace of the one Man, Jesus Christ, overflow to the many. The gift is not like *that which* came through the one who sinned; for on the one hand the judgment arose from one *offense*, resulting in condemnation, but on the other hand the gracious gift arose from many offenses, resulting in justification. For if by the offense of the one, death reigned through the one, much more will those who receive the abundance of grace and of the gift of righteousness reign in life through the One, Jesus Christ.

So then, as through one offense the result was condemnation to all mankind, so also through one act of righteousness the result was justification of life to all mankind. For as through the one man's disobedience the many were made sinners, so also through the obedience of the One the many will be made righteous.

The Bible uses *types*[4] to point forward in prophetic ways, without using explicit prophetic language. Usually these types show in shadow form how a previous event, symbol or character prepared the way for a later substantial truth. In Romans 5, we learn something so intriguing that at first it is hard to understand. Paul tells us Adam was a *type* of Jesus. Has Paul read Genesis lately? Does he know Adam brought sin into the world and Jesus was perfect and sinless? Paul is acutely aware. The way in which Adam was a type of Jesus is extremely important for helping us understand how the Bible deals with sin and how the Bible then deals with salvation.

If we work our way backward, then the argument goes like this: If people could be made righteous through one man, Jesus, then those same people could be made unrighteous through one man, Adam. If

---

4   For example, the tabernacle and the temple, the Passover, Jonah in the fish for three days, etc. These and many other symbols are examples which point foward and culminate in Jesus Christ.

people could be represented by proxy so that Christ's obedience would be theirs, then those same people could be represented by proxy so that Adam's disobedience would be theirs. In fact, if in Christ innocence could be imputed[5] to all whom Jesus represents, then it is true that in Adam guilt is imputed to all whom he represents—and, the clear implication is this: Adam represents us all. In this way, Adam was a type of Christ, in that he stood as *representative head* of the first creation, just as Jesus stands as *representative head* of the new creation. When Christ died, those in Christ died with him; so it is when Adam sinned, those in Adam sinned with him.

EXPLANATION

"God originally created man in his own image, and free from sin..."

It really is amazing that God wanted to have human beings image him! They were called to fill the earth with his glory. Human beings were created righteous, good and blessed by God. This means humans were pure in mind, oriented in affections and unmixed in will. They walked in innocence, enjoyed God and had perfect harmony together. Human beings, having been made in God's image, had the unique privilege of reflecting the communicable attributes of God.[6]

"but, through the temptation of Satan, he transgressed the command of God..."

It is important for us to remember that God had given Adam and Eve the opportunity to eat from any tree in the garden, including the Tree of Life. God was extremely gracious and good to them in offering them so much and personally caring for them. He simply gave them one small prohibition. And it was this prohibition that would eventually undo them. We aren't sure how long Adam and Eve lived in this state

---

5 This means to credit, attribute or assign. This language is extremely important for Christian theology, since the entire Christian gospel revolves around the life, death and resurrection of Jesus in our place.

6 For more on communicable and non-communicable attributes, see Article II.

of innocence, but from the way the text reads, it doesn't seem like they enjoyed it for very long. Satan, that serpent of old, lied to Eve and deceived her. She took the fruit and ate it, the one thing God had told them not to do. And she gave the fruit to Adam and he ate it, plunging all of humanity with him into the depths of sin and death. We learn then, that the heart of sin is a *distrust* of God, and the substance of sin is *breaking* God's commands.

"and fell from his original holiness and righteousness..."

What Adam and Eve had enjoyed by way of fellowship with God and consecration to God, was immediately lost. The word *Fall* is appropriate because the dignity of the higher holy life was traded for the shame of the murky grime of sin. The Fall meant man had no hope of return. Neither repentance nor a second chance would do. Holiness and righteousness, according to the standard of God, must have no hint of imperfection.

"whereby his posterity inherit a nature corrupt and wholly opposed to God and his law..."

The first major problem involved in the Fall is that Adam—and all those born in him—would receive a fallen nature. This corrupt nature involved a corrupt mind, will and affections. The first transgression of God's law was a shadow of what was to come for all of humanity. By nature, human beings misunderstand God's commands as either unimportant or abusive. And what might be even worse, all human beings, born into Adam's fallen nature, find themselves at odds with God himself. There is no peace between God and humanity.

"are under condemnation..."

The second major problem involved in the Fall is God had clearly explained the consequence of transgressing his commands. The consequence was death. The criminal guilt of humankind finds the just penalty of God executed without relief. God is angry and his justice demands punishment.

"and as soon as they are capable of moral action, become actual transgressors."

In view of the corrupt nature of humanity, it is inevitable that having been born at enmity with God, all human beings are destined to commit real acts of transgression. Every human being following in the way of their father Adam breaks God's law. We are by nature children of wrath,[7] and we confirm our just condemnation by the actual sins we commit. We all sin because we are all sinners.

MISCONCEPTIONS

We are living in a time when the questions of humanity have never been greater. *Who are we? What were we made for? How do we operate? Are we accountable to anything or anyone outside of ourselves?* The misconceptions related to the Fall attempt to answer these questions, and questions like these.

The first major misconception is *we can establish our own identity.* We live in a time when the greatest burden on our shoulders is determining who we are. But, in the Bible we learn it is God who tells us who we are. We were made by him and for him. We were made to reflect him and enjoy him. We were made male and female. We were made to be holy, righteous and blessed. When Eve was deceived by Satan, he attacked her at the level of *identity.* He said to her, "For God knows that on the day you eat from it your eyes will be opened, and you will become like God, knowing good and evil."[8] He told her she needed to do something to be like God, but if she had been firm in her identity—who God created her to be—then she would have known she was already like God. In fact, she was made in his likeness. If we could learn to enjoy our God-given identity, then one of the greatest burdens of this stressed-out generation would be put to rest.

Another important misconception is the belief that *we are basically good people.* It is funny how most people will acknowledge they aren't perfect. But, there is always someone else to blame, some life circumstances to point to or some life experience to explain away our shortcomings. The idea is if you put yourself in the right situations, possess the right education and catch all the right breaks (which all of us truly

---

7 Ephesians 2:3.
8 Genesis 3:5.

deserve!), then we basically would all be good and helpful citizens who put others first and seek world peace. The problem is neither life experience nor the Bible corroborate this story! What we find is self-pity, self-righteousness, self-sufficiency, self-centredness, self-worship... you get the picture! And it is even our own selfishness that keeps us from seeing our sins for what they truly are: not mainly about us, but about *rebellion* against a gracious God. Total depravity does not mean we are all *as bad as we could be*, and it also does not mean there isn't a general sense of common good which sinners enjoy under God's sovereign hand. But it does mean that, in the sight of a holy God, even our best deeds are laced with sinful motives and desires.

A third misconception is the idea that *because God is so loving, he doesn't really care what we do*. In reality, this pits God's attributes against each other. As we have seen in Article II, God's attributes don't work that way. God doesn't choose to love *at the expense of* his wrath, and God doesn't choose to show mercy *at the expense of* his justice. God hates sin, and contrary to popular opinion, the Bible actually says that, "You hate all who do injustice."[9] God doesn't hate the sin, but love the sinner, he hates the sin *and* hates the sinner. This does not mean God cannot simultaneously love sinners, he does.[10] But, his natural reflex to sinners is anger; that is what it means when it says, "we were by nature children of wrath."[11] Who we are as people, incites anger in God. God's grace in Christ Jesus does not lower his standard and it does not diminish his justice—it establishes his standard and satisfies his justice, which is why Jesus died a gruesome death on the cross.

A final misconception deals with *how sin relates to the image of God during the state of sin*. There are actually two mistakes we can make at this point. The first is to say, sin means we no longer possess the image of God. This is not true. Human beings still have the capacity to reflect God and to know God. The dignity of being a person who is made for God's glory is outstanding. The other mistake we can make is to say, sin has had no effect on the image of God in man. Clearly, part of the

---

9 Psalm 5:5.

10 We must remember God relates to our sin in both natural and sovereign ways. According to his nature, he hates sinners, but according to his sovereign grace, he loves sinners.

11 Ephesians 2:3.

image of God in humanity was the original holiness and righteousness that were lost in the Fall. That is why, at times, the Bible describes salvation as being formed into God's image or formed into Christ's image.[12] If we had not fallen from God's image in the first place, then why would we need to be remade after his likeness by his Spirit? So, regarding human dignity and God-given identity, it is right for us to think of ourselves as made in God's image. But we must also remember this image has been marred. We do not fully reflect God the way he intended until we are made anew in Christ.

---

12 2 Corinthians 3:18.

APPLICATION

Article VI: The Fall of Man

God originally created man in his own image, and free from sin; but, through the temptation of Satan, he transgressed the command of God, and fell from his original holiness and right-eousness; whereby his posterity inherit a nature corrupt and wholly opposed to God and his law, are under condemnation, and as soon as they are capable of moral action, become actual transgressors.

---

1. **Because we are made in God's image, it means abortion is murder.**
   When we take the life of an unborn child, we are killing someone who reflects God. Being made in the image of God means we do not live in a utilitarian world, where we judge the value of someone's life by how much contribution they make to society. The value placed on someone's life comes from the very heart of God, not from that person's ability to talk, move or provide for themselves.

2. **Because we are made in the image of God, it means marriage is between one man and one woman for a lifetime.**
   And, it means sex is God's good gift to be enjoyed in marriage. God gets to tell us what to do with our bodies, and he gets to tell us the who, what, when and where that relate to those who are joined together in covenant relationship. Telling us what to do and who to love is God's wonderful love for us. He knows what is best for he made us.

3. **Because we are made in the image of God, it means no one is "born gay."**
   Homosexuality is a sad consequence of life in a fallen world. The Bible actually says sexual desire for someone of the same gender is part of the curse all human beings live under. This curse manifests itself in

our lives in different ways, but this is one of the ways our corrupt nature reveals itself. It may very well feel like a person was born with these desires, but that feeling neither validates it nor justifies it. There are many things God hates that feel good, right and natural to us in our state of corruption. It is a very sad thing when a society celebrates what God condemns. As the church, we must be prepared to graciously welcome those who have experienced the curse of their sin in this way by pointing them to the gospel of Jesus Christ and to the wonderful picture of life lived in God's image.

4. *Because we are made in the image of God, it means there is absolutely no tolerance for racism, classism, prejudice, sexism, etc.*

All people come from the same family. Our significance, worth, value, dignity and opportunity have nothing to do with where we are from, what colour the pigmentation of our skin is or in what socio-economic class we find ourselves. God is thrilled about our differences and desires for us to learn to embrace exactly who he has made us to be. Our languages, customs and cultures are important to him because in him we all live and move and have our being.[13] We hold in balance the fact God does not look at the outward appearance but at the heart, with the fact that God is not "colour blind." The glimpse we get of the future is this,

> After these things I looked, and behold, a great multitude which no one could count, from every nation and *all* the tribes, peoples, and languages, standing before the throne and before the Lamb, clothed in white robes, and palm branches *were* in their hands; and they *cried out with a loud voice, saying,
>
> > "Salvation *belongs* to our God who sits on the throne, and to the Lamb."[14]

In this sense, what it means for God to look at the heart is not that he does not see or find delight in our respective cultures, it simply

---

13 Acts 17:28.
14 Revelation 7:9–10.

means he has his own set of judgments and they are perfect according to his standard.

5. **Because we are totally depraved, it means we call sin what it is and do not minimize its damning effects.**
We boldly admit our sin is rebellion against God. We don't just "mess up" or "struggle." We have missed God's mark and have become criminals in his kingdom. We are in constant need of the cleansing cross-work of Jesus.

6. **Because we are totally depraved, we recognize our own need and call others to repentance.**
The church understands the reality of this confession. The church's existence is based on mercy, and if it is based on mercy then it is riddled with sin. This allows the church to both confidently and humbly call others to repentance. When we ask others to turn from their sin and turn to God, we aren't asking them to do anything we ourselves are not doing.

7. **Because we are totally depraved, we don't see sin in tiers.**
There is no such thing as *serious sins* and *trivial sins*. *All* sins are against God, which makes them worthy of infinite punishment. It is right for us to understand the effects different actions can have on other people. But we move in extremely dangerous waters when we begin to laugh at *small sins* and gawk at *big sins*. Christians should take *all sin* as seriously as God does.

8. **Because we are totally depraved, we look totally and completely outside of ourselves for salvation.**
If we are to be made right with God, we need someone to intervene on our behalf. Our corrupt nature is not something we can reverse, and the condemnation we are under is not something we can withstand or avoid. If we are to be renewed and justified, someone—God himself—must come to our rescue. It is to this hope, we turn to next.

VII

The Mediator

Jesus Christ, the only begotten Son of God, is the divinely appointed mediator between God and man. Having taken upon himself human nature, yet without sin, he perfectly fulfilled the law; suffered and died upon the cross for the salvation of sinners. He was buried, and rose again the third day, and ascended to his Father, at whose right hand he ever lives to make intercession for his people. He is the only Mediator, the Prophet, Priest and King of the Church, and Sovereign of the Universe.

The Mediator

INTRO + OVERVIEW

When it comes to *persons, natures, wills* and *minds* in the realm of Christian theology, it might be easy for many of us to check out. We may be tempted to think, *Does it really matter how technically we think, believe and talk about who Jesus is?* On one level, our problem is pretty simple: we have turned from God. And the solution is pretty simple as well: Jesus came to save us. But, on another level, once we have encountered the full-orbed perspective of our sin whereby we find ourselves guilty before a holy God and corrupt in mind, will, affections and actions, we realize the complex reality of our sin demands an explanation of our salvation that meets the complexity of our problem and responds with clarity. Can we really afford to be haphazard with something as important as eternal life? Shouldn't we seek to be as thorough in our understanding of Jesus as we have been in our understanding of ourselves?

Jesus is 100 percent God and 100 percent man, as the popular saying goes. But what exactly does that even mean? In what sense is Jesus 100 percent God, and in what sense is Jesus 100 percent man? These are the questions that lead us to care about persons, natures, wills and minds. And these terms lead us to the conceptions of many of the greatest heresies in the history of the church—false teachings that aren't out on the periphery of our faith but so much at the heart of Christianity they are the difference between life and death. If it is true that Jesus is the way, the truth and the life, and that no one comes to the Father except through him,[1] then we better make sure we are talking about the right Jesus. And just like in Article III on the Trinity, the church of ages past has not left us to reinvent the wheel in every generation, but instead has left us a creed to help us find our way forward.

---

1   John 14:6.

When the fourth century dispute with Arius was over,[2] the church came to a clear articulation of the fact that Jesus was not merely *like* God, but he *was* God. However, soon after the Nicene Creed was established, a new question came forward. It is one thing to affirm Jesus is *God*, but in what sense is he *man*? And how does the deity of Jesus relate to the humanity of Jesus? In other words: *Who does Jesus have to be to accomplish our salvation?*

The humanity of Jesus

One idea came from a man named Apollinaris. It is probably slightly over simplified, but he basically taught that Jesus was a man who had a body, but his body was controlled by a divine mind. Essentially, he posited, Jesus was part man and part God. Another idea came from a man named Eutyches. In his conception, the God-ness and the man-ness of Jesus combined to make him a unique kind of being. We might think of Jesus as a type of hybrid between God and man. A final major hypothesis came from a man named Nestorius. Nestorius wanted to keep the deity and humanity of Jesus separate. However, in his attempt to protect the God-ness of Jesus and the man-ness of Jesus, he basically split Jesus into two different persons altogether.

Now, while all three of these ideas are very different, they all fall apart under the same pressure. The fourth-century church father Gregory of Nazianzus put it this way, "For that which He has not assumed He has not healed."[3] In other words, God alone saves, but for Jesus to save humanity, he must be *all* that it means to be human. So, the problem with Apollinarius's view was if Jesus had adopted a divine mind, then the rest of our human nature is still lost and corrupt. Remember, the mind, will, affections, body, actions, etc. were all affected and corrupted by sin. The problem with Eutyches's view was that in turning Jesus into some sort of God-man hybrid, he saw Jesus as *neither* God *nor* man! He envisioned a *third* nature, which was neither God's nature nor man's nature. And the problem with Nestorius's view was in separating the nature of God and the nature of man to the extreme, he took salvation out of the hands of God alone. After all, the

---

2   See Article III: The Trinity.

3   Gregory of Nazianzus, *Critique of Apollinarius and Apollinarianism*; see https://earlychurchtexts.com/public/gregoryofnaz_critique_of_apolliniarianism.htm.

Bible itself doesn't shy away from proclaiming, "the church of God which He purchased with His own blood."[4] When Jesus died on the cross, God died on the cross. Certainly, careful nuance is appropriate, but Nestorius sought too eagerly to remove the provocation of the cross. He failed to realize humanity needed reconciliation with God, and in the very person of Jesus Christ, God and man were indeed reconciled. Jesus united the two natures into his one person, thereby revealing God, saving man and healing all who were corrupted by sin.

This means Jesus is *one person* who possesses *two natures, two wills* and *two minds*. And yet, when Jesus acts, he acts as one person, so that we can't divide Jesus or act like he operates as two different people. Whatever it means to be God, Jesus is; whatever it means to be man, Jesus is. Furthermore, if God were to be a man (which in Jesus he is), then that man would act and live as Jesus acts and lives. He is God *revealed*. As another fourth century church father, Athanasius, says poetically, Jesus is the "unfolded Godhead of the Word."[5]

It was necessary for our salvation for Jesus to be fully God and fully man. When he offered himself up for our sins, only a sinless sacrifice could meet God's requirements. At the same time, Jesus must actually be a man so that he could represent us. If Jesus had not been God, he would not have been *worthy*, and if Jesus had not been man, he would not have been *qualified*.

The Council of Chalcedon

In A.D. 451, the church came together in a similar way as had happened in A.D. 325. This time, the council dealt with how the person of Jesus Christ possessed both God's nature and human nature. The council was called the Council of Chalcedon, and the document or creed it produced has come to be known as the *Chalcedon Definition*. It reads as follows:

Therefore, following the holy fathers,
we all with one accord teach men
to acknowledge one and the same Son, our Lord Jesus Christ,
at once complete in Godhead and complete in manhood,

---

4   Acts 20:28.
5   Athanasius, *On the Incarnation.*

truly God and truly man,
consisting also of a reasonable soul and body;
of one substance with the Father as regards his Godhead,
and at the same time of one substance with us
as regards his manhood;
like us in all respects, apart from sin; as regards his Godhead,
begotten of the Father
before the ages, but yet as regards his manhood begotten,
for us men and for our salvation, of Mary the Virgin,
the God-bearer;
one and the same Christ, Son, Lord, Only-begotten,
recognized in two natures, without confusion,
without change, without division, without separation;
the distinction of natures being in no way annulled by the union,
but rather the characteristics of each nature being preserved
and coming together to form one person and subsistence,
not as parted or separated into two persons,
but one and the same Son and Only-begotten God the Word,
Lord Jesus Christ;
even as the prophets from earliest times spoke of him,
and our Lord Jesus Christ himself taught us,
and the creed of the fathers has handed down to us.

A few things are worth noting. The definition begins by agreeing
with the previous definition laid down in the Nicene Creed. Jesus is
truly God and truly man. This means everything uniquely true about
God is true about Jesus, eternally. Jesus has in and of himself all perfections, and he is infinite in them all.

The definition aimed itself at the complexity and the clarity necessary for our salvation when it deemed Mary the Virgin, "the God-bearer." This was not added into the definition by accident. This was a sort
of litmus test of orthodoxy. If someone could not agree Mary was the
God-bearer, then it showed they did not understand who Jesus was.
When Jesus Christ was conceived of the Holy Spirit in the womb of
the Virgin Mary, God himself, in the person of Jesus, was conceived.
To remove the eternal Word of God from the womb, was to divide the
person of Jesus in half, the very mistake Nestorius had made. This did
not mean Mary created God, but it did mean she brought forth God

from her womb in Jesus. A divided Christ was no Christ at all.

The definition explicitly states we should recognize Jesus in two natures. The word *recognize* is very helpful. When we read the Bible, we can't help but recognize Jesus is man, but not *merely* man. We recognize him in two natures, 100 percent God and 100 percent man.

Finally, the Chalcedon Definition provides "guard rails" for understanding Jesus. It is true Jesus possesses *two distinct natures*. The fact he is *one person* does not sabotage either of the natures. At the same time, what is *distinct* in the characteristics of each nature, is *united* in one person. Jesus is not two persons, and he is not divided. So while God is three persons who share one divine nature, Jesus is one person who possesses two natures. Just as God is not three natures, Jesus is not two persons. He is one unified person who eternally has been a partaker in the divine nature, but who—for us and for our salvation—has taken to himself our human nature.

Do you remember when we considered God's communicable and non-communicable attributes in Article II? There are some attributes unique only to God, and there are other attributes God can give or communicate to us. Using this same principle, we can understand how it is Jesus is one person who possesses two natures. What is true of each nature can rightly be ascribed to the one person Jesus Christ, even though the two natures don't pass attributes back and forth. That is why we can say God died on the cross, because while the divine nature did not die, the person Jesus who possesses the divine nature did die on the cross. Jesus is everything it means to be God and everything it means to be man. This is astounding! He alone is able to save us and he alone is worthy of our worship.

SCRIPTURAL FOUNDATIONS

Deuteronomy 18:15-19

"The LORD your God will raise up for you a prophet like me from among you, from your countrymen; to him you shall listen. *This is* in accordance with everything that you asked of the LORD your God at Horeb on the day of the assembly, saying, 'Do not let me hear the voice of the LORD my God again, and do not let me see this great fire anymore, or I will die!' And the LORD said to me, 'They have spoken well. I will raise up for them a prophet from among their countrymen like you, and I will put My words in his mouth, and he shall speak to them everything that I command him. And it shall come about that whoever does not listen to My words which he speaks in My name, I Myself will require *it* of him."

One of the remarkable things about this article on the Mediator is it points us to different offices or titles which are fulfilled in Jesus. But it is not as if Jesus simply showed up on the scene and reinterpreted those roles. Jesus was predicted as the fulfilment of these offices long before he was born. In this passage in particular, Jesus is predicted to come as a prophet. A prophet is someone who speaks for God. This prophet will be like Moses in some ways, but greater than Moses in other ways.

2 Samuel 7:8–17

"Now then, this is what you shall say to My servant David: 'This is what the LORD of armies says: "I Myself took you from the pasture, from following the sheep, to be leader over My people Israel. And I have been with you wherever you have gone, and have eliminated all your enemies from you; I will also make a great name for you, like the names of the great men who are on the earth. And I will establish a place for My people Israel, and will plant them, so that they may live in their own place and not be disturbed again, nor will malicious people oppress them anymore as previously, even from the day that I appointed judges over My people Israel; and I will give you rest from all your enemies. The LORD also declares to you that the LORD will make a house for you. When your days are finished and you lie down with your fathers, I will raise up your descendant after you, who will come from you, and I will establish his kingdom. He shall build a house for My name, and I will establish the throne of his kingdom forever. I will be a father to him and he will be a son to Me; when he does wrong, I will discipline him with a rod of men and with strokes of sons of mankind, but My favor shall not depart from him, as I took *it away* from Saul, whom I removed from you. Your house and your kingdom shall endure before Me forever; your throne shall be established forever.'"" In accordance with all these words and all of this vision, so Nathan spoke to David.

In similar fashion to the office or role of prophet, it was predicted that Jesus would fulfil the promise of an eternal king. This passage focuses the search for the Messiah on the lineage of David, and it seems to have a dual fulfilment. On the one hand, David's son Solomon can be seen in this Scripture. He did in fact build the house for God David had dreamed of. But this text outstrips Solomon—it puts more of a load on his life than he could handle. Israel had many kings, but only for King Jesus will God establish the throne of his kingdom *forever.*

Isaiah 53

Who has believed our report?
And to whom has the arm of the LORD been revealed?
For He grew up before Him like a tender shoot,
And like a root out of dry ground;
He has no *stately* form or majesty
That we would look at Him,
Nor an appearance that we would take pleasure in Him.
He was despised and abandoned by men,
A man of great pain and familiar with sickness;
And like one from whom *people* hide their faces,
He was despised, and we had no regard for Him.

However, *it was* our sicknesses *that* He Himself bore,
And our pains *that* He carried;
Yet we ourselves assumed that He had been afflicted,
Struck down by God, and humiliated.
But He was pierced for our offenses,
He was crushed for our wrongdoings;
The punishment for our well-being *was laid* upon Him,
And by His wounds we are healed.
All of us, like sheep, have gone astray,
Each of us has turned to his own way;
But the LORD has caused the wrongdoing of us all
To fall on Him.

He was oppressed and afflicted,
Yet He did not open His mouth;
Like a lamb that is led to slaughter,
And like a sheep that is silent before its shearers,
So He did not open His mouth.
By oppression and judgment He was taken away;
And as for His generation, who considered
That He was cut off from the land of the living
For the wrongdoing of my people, to whom the blow *was due?*
And His grave was assigned with wicked men,
Yet He was with a rich man in His death,
Because He had done no violence,
Nor was there any deceit in His mouth.

But the LORD desired
To crush Him, causing *Him* grief;
If He renders Himself as a guilt offering,
He will see *His* offspring,
He will prolong *His* days,
And the good pleasure of the LORD will prosper in His hand.
As a result of the anguish of His soul,
He will see *it* and be satisfied;
By His knowledge the Righteous One,
My Servant, will justify the many,
For He will bear their wrongdoings.
Therefore, I will allot Him a portion with the great,
And He will divide the plunder with the strong,
Because He poured out His life unto death,
And was counted with wrongdoers;
Yet He Himself bore the sin of many,
And interceded for the wrongdoers.

Jesus was predicted as a *prophet* greater than Moses and an eternal *king* from the lineage of David, but he was also predicted as the one who would make a healing sacrifice on behalf of his people. In that sense, Jesus fulfiled the office of the *priest*. The difference between all of the other priests and Jesus was instead of needing to offer a sacrifice for himself like the other priests did, Jesus *himself* was the sacrifice. He offered up himself as an offering to God. Jesus did this on behalf of other people. The piercing, crushing, chastening and scourging Jesus experienced unto death are to be understood as an effective sacrificial offering, which healed and absorbed God's wrath toward sinners.

John 1:1–5,14–18

In the beginning was the Word, and the Word was with God, and the Word was God. He was in the beginning with God. All things came into being through Him, and apart from Him not even one thing came into being that has come into being. In Him was life, and the life was the Light of mankind. And the Light shines in the darkness, and the darkness did not grasp it....

And the Word became flesh, and dwelt among us; and we saw His glory, glory as of the only *Son* from the Father, full of grace and truth. John testified about Him and called out, saying, "This was He of whom I said, 'He who is coming after me has proved to be my superior, because He existed before me.'" For of His fullness we have all received, and grace upon grace. For the Law was given through Moses; grace and truth were realized through Jesus Christ. No one has seen God at any time; God the only *Son*, who is in the arms of the Father, He has explained *Him*.

One of the names given to the eternal Son of God is the *Word*. The Word is God and the Word was with God from all eternity. John helps us understand the divine relationship between the persons of the Godhead. We learn that God created all things through the Word. The Word is life and light, he is very God. And then John tells us the Word—the eternal Son of God—became flesh. This is John's way of telling us the Son of God assumed a human nature. The one person, Jesus, was simultaneously the Word *and* flesh—God and man. When Athanasius said Jesus is the "unfolded Godhead of the Word,"[6] he was simply restating what John is telling us here: in Jesus, the mystery of God is revealed. This is where we get the term *incarnation*. Jesus is God incarnate or, we might say, Jesus is God enfleshed or embodied. So, as we witness Jesus-in-the-flesh, we see the glory of God revealed.

---

6   Athanasius, *On the Incarnation.*

1 Corinthians 15:1-4

Now I make known to you, brothers *and sisters*, the gospel which I preached to you, which you also received, in which you also stand, by which you also are saved, if you hold firmly to the word which I preached to you, unless you believed in vain. For I handed down to you as of first importance what I also received, that Christ died for our sins according to the Scriptures, and that He was buried, and that He was raised on the third day according to the Scriptures.

Things of first importance carry special significance. Here, Paul is reminding the church what should be of first importance to us: *the gospel*. And the gospel in summarized form is the death of Jesus for our sins, the burial Jesus and the resurrection of Jesus, all according to the Scriptures. While all of our articles and doctrines are vitally important, the Bible gives supreme importance to the central truth of the person and work of Jesus in salvation. This is the heart of the Bible and the lifeblood of Christianity.

1 Timothy 2:1-7

First of all, then, I urge that requests, prayers, intercession, *and* thanksgiving be made in behalf of all people, for kings and all who are in authority, so that we may lead a tranquil and quiet life in all godliness and dignity. This is good and acceptable in the sight of God our Savior, who wants all people to be saved and to come to the knowledge of the truth. For there is one God, *and* one mediator also between God and mankind, *the* man Christ Jesus, who gave Himself as a ransom for all, the testimony *given at* the proper time. For this I was appointed as a preacher and an apostle (I am telling the truth, I am not lying), as a teacher of the Gentiles in faith and truth.

The Scriptures are clear: Jesus is the only possible way, connection or intermediary between God and human beings. Since there is only one God, we must come to him on his terms. The terms of the one God are that we must know him through knowing Jesus. When we know Jesus, we know God. There is no other way for sinners to be justified before

God, and there is no other way for sinners to be reconciled to God. If the doctrine of sin means we are born enemies of God, then all people are dependent on Jesus as our reconciling mediator.

Hebrews 2:17–18

> Therefore, in all things He had to be made like His brothers so that He might become a merciful and faithful high priest in things pertaining to God, to make propitiation for the sins of the people. For since He Himself was tempted in that which He has suffered, He is able to come to the aid of those who are tempted.

The reality of Jesus Christ as Mediator is not a past tense office or role for Jesus. *Right now*, the resurrected, glorified and ascended Jesus sits at the right hand of the Father as our Mediator. Since Jesus took to himself a human nature, lived as a man, was tempted as we are, suffered and died, he is able to help us in our own temptations and suffering. Jesus is our present tense Mediator, representing us before God. Jesus doesn't argue our case on the basis of *our* good works or righteousness, he argues our case and comes to our aid on the basis of *his* righteousness and *his* propitiating[7] work.

EXPLANATION

"Jesus Christ, the only begotten Son of God, is the divinely appointed mediator between God and man..."
Simply put, there is only one true Son of God. He has eternally been the Son of the Father. As the Son of God, he participates in the divine nature with the Father and the Spirit. God has determined that it is through the Son, Jesus, that God and humans experience relationship. The all-wise God has determined for his Son to *reveal* God to men and to *represent* men and women to God.

---

7   *Propitiation* is not a word we use in our everyday speech, but it is a helpful word. It means to appease anger or to satisfy wrath. In this case, Jesus offered himself up to satisfy God's holy wrath toward sinful human beings.

"Having taken upon himself human nature, yet without sin..."
The reason Jesus is the perfect mediator between God and man is because through the incarnation, Jesus is both God and man. Jesus assumed a human nature, adding it to his eternal divine nature. The Son of God has eternally been his own distinct person, and now the one person, Jesus, possesses the divine and human natures forevermore. Jesus did not assume a *corrupt* nature, but he did assume a fully *human* nature. It is not native to human nature to be corrupt, but now in Adam, all humans are born into his corrupt nature. Jesus did become everything it means to be human, but he was not born a sinner. Jesus did become sin for us on the cross, but not because he sinned. Rather, he became sin so that he could make atonement for our sins. Jesus was not born with a corrupt mind, will and affections. He was, however, tempted in every way we are, but where Adam (and all of us in Adam) failed to withstand temptation, Jesus succeeded and obeyed God with joy. It was necessary for our salvation that Jesus be truly human and fully righteous.

"He perfectly fulfilled the law..."
The fact that Jesus fulfilled the law has multiple levels of meaning. On the one hand, at the most basic level, this means Jesus lived out the embodiment of God's law. With regard to the eternal and moral aspect of God's law, reflecting the character and attributes of God, Jesus lived a life perfectly in line with God's standard. A second look at this concept reveals Jesus satisfied *all* of the demands of God's law. For example, the sacrificial death necessary for atonement and the priestly offerings required to enter God's presence were both met in Jesus on the cross. In that sense, Jesus not only embodied the moral aspect of the law, but he endured the covenant curses revealed in the law. In addition, the New Testament refers to the law as a prophetic document. All the law pointed toward, with prediction, prophecy and promise, was fulfilled in Jesus. He was the end—the goal—of the law. Jesus is the substance of all the shadowy promises found in the law.

"suffered and died upon the cross for the salvation of sinners."
Jesus did not just die for our salvation, he died a gruesome, suffering-filled death. The suffering and death sinners deserve is the worst

punishment possible, for treason against a holy God. Death by crucifixion was not like dying in your sleep, and it was not even like being shot, stabbed or decapitated. Death on a Roman cross was the most painful and excruciating death possible. It included piercing, muscle, joint and bone tearing, and eventually suffocation. The death Jesus died was the worst death with the most suffering. When Jesus took death head on, he took on the worst and most shameful form of death.

"He was buried, and rose again the third day..."

After death, Jesus experienced what all human beings experience, returning to the dust from which we are made. His body and soul were separated. His body was buried and his soul went to rest with God. But Jesus did not remain dead. Jesus was not the first person who had been raised from the dead, but Jesus was the first person to *conquer* death. He was the first person who was raised from the dead never to die again. Jesus defeated death, Satan and hell, by rising triumphantly to life. Although still human, Jesus was glorified.

"and ascended to his Father, at whose right hand he ever lives to make intercession for his people."

After Jesus rose from the dead, he spent forty days appearing to his disciples and verifying his resurrection. Biblical records indicate Jesus appeared to over 500 people. After spending this time with them, Jesus ascended back to the Father in heaven from where he had come—only now, as God *and* man. Jesus, as High Priest forever, no longer works toward the atonement, but he does minister in his priestly duties, leading, helping, saving, protecting, defending and interceding on behalf of his people.

"He is the only Mediator, the Prophet, Priest and King of the Church..."

It is vitally and critically important for us to acknowledge Jesus as the way, the truth and the life. No one can come to God except through his mediation. He is the only one who represents God to the church, and he is the only one who represents the church to God. He serves in this mediatorial role as Prophet (one who speaks for God), King (one who rules on behalf of God) and Priest (one who represents people to God).

"and Sovereign of the Universe."

Jesus accomplished what Adam failed to do. Jesus secured dominion over all the earth. When Jesus exclaimed all authority in heaven and on earth had been given to him,[8] he made that exclamation as the man Jesus Christ. As God, Jesus had always exerted authority with his divine nature, but now, through his living, dying and rising as a man, Jesus was given all authority over heaven and earth. Jesus is the victorious vice-regent who fills the earth with the image of God.

MISCONCEPTIONS

Since we have already looked at some of the heresies involved with who Jesus is, we aren't going to spend time here covering those. Obviously, with someone as influential and controversial as Jesus Christ, there are going to be endless misconceptions. However, what we can do here is look at how *we like to treat Jesus like a buffet.* Many of us like *aspects* of who Jesus is, but we neglect other aspects. We must work hard to make sure we have put our faith in the *real* Jesus.

With that in mind, let's consider three misconceptions or dangers. First, we can overemphasize the *priestly role* of Jesus, to the exclusion of Jesus as Prophet and King. When we do this, we might create the "lovey-dovey" Jesus. We love the fact Jesus offered himself up for us. It shows us how important *we* are. It means Jesus will always forgive us and never be mad at us for anything. The problem with this view is Jesus is also a *prophet* who challenges our idols and calls us to the carpet on our view of reality. And, Jesus is also a *king* who demands our obedience. If we overemphasize Jesus as Priest to the exclusion of Jesus as Prophet and King, we create a false Jesus who looks more like the modern god of tolerance.

A second misconception or danger is when we overemphasize the *prophetic role* of Jesus, to the exclusion of Jesus as Priest and King. When we do this, we might create an angry Jesus. He convicts us at every turn. He constantly challenges our empty religion. He pierces our hearts with his amazing teaching, always calling us to more. The

---

8   Matthew 28:18.

problem with this view is Jesus is also a priest who gave himself up for us out of love. And, Jesus is a king who is humble and lowly in heart, exhibiting astounding gentleness, kindness, patience, joy and self-control. If we overemphasize Jesus as Prophet, to the exclusion of Jesus as Priest and King, we create a false Jesus, who looks more like the modern god of resistance.

A final misconception or danger is to overemphasize the *kingly role* of Jesus, to the exclusion of Jesus as Priest and Prophet. When we do this, we might create a domineering Jesus. He puts heavy demands upon our lives. He leads from the top down. He is all about stream-lining, efficiency, accountability and results. The problem with this view is Jesus is also a priest who won by losing, led by serving and executed his power through weakness. And, Jesus is also a prophet who speaks tender, loving and caring promises to his people. If we overemphasize Jesus as King, to the exclusion of Jesus as Priest or Prophet, we create a false Jesus who looks more like the modern god of power.

These misconceptions are just as important for us to be aware of as any Christological heresies. All misconceptions about Jesus are danger-ous, but these misconceptions are especially dangerous because they display our deep selfishness, which leads us to pick and choose how and why we follow Jesus. We must be vigilant not to mold our version of Jesus into mirror images of ourselves.

APPLICATION

Article VII: The Mediator

> Jesus Christ, the only begotten Son of God, is the divinely appointed mediator between God and man. Having taken upon himself human nature, yet without sin, he perfectly fulfilled the law; suffered and died upon the cross for the salvation of sinners. He was buried, and rose again the third day, and ascended to his Father, at whose right hand he ever lives to make intercession for his people. He is the only Mediator, the Prophet, Priest and King of the Church, and Sovereign of the Universe.

---

1. We should listen to Jesus above all other words.
We are constantly being bombarded with messages. We have so many different opinions trying to persuade us how to live our lives, in whom to put our trust and what kinds of things we should support and delight in. If Jesus is the only mediator between God and man, then we should be listening to Jesus more closely than anything or anyone else. And all other messages we hear should be evaluated by Jesus Christ.

2. We should trust Jesus as a sufficient sacrifice for our guilt.
We cannot make ourselves right before God by our own merits. Our own righteousness has been ruined through the Fall. Jesus does everything necessary to save us. If we are to be made right with God and be reconciled to God, we must trust in the passive righteousness of Jesus alone. Any mixing of our own works or efforts renders void the sufficient, once-for-all sacrifice of Jesus.

3. We should follow Jesus as our only viable leader.
We were made to be followers, which means all of us, even the best leaders among us, will be following someone. If Jesus is the way, the truth and the life, then it makes no sense to follow anyone else. Jesus is the most humble, most wise, most gracious and most

straight-forward leader who has ever existed. We are called to be his disciples, and that means following him.

4. *We should proclaim Jesus as the only way to God.*

The message of Christianity is the message of Christ. Jesus is *exclusively* the only possible way for sinners to be reconciled to God. It isn't just that he is *able*, it is that without him we are *unable*. That means we are compelled to proclaim Jesus and to proclaim him as the *only* mediator between God and man.

5. *We should worship Jesus as eternal God and worthy Sovereign.*

Jesus is worthy of our worship because he is God, and Jesus is worthy of our worship because of all he has accomplished for us in his life, death and resurrection. While we are not called to pay him back for the sacrifice he made for us, we do owe everything to him out of gratitude. We should praise and boast in Christ alone. He deserves all honour and glory, forever and ever.

VIII

Regeneration

Regeneration is a change of heart, wrought by the Holy Spirit, who quickens the dead in trespasses and sins enlightening their minds spiritually and savingly to understand the Word of God, and renewing their whole nature, so that they love and practice holiness. It is a work of God's free and special grace alone.

Regeneration

INTRO + OVERVIEW

I n the last two articles we have been dealing with how God created the world good, how sin corrupted everything and how Jesus was sent on a mission to become the redeeming Mediator between God and man. As we turn now to different kinds of articles, a helpful distinction is in order. The gospel is deep and full, and at the same time, it is clear and simple. There are so many different things we could say the gospel is. The gospel is salvation, the gospel is the gift of righteousness, the gospel is the news about Jesus, the gospel is the announcement of the kingdom of God, the gospel is reconciliation, the gospel is…many things.

Distinguishing between the history of salvation and the order of salvation

What will help us make sense of the gospel, both its simplicity and its complexity, is clarifying between the *history* of salvation and the *order* of salvation. The *history of salvation* is the events—events like the incarnation, the death of Jesus, the resurrection of Jesus, the ascension of Jesus, etc.—that make up the basic story of the gospel. The *order of salvation* is the application—applications like justification, sanctification, perseverance, glorification, etc.—that make up the benefits, new realities and new identities of the gospel.

There are at least three reasons this distinction is helpful because the story, like any story, is infused with meaning and significance. First, this distinction is helpful because it helps us navigate what we mean when we use the phrase, "The gospel is_____." The story of the gospel is *one story,* and its basic core is that Jesus came, lived, died and rose from the dead. However, the gospel is more than that, because even those historical details need to be explained. For example, think about this sentence: Jesus died. We, because we have had some exposure to who Jesus is and what his death might mean, (probably) immediately associate a certain meaning to that sentence. But imagine if you had never heard anything about Jesus and did not know anything about what the Bible says about him. Jesus died. George Washington died. Martin Luther King Jr. died. These are historical facts with no explanation. The story of salvation says, Jesus died. The order of salvation helps us answer the question, "So what?" So the order of salvation might say, Jesus died so we might be declared righteous before God. That is the order of salvation because it gives a specific significance to the historical event we call justification (Article XI).

Second, distinguishing between the history of salvation and the order of salvation is helpful because through it we learn the difference between *salvation accomplished* and *salvation applied.* The history of salvation happens externally to us. In other words, we have no part in it. It is what God has done in Christ to save. And while the order of salvation is not to be seen as "our part" in salvation because it is still the work of God, the order of salvation is where the history of salvation intersects with our lives. The order of salvation explains how this gospel story, which is external to us, becomes our own story, challenging, changing and reorienting our very lives. The order of salvation makes the objective gospel subjective. And it is more than just our response to the gospel, it is God working out the historical gospel in our lives. That is why we still sometimes say, "The gospel is_____," when we speak of the order of salvation, because it is only good news to us when God graciously applies the work of Christ in our lives. To put it simply, the order of salvation is the Holy Spirit applying in us the history of salvation, which Jesus accomplished for us.

Third, the distinction is helpful because it helps us remember that the story and the order are both vital. It is easy for us to focus on the story only, and so forget the rich depth of meaning in the gospel, and it is just as easy to get caught up in the meaning of the story and forget there were real historical events which gave credence to those gospel truths. We make the order of salvation stale if we forget the history of salvation, and we become shallow in our view of the history of salvation if we neglect to reflect and actively believe the order of salvation. What Jesus did and what that means for us are both vital for walking with God.

While the last few articles have focused mainly on the *history* of salvation, as we look at this article on regeneration,[1] we enter the vicinity of the *order* of salvation.

The need for regeneration

Regeneration is the first, fundamental and decisive change by which the Holy Spirit makes a person a new creation in Christ. Before we break down this definition, let's take a brief look at what total depravity has done to us, so we can understand why regeneration is so important.

One of the Scriptures where the word *regeneration* appears is Titus 3. Paul begins by saying,

> For we too were once foolish, disobedient, deceived [the mind], enslaved to various lusts [the will] and pleasures [the affections], spending our life in malice and envy, hateful, hating one another [actions] (Titus 3:3).[2]

Total depravity means we have *corrupt minds*. We are foolish and deceived. We think we know what is best, but because our minds are rotten, we *think* wrong. Total depravity also means we have *corrupt wills*. We *choose* wrong. And this is no little thing because we are actually a slave to our wrong choosing. Sin enslaves us so even when we make free choices, those free choices are controlled by and rushing toward sin. Total depravity also means we have *corrupt affections*. We move toward the wrong things *with delight*. We enjoy things that kill us and hate things meant for our good. And all of this together, corrupt minds, wills and affections, produces all kinds of *corrupt actions* in and out from us. Because we are totally depraved, disobedience, malice, envy, hatred, etc. are inevitable in our lives.[3]

Out of this context of total depravity, the Scripture leads us toward the *need* for regeneration. We don't just need a new start, we need a new life. Paul continues,

---

1   Think about a generator. It provides power to your house if the power goes out. It is a life-giving force. So, *regeneration* simply means *to revive* or *to give life back to something*.

2   Parentheses by the author.

3   See Article VI: The Fall of man.

But when the kindness of God our Savior and *His* love for mankind appeared, He saved us, not on the basis of deeds which we did in righteousness, but in accordance with His mercy, by the washing of regeneration and renewing by the Holy Spirit, whom He richly poured out upon us through Jesus Christ our Savior, so that being justified by His grace we would be made heirs according to *the* hope of eternal life (Titus 3:4-7).

Now, there is *much* more here than just the article of regeneration, but we see briefly the distinction between the history of salvation and the order of salvation. The history of salvation, according to Titus 3, is that "when the kindness of God our Savior and His love for mankind appeared, He saved us." But how does this salvation meet us in our lives? "By the washing of regeneration and renewing by the Holy Spirit." Again, there is more here, but this is the answer to our total depravity. Our total corruption demanded a total renewal; in Christ, that is what we receive.

As we close out this section, let's look back at our initial definition of regeneration. Regeneration is the first, fundamental and decisive change by which the Holy Spirit makes a person a new creation in Christ. Regeneration is *first* because it is the first thing we need for our transformation. Before we can believe, repent or be made holy, God must change us. A person cannot believe in Christ with a totally depraved will. They will not—they *cannot*—choose Jesus until their will has been renewed. A person cannot repent of sin and turn to God with a totally depraved mind and totally depraved affections. They will not—they *cannot*—submit to God's law until their mind and affections have been renewed. Regeneration must be first because we are totally dependent upon God in salvation. God must work new life in us, if we are to be found in Christ.

Regeneration is *fundamental* because it changes us at our core. Regeneration doesn't mean some part of us, out on the periphery of our lives, gets touched with holiness, it means we are given a new and radically different spiritual life. This new life works itself out through our minds, our wills, our affections and our actions. Regeneration, the new life we receive, isn't synonymous with glorification (our final perfected life in Christ), but just like total depravity, regeneration *affects every area* of our lives. Since we experience a fundamental change, that fundamental change affects our whole being.

Regeneration is *decisive* because once we are changed by the Spirit of God at the core of our being, there is no going back. When the Holy Spirit revives us, it is impossible for us to die again. Regeneration is a one time event, and if it happens to us, then that settles it. Once regenerated, we are no longer *dead* in our sins, but are instead *alive* to God because we now possess Holy Spirit life.

Finally, it is vitally important for us to affirm regeneration is a work of God alone. Particularly, the Holy Spirit is emphasized as the agent of regeneration. This regenerative act contains no amount of help on our part whatsoever. Regeneration is totally of free grace. The image regeneration resembles is that of the first creation, when God merely spoke creation into existence. Just as Jesus was raised from the dead, through regeneration, the same Spirit who raised Jesus up raises sinners from death to life as well.[4] Just as Christ was raised as the first fruits of a new creation, through regeneration the Holy Spirit implants Christ's new creational life in us.[5] Because of sin, we are just as helpless and lifeless as the dust which God used to create Adam. But just like God breathed his breath of life into Adam,[6] the Holy Spirit breathes the new resurrected life of Christ into us.[7] Adam was God's created being; in Christ, we are God's new-created beings.

SCRIPTURAL FOUNDATIONS

Deuteronomy 30:1–10

> "So it will be when all of these things have come upon you, the blessing and the curse which I have placed before you, and you call *them* to mind in all the nations where the LORD your God has scattered you, and you return to the LORD your God and obey Him with all your heart

---

4   See Romans 8:11.
5   See 1 Corinthians 15:20–23.
6   Genesis 2:7.
7   John 20:22.

and soul in accordance with everything that I am commanding you today, you and your sons, then the LORD your God will restore you from captivity, and have compassion on you, and will gather you again from all the peoples where the LORD your God has scattered you. If any of your scattered *countrymen* are at the ends of the earth, from there the LORD your God will gather you, and from there He will bring you back. The LORD your God will bring you into the land which your fathers possessed, and you shall possess it; and He will be good to you and make you more numerous than your fathers."

"Moreover, the LORD your God will circumcise your heart and the hearts of your descendants, to love the LORD your God with all your heart and all your soul, so that you may live. And the LORD your God will inflict all these curses on your enemies and on those who hate you, who persecuted you. And you will again obey the LORD, and follow all His commandments which I am commanding you today. Then the LORD your God will prosper you abundantly in every work of your hand, in the children of your womb, the offspring of your cattle, and in the produce of your ground, for the LORD will again rejoice over you for good, just as He rejoiced over your fathers; if you obey the LORD your God, to keep His commandments and His statutes which are written in this Book of the Law, if you turn to the LORD your God with all your heart and soul."

Here, Moses speaks to God's people using the image of circumcision. This was not a foreign concept to the people who had received this sign from God. But here, instead of Moses talking about a circumcision of the flesh, he speaks of a *circumcision of the heart*. It is the acknowledgment that transformation of sinful humanity must take place from the inside out. God must strike a blow to the very core of our being, if we are to be transformed by him. The result of this heart circumcision is a love for God which leads to life. Regeneration, then, is heart surgery, and it is a matter of life and death.

Ezekiel 36:24-32

For I will take you from the nations, and gather you from all the lands; and I will bring you into your own land. Then I will sprinkle clean water on you, and you will be clean; I will cleanse you from all your filthiness and from all your idols. Moreover, I will give you a new heart and put a new spirit within you; and I will remove the heart of stone from your flesh and give you a heart of flesh. And I will put My Spirit within you and bring it about that you walk in My statutes, and are careful and follow My ordinances. And you will live in the land that I gave to your forefathers; so you will be My people, and I will be your God. Moreover, I will save you from all your uncleanness; and I will call for the grain and multiply it, and I will not bring a famine on you. Instead, I will multiply the fruit of the tree and the produce of the field, so that you will not receive again the disgrace of famine among the nations. Then you will remember your evil ways and your deeds that were not good, and you will loathe yourselves in your own sight for your wrongdoings and your abominations. I am not doing *this* for your sake," declares the LORD God; "let *that* be known to you. Be ashamed and humiliated for your ways, house of Israel!"

Regeneration deals mainly with the corrupting power of sin. Our idolatry has led us into filth; in regeneration we are cleansed. Our fallen nature is void of life and our heart is a heart of stone, but in regeneration our heart is replaced with a living heart. In fact, it isn't just a new spirit we receive, God puts *his* very Spirit within us. Our new spiritual life is Holy Spirit life because it is given by virtue of his presence and activity. The state of sin enslaved us to acts of sin, but in regeneration the Holy Spirit causes us to walk in God's ways. When we were dead in our sins, we might have had a sense of shame or guilt, but it wasn't the appropriate kind of guilt which sees God as the target of our crimes.[8] Once we are regenerated, we receive a new mind and we now see life differently. When we see all of our sin as rebellion against a holy, precious and benevolent God, we remember our evil deeds in a new and different way. We see our sin for what it truly is, and loathe ourselves for it. Finally, in sin we exchanged the glory of God for the good things God had made. Now, through regeneration, we come to understand all of creation, all of life and even our own salvation, is not ultimately about us—it is God who is the main character of the story, and he is right in acting for his own name's sake. Only through regeneration can we rejoice at this thought!

---

8   See Psalm 51.

John 3:1-3

> Now there was a man of the Pharisees, named Nicodemus, a ruler of the Jews; this man came to Jesus at night and said to Him, "Rabbi, we know that You have come from God *as* a teacher; for no one can do these signs that You do unless God is with him." Jesus responded and said to him, "Truly, truly, I say to you, unless someone is born again he cannot see the kingdom of God."

This is probably one of the most important Scriptures for explaining what happens to a person when they are saved. So much so, the term *born again* has become a shorthand phrase for a person who is a Christian. Regeneration should be envisioned as a second birth. It is that radical, that fundamental and that transformational; it carries with it the imagery of someone becoming a totally new person. No wonder Nicodemus was so confused when Jesus said this to him! Because sin has so affected our mind, will and emotions, our spiritual sight is completely wrecked. By nature, we are spiritually blind. Regeneration, then, is a prerequisite for someone to even see the kingdom of God. To be given new eyes to see the things of God, we must undergo a comprehensive and decisive transformation so all encompassing that Jesus expresses it as a *new birth*.

2 Corinthians 4:3-7

> And even if our gospel is veiled, it is veiled to those who are perishing, in whose case the god of this world has blinded the minds of the unbelieving so that they will not see the light of the gospel of the glory of Christ, who is the image of God. For we do not preach ourselves, but Christ Jesus as Lord, and ourselves as your bond-servants on account of Jesus. For God, who said, "Light shall shine out of darkness," is the One who has shone in our hearts to give the Light of the knowledge of the glory of God in the face of Christ.
>
> But we have this treasure in earthen containers, so that the extraordinary *greatness* of the power will be of God and not from ourselves.

Those who are unregenerated, dead in their sins, cannot see the beauty of the gospel. They can hear it over and over, but they will not receive it. It is as if a veil hovers over the gospel, so the message is obscured and hidden. But, our call is to preach Christ and to live as bond-servants for the sake of Jesus, and trust the Holy Spirit to perform his life-giving work. When the Spirit brings a person from death to life, it is like day one of creation, when God spoke and there was light. We are completely dependent on the Spirit for regeneration, and he deserves all the glory for it. When a person dead in their sins is enlightened by God to see and believe the gospel of the glory of Christ, it is nothing less than a miracle!

Ephesians 2:1-10

And you were dead in your offenses and sins, in which you previously walked according to the course of this world, according to the prince of the power of the air, of the spirit that is now working in the sons of disobedience. Among them we too all previously lived in the lusts of our flesh, indulging the desires of the flesh and of the mind, and were by nature children of wrath, just as the rest. But God, being rich in mercy, because of His great love with which He loved us, even when we were dead in our wrongdoings, made us alive together with Christ (by grace you have been saved), and raised us up with Him, and seated us with Him in the heavenly *places* in Christ Jesus, so that in the ages to come He might show the boundless riches of His grace in kindness toward us in Christ Jesus. For by grace you have been saved through faith; and this *is* not of yourselves, *it is* the gift of God; not a result of works, so that no one may boast. For we are His workmanship, created in Christ Jesus for good works, which God prepared beforehand so that we would walk in them.

This is salvation applied! This is how God takes the objective work of Christ and brings it to bear upon our lives. When the work of Christ is applied to us, we are raised from death to life, through regeneration. And notice, this life given by God is not in *response* to any good thing we put forward—no good thing of the mind, will or affections. Paul goes to great pains to remind us that God's life giving activity, because it is an act of grace, is exercised upon us "even when we were dead in our wrongdoings." While there is so much more we could say here, let us focus our attention on the last sentence of this glorious paragraph. Through regeneration we are "created in Christ Jesus." The resurrection of Jesus is the foundation of regeneration because through the resurrection Jesus inaugurated a new creation—he himself being the first fruits. Before regeneration, we belonged to Adam, the first man. We are all citizens of the first creation, cursed and destined to perish. But, through regeneration, we are *re*-created in Christ, the last man. We aren't just citizens of a new creation, we ourselves *are* a new creation, since by the Spirit we are united to the One who is the new creation.

1 John

If you know that He is righteous, you know that everyone who practices righteousness also has been born of Him (1 John 2:29).

No one who has been born of God practices sin, because His seed remains in him; and he cannot sin *continually*, because he has been born of God (1 John 3:9).

Beloved, let's love one another; for love is from God, and everyone who loves has been born of God and knows God (1 John 4:7).

Everyone who believes that Jesus is the Christ has been born of God, and everyone who loves the Father loves the *child* born of Him (1 John 5:1).

For whoever has been born of God overcomes the world; and this is the victory that has overcome the world: our faith (1 John 5:4).

We know that no one who has been born of God sins; but He who was born of God keeps him, and the evil one does not touch him (1 John 5:18).

This string of verses from 1 John reveal a whole book of the Bible dedicated to helping us understand what it means to be born of God— to possess the life of God through regeneration. Regeneration produces righteousness in us because God is righteous. Regeneration means sin is a contradiction in us because life in the Spirit is contrary to a life of sin. Regeneration produces love in us because God is love. Regeneration produces faith in us because through this new Holy Spirit life we see the beauty and worth of Jesus. Regeneration causes us to overcome the world because we are born of a life greater than the world—we are born of God himself. Regeneration does not mean a Christian cannot or will not sin. In fact, we know from other Scriptures, like Romans 7 and Galatians 5, Christians continue to sin. We are called to fight against sin until the day we die. However, John is using such striking language to show us the radical nature of the change the Holy Spirit works in our lives. All kinds of new things come out of our lives and all kinds of old things exit the picture, when the Holy Spirit make us new in Christ.

EXPLANATION

"Regeneration is a change of heart wrought by the Holy Spirit..."

At the most basic level, we are referring to a change at the core of our being. This change is not something we bring upon ourselves. Instead, it is something that happens to us. Regeneration is the person of the Holy Spirit applying the work of Christ, according to the election of the Father. All those whom the Father has chosen before the foundation of the world[9] will experience regeneration by the Holy Spirit.

"who quickens the dead in trespasses and sins..."

This change is a change from death to life. It is not an incremental change. Regeneration is not something changing us from worse to better. Regeneration is not mere improvement. Regeneration creates something new. It is a miracle of life out of someone who was spiritually dead.

---

9   Ephesians 1:4.

"enlightening their minds spiritually and savingly..."
Just like total depravity affects the mind's ability to understand the things of God, so regeneration allows a person to understand spiritual things. This new ability to perceive the things of God is the work of the Holy Spirit. It is not a deeper insight, it is a *new ability* altogether. This spiritual enlightenment is necessary for salvation. To *enter* the kingdom of God, we need to be able to *see* the kingdom of God. When the Holy Spirit works this new life in us, he imparts the knowledge of salvation.

"to understand the Word of God..."
An unregenerate person who was bored to death by the Bible, after regeneration is thrilled by it. A person who was totally uninvolved and uninterested in the Word of God, is now dying to get more of it. There is a genuine understanding, a communion with God through his Word.

"and renewing their whole nature..."
If we remember how sin corrupted the whole nature of man, then we know salvation must include a renewal of the whole nature of man. Through regeneration, we are no longer objects of wrath according to our nature. We are no longer slaves to the passions, lusts and pleasures of the world. We are not a different person, but what we are has undergone a change. We have been generated from a new source. There has been a cleansing renovation. The new creational activity of the Spirit, inaugurated by the resurrection of Jesus, has been implanted in us.

"so that they love and practice holiness."
This first, fundamental and decisive act of regeneration changes our disposition toward God. This means the appetites and actions of our lives change as well. This is not instant sanctification,[10] or instant glorification.[11] The Fall of man does not mean we are as bad as we possibly could be, but it does mean every area of our life is affected by the Fall. Regeneration doesn't mean we are instantly as holy as we will be, but it does mean every *area* of our life is affected by this new resurrection life.

---

10 The process of becoming holy. See Article XII.

11 Our final state when we are bodily resurrected and perfected in Christ. See Article XIX.

"It is a work of God's free and special grace alone."
God alone is the source of regeneration. He is doing this, not because
of anything we do, or have done, and he is doing this specifically in
individuals hearts. When any Christian is asked, "Why are you a
Christian?" The only correct response is, "Because while I was dead
in my trespasses and sins, God made me alive together with Christ."[12]
And it doesn't matter if we are like John the Baptist (when this happened to him in his mother's womb according to Luke 1:15), or if we
were six years old (and can't remember a time when we didn't believe
in Jesus), or if we are on our deathbed (and will have lived our whole
life dead in our sins until the last moment when God's Spirit breathes
life into us)—this work of God is a miracle of grace! Regeneration
is as miraculous as when God created the universe out of nothing.

MISCONCEPTIONS

There are many different misconceptions related to regeneration, but
we will focus on three. All three of these errors misunderstand
regeneration in the same place—they each see regeneration as brought
about by something other than God. The first misconception is, "I am
a Christian because of my family." Many people falsely believe spiritual
life can be handed down through family members. But we don't receive
spiritual life from our family. Each individual must have their *own*
experience of regeneration because we are all born into Adam and
into his corrupt nature—whether or not we have parents who have
been born again.

The second misconception is, "I am a Christian because of my
country of origin." Just like the misunderstanding of how family might
aid us in receiving spiritual life, there is also a misunderstanding that
being born in a certain place or as a citizen of a certain country would
aid us in receiving spiritual life. There is no such thing as a Christian
nation. God is the God of all nations. Every *person* of every nation must
themselves experience the regenerating power of the Holy Spirit, if
they are to come into fellowship with Christ.

---

12 See Ephesians 2:5.

The final misconception is, "I am a Christian because of my baptism." While baptism is an extremely important aspect of our obedience to Jesus,[13] we don't receive a new birth from the church or from any of the ordinances of the church. It is God and God alone who brings a sinner from death to life. Baptism is an important response to regeneration, but it in no way causes it. We should not put our hope in family, country or baptism with regard to life in Christ—if we make any of these false steps, our mistake would prove fatal.

---

13 So important, in fact, we will spend all of Article XV exploring it.

APPLICATION

Article VIII: Regeneration

Regeneration is a change of heart, wrought by the Holy Spirit, who quickens the dead in trespasses and sins enlightening their minds spiritually and savingly to understand the Word of God, and renewing their whole nature, so that they love and practice holiness. It is a work of God's free and special grace alone.

---

1. *As those born of God, we are reminded to take seriously and get excited about life.*

   We looked at many passages in 1 John where the born again life is described. We should pursue faith in Christ, righteousness, love and turning from sin. It is a privilege to get to enjoy and embody the very life of God. We get to experience eternal life now, because of regeneration.

2. *Regeneration reminds us we are changed from the inside out.*

   We will spend an entire article talking about sanctification, which is how those in Christ are changed, but even in regeneration we are reminded true change must happen from the inside out. This means we should take seriously keeping watch over our souls.

3. *On a relational level, other people change from the inside out as well.*

   When thinking about evangelism, discipleship, parenting, counselling, etc., regeneration reminds us *all life change*, for anyone, must be from the inside out. This means prayer is an essential component to any kind of ministry, in the home, in the world and in the church. We cannot change people, not at their core where it really counts—but God can—and he does!

4. Regeneration reminds us to regard no one according to the flesh.

In 2 Corinthians 5:17, Paul writes, "Therefore if anyone is in Christ, *this person is* a new creation; the old things passed away; behold, new things have come." This is a statement of regeneration. The new-creational life of God has come into a person's life—and we should get excited about being a new creation!

However, this text is not about our own *self identity*. The text starts in verse 16, "Therefore from now on we recognize no one by the flesh; even though we have known Christ by the flesh, yet now we know *Him in this way* no longer." In other words, because regeneration is a reality, we should no longer judge others and relate to them based on their old, dead self. And why is that? Because "if anyone is in Christ, *this person is* a new creation; the old things passed away; behold, new things have come." We should be treating other people like they are born again because they *are* a new creation. We all want to be regarded based on our newness in Christ, wrought by the Spirit. Paul's point is this: if that is how *you* want to be seen—as a new creation—then that is how you should see *others*.

IX

—

Repentance

Repentance is an evangelical grace, wherein a person being by the Holy Spirit, made sensible of the manifold evil of his sin, humbles himself for it, with godly sorrow, detestation of it, and self-abhorrence, with a purpose and endeavour to walk before God so as to please him in all things.

Repentance

INTRO + OVERVIEW

I n Sinclair Ferguson's book *The Whole Christ*, he launches into a discussion about grace, the law and the gospel, by introducing us to a historical moment. It was the year 1717, and a pastor-to-be was faced with a very difficult and tricky decision. He was asked by his ordination board to either approve or deny the following statement:

> I believe that it is not sound and orthodox to teach that we forsake sin in order to our coming to Christ, and instating us in covenant with God.

After sharing the statement, Ferguson then adds, "Turn the question over in your own mind. How would you respond? Do you agree that 'it is not sound and orthodox to teach that we forsake sin in order to our coming to Christ?'"[1] So, how would you respond? Ferguson acknowledges the statement is a bit of a trap. Even so, the answer we give, if we really understand what is being said, reveals at a core level what we think of grace, the gospel and this all important doctrine we turn now to discuss, repentance.

Repentance is an extremely misunderstood concept. Many of us haven't thought very hard about the relationship between the gospel and repentance. *Does repentance prepare us for salvation? Is repentance a distortion of the salvation in the gospel? Does repentance really matter at all?* Many of us profess Jesus gives us salvation as a free gift, but we also assert repentance is necessary. So, how do these things relate and what is the right answer to the tricky statement above?

---

1   Sinclair B. Ferguson, *The Whole Christ: Legalism, Antinomianism, and Gospel Assurance—Why the Marrow Controversy Still Matters* (Wheaton: Crossway, 2016), 28.

To try and make sense of this and answer some of these questions, we are going to look at six helpful categories related to repentance.

1. The cause of repentance

The *cause* of repentance is the person of the Holy Spirit. God leads us in returning to him. God leads us in forsaking sin. God grants repentance.[2] We ought to pray for the power and grace of God to repent. So, herein is one similarity between salvation and repentance— they are both gifts of God, applied through the work of the Spirit in our lives.

2. The nature of repentance

The *nature* of repentance is relational. We should think of repentance, the forsaking of sin and returning to God, as the restoration of a relationship. God is a person whom we have offended by sin and through repentance we are invited to come back to be refreshed in his presence. Repentance is about proximity, it is about closeness and it is about being where God is.

3. The outcome of repentance

The *outcome* of repentance is a new endeavour. Repentance brings about new actions, new desires and new direction. Repentance is reflected in the aims of our life. Repentance sets us on a new path and launches us on a new journey. Repentance sets our face toward God.

4. The extent of repentance.

The *extent* of repentance is pervasive. Repentance works with the specifics of sin and the generalities of sin. Repentance acknowledges particular sins, and it addresses sin at large. The influence of repentance is widespread—it permeates into *all* of life. Repentance is a lifelong experience, and it is experienced in all of life.

5. The place of repentance

The *place* of repentance is a response to regeneration. It is only after a person has experienced, "a change of heart, wrought by the Holy Spirit, who quickens the dead in trespasses and sins enlightening their

---

2   See 2 Timothy 2:25.

minds spiritually and savingly to understand the Word of God,"[3] that repentance can flow from the heart and into the life. A living heart knows the horror of sin which a dead heart could never know. A living heart sees the beauties of God which a dead heart could never see. A living heart desires a relationship with God which a dead heart could never desire.

6. The context of repentance

The *context* of repentance is the gospel. Repentance doesn't happen outside or alongside the gospel. Repentance happens underneath the umbrella of the gospel. Repentance is a response to the gospel. Repentance is a gift of the gospel. Repentance is a grace secured through the gospel. Were there no substitutionary life, death and resurrection of Jesus, repentance would be meaningless. No amount of repentance could make up for the sins we have committed, and no amount of repentance could make us desirable in God's eyes. As the hymn, "Rock of Ages, Cleft for Me," by Augustus Toplady, so clearly expresses:

> Could my zeal no respite know,
> Could my tears forever flow,
> All for sin could not atone,
> Thou must save, and Thou alone.

With these categories in mind, we come back to the delicate statement we opened with. Will we affirm or deny? How should we respond to the trick question? With a right understanding of repentance, we should approve! Repentance is an *outworking* of coming to Christ, not a *qualification* for coming. Repentance is the lifelong process of forsaking sin and turning to God, but to make repentance necessary in order to "coming to Christ" would make, our turning, not Christ's dying, the warrant for our salvation. Repentance is vital, but it is included in the free gift of life bestowed on us in Christ through the Spirit. It is not a pre-condition to receive the life offered to us in Jesus. If we could turn from our sin without first coming to Christ, there would be no need for Christ. If forsaking sin was a prerequisite for God's grace in our lives, no one would know the grace of God.

---

3   Ssee Article VIII: Repentance.

Before we press on in the Scriptures, to be clear, let me clearly answer some of those earlier questions. *Does repentance prepare us for salvation?* No. Nothing can prepare us for salvation. God saves us while we are dead in our trespasses and sins. *Is repentance a distortion of the salvation in the gospel?* No. Repentance flows from salvation in the gospel. When we attempt to repent outside of the context of the gospel, we distort the salvation in the gospel. *Does repentance really matter at all?* Yes. Repentance is one of the crowning jewels of the gifts given to us in Christ. Forsaking sin and turning to God—repentance— is a painfully joyful grace of God. No person who does not forsake sin and turn to God will enter the kingdom of God,[4] but this forsaking and turning is experienced *within* God's covenant grace, not as a qualification to obtain it.

SCRIPTURAL FOUNDATIONS

Exodus 9:27-35

Then Pharaoh sent for Moses and Aaron, and said to them, "I have sinned this time; the LORD is the righteous one, and I and my people are the wicked ones. Plead with the LORD, for there has been enough of God's thunder and hail; and I will let you go, and you shall stay no longer." Moses said to him, "As soon as I go out of the city, I will spread out my hands to the LORD; the thunder will cease and there will no longer be hail, so that you may know that the earth is the LORD's. But as for you and your servants, I know that you do not yet fear the LORD God." (Now the flax and the barley were ruined, for the barley was in the ear and the flax was in bud. But the wheat and the spelt were not ruined, for they *ripen* late.) So Moses left the city from *his meeting* with Pharaoh, and spread out his hands to the LORD; and the thunder and the hail stopped, and rain no longer poured on the earth. But when Pharaoh saw that the rain and the hail and the thunder had stopped, he sinned again and hardened his heart, he and his

---

4   Repentance is a *necessary consequence* of regeneration.

servants. So Pharaoh's heart was hardened, and he did not let the sons of Israel go, just as the LORD had spoken through Moses.

This text is important because it shows us a type of interaction with sin and remorse that falls short of true repentance. We should marvel Pharaoh confesses his sin! We should marvel Pharaoh confessed God to be the righteous one! We should marvel Pharaoh confesses himself and his people to be utterly wicked! We should marvel Pharoah seems to have set his face toward a new endeavour in light of God's heavy hand upon him! This seems so genuine and so promising—and yet Moses is not impressed. Moses knows Pharaoh's remorse is driven by selfishness; his remorse is only in order to get a better lot in life; his remorse will not end in a new endeavour. Moses knows there has not been a regenerative change of heart leading to the true fear of God in Pharaoh. Pharaoh just wants his life back. As soon as he gets what he wants, Pharoah hardens his heart once again. At every level and measured by all the categories we have examined, this falls short of true repentance. O, how often do we all settle for what falls short of true repentance!

Isaiah 55:6-9

> Seek the LORD while He may be found;
> Call upon Him while He is near.
> Let the wicked abandon his way,
> And the unrighteous person his thoughts;
> And let him return to the LORD,
> And He will have compassion on him,
> And to our God,
> For He will abundantly pardon.
> "For My thoughts are not your thoughts,
> Nor are your ways My ways," declares the LORD.
> "For as the heavens are higher than the earth,
> So are My ways higher than your ways
> And My thoughts than your thoughts.

Many times repentance is cast in a negative light. It is associated with doom and gloom, hell, fire and brimstone preaching. The reason repentance is represented in this way is because it is stripped of its *gospel context*. When repentance is set forward as a *qualification* for coming to Christ, it becomes cold, lifeless and burdensome. But within the context of grace, repentance is the most wonderful invitation. In these verses, God has made himself available. God has, on his initiative, drawn near to sinners. Repentance is set forward as the opportunity of a lifetime—to leave behind the foolish ways and dumb thoughts of our sinfulness and enter the heavenly highways and thoughts of God. Repentance is the invitation to get to think and act like God—the God in whose image we were originally made.

Matthew 12:38-45

Then some of the scribes and Pharisees said to Him, "Teacher, we want to see a sign from You." But He answered and said to them, "An evil and adulterous generation craves a sign; and so no sign will be given to it except the sign of Jonah the prophet; for just as JONAH WAS IN THE STOMACH OF THE SEA MONSTER FOR THREE DAYS AND THREE NIGHTS, so will the Son of Man be in the heart of the earth for three days and three nights. The men of Nineveh will stand up with this generation at the judgment, and will condemn it because they repented at the preaching of Jonah; and behold, *something* greater than Jonah is here. *The* Queen of *the* South will rise up with this generation at the judgment and will condemn it, because she came from the ends of the earth to hear the wisdom of Solomon; and behold, *something* greater than Solomon is here.

"Now when the unclean spirit comes out of a person, it passes through waterless places seeking rest, and does not find it. Then it says, 'I will return to my house from which I came'; and when it comes, it finds *it* unoccupied, swept, and put in order. Then it goes and brings along with it seven other spirits more wicked than itself, and they come in and live there; and the last *condition* of that person becomes worse than the first. That is the way it will also be with this evil generation."

At first, it might seem like the two parts of this Scripture aren't paired well together. Matthew seems to be arranging his material with no helpful order in mind. But when we think a little deeper about the true nature of repentance, we realize they are inseparable. The book of Jonah is well known for its supernatural events, irony and infamously flamboyant main character, Jonah. Jonah is without a doubt the worst prophet in Israel's history—and yet God uses him to bring about the greatest revival recorded in human history! Jesus points to Jonah and the people who repented at his preaching, and says they will be a witness against his generation at the final judgment because they actually repented.

And then, it seems, Jesus changes the subject to demonology. But, the last sentence is the clue to understanding how these teachings fit together. Jesus says, "That is the way it will also be with this evil generation." Demonology is actually an illustration of what he has been talking about. The same generation convicted by the people of Nineveh, have gone through an experience mirroring this illustration. John the Baptist came and preached repentance to the generation and many of them purged sins and swept the houses of their lives. But they didn't realize John the Baptist was a preparatory prophet. So whatever repentance the people thought they had experienced, it wasn't true repentance because while forsaking sin, the people didn't turn to God through Jesus Christ. They may have gotten rid of some sins because of the preaching of John, but they hadn't welcomed Christ to take up residence in their hearts. Now the demon was going to return, and bring its friends. These people were worse off than if John had never led them toward repentance in the first place. True repentance isn't just about purging bad things from our lives. It's about joyfully embracing the necessary changes and turnings which come from a relationship with God through Jesus Christ.

Romans 2:1-4

Therefore you have no excuse, you *foolish* person, everyone *of you* who passes judgment; for in that *matter in* which you judge someone else, you condemn yourself; for you who judge practice the same things. And we know that the judgment of God rightly falls upon those who practice such things. But do you suppose this, you foolish person who passes judgment on those who practice such things, and *yet* does them *as well*, that you will escape the judgment of God? Or do you think lightly of the riches of His kindness and restraint and patience, not knowing that the kindness of God leads you to repentance?

Many of us falsely believe the way toward repentance is through fear and condemnation. Certainly, the sense of fear and the threat of condemnation have their place as real and legitimate motivating factors for change in our lives, but they are not ultimate. Paul reminds the Romans we can't judge people or bully people into forsaking sin and turning to God—that, after all, is not how God moved us. Ultimately, the reason people are led to repentance is the kindness of God. His grace, his love and his welcoming heart draw people away from sin and deeper into Christ. Harshness is not God's way for motivating change in us, so why should it be ours?

2 Corinthians 7:8-12

For though I caused you sorrow by my letter, I do not regret it; though I did regret it—*for* I see that that letter caused you sorrow, though only for a while—I now rejoice, not that you were made sorrowful, but that you were made sorrowful to *the point of* repentance; for you were made sorrowful according to *the will of* God, so that you might not suffer loss in anything through us. For the sorrow that is according to *the will of* God produces a repentance without regret, *leading to* salvation, but the sorrow of the world produces death. For behold what earnestness this very thing, this godly sorrow, has produced in you: what vindication *of yourselves*, what indignation, what fear, what longing, what zeal, what punishment of wrong! In everything you demonstrated yourselves to be innocent in the matter. So although I wrote to you, *it was* not for the sake of the offender nor for the sake of the one offended, but that your earnestness in our behalf might be made known to you in the sight of God.

While sorrow is not the end of repentance, sorrow is an important and necessary aspect of repentance. Sorrow leads people in different directions. Those who are dead in sin, and have not experienced the regenerating life of the Holy Spirit, cannot experience godly sorrow. The sorrow they feel for the bad things they have done or the sins they have committed, only leads to death. But God has an important design in sorrow for those who have been given new life in the Spirit. It is a sorrow that *drives* true repentance. This sorrow "produces a repentance without regret" and an earnestness to forsake sin and draw near to God. Sorrow alone is not true repentance, but true repentance is driven by godly sorrow.

2 Peter 3:8–15

But do not let this one *fact* escape your notice, beloved, that with the Lord one day is like a thousand years, and a thousand years like one day. The Lord is not slow about His promise, as some count slowness, but is patient toward you, not willing for any to perish, but for all to come to repentance.

But the day of the Lord will come like a thief, in which the heavens will pass away with a roar and the elements will be destroyed with intense heat, and the earth and its works will be discovered.

Since all these things are to be destroyed in this way, what sort of people ought you to be in holy conduct and godliness, looking for and hastening the coming of the day of God, because of which the heavens will be destroyed by burning, and the elements will melt with intense heat! But according to His promise we are looking for new heavens and a new earth, in which righteousness dwells.

Therefore, beloved, since you look for these things, be diligent to be found spotless and blameless by Him, at peace, and regard the patience of our Lord as salvation; just as also our beloved brother Paul, according to the wisdom given him, wrote to you.

We have already examined this text in Article V: Election, but we looked at it primarily from the perspective of argumentation. Here, we want to look at it from the perspective of *devotion*. Just like Paul argued in Romans 2, God's patience is his heart in repentance. The reason it seems God is taking his time is because he is, by nature, not in a hurry. God has nowhere to run off to, no task to get back to and no problem to attend to—he is content, and at rest in his patient providence. Balanced with this, Peter wants us to remember there will be a day which arrives like a thief in the night. While it seems to the world as though God has fallen asleep, he will come to call us to account. Repentance is what God's people do to remain vigilant in the tension of God's patience, on the one hand, and the day of the Lord, on the other. The relational context for repentance is within the grace of the gospel, but the embodied context of repentance is within the *diligent waiting* on the coming day of God. Let us be diligent to be found in him—his patience is our salvation.

EXPLANATION

"Repentance is an evangelical grace..."

From the outset, we establish repentance as an evangelical[5] grace. In other words, it flows out from the gospel. Repentance belongs to the order of salvation and is part of the application of redemption. Repentance is something we do not deserve. Repentance is better than what we should experience. Forsaking sin is just as much a gospel jewel, and is just as much outside our control, as pardon for sin. The Spirit of God works repentance in us, and he does it as an outworking of the finished work of Christ.

"wherein a person being by the Holy Spirit made sensible of the manifold evil of his sin..."

Before a person can repent, they must become aware of sin. This means becoming aware of the manifold evil of sin, the reality that sin is far worse, far deeper and far more offensive than we ever imagined. Certainly all people feel remorse and sorrow for certain acts which they have committed, but this is not true repentance. The Holy Spirit presses the truth and the horror of our sin into our minds—not just our sinful *acts*, but our sinful *state*. We come to understand that nothing we ever did was without sin, all that we are has been marred by sin and there has not been a day in our lives when we loved God or our neighbour to the degree God's law requires. We stop playing the victim and we start acknowledging our utter wickedness before God. The first sign the Spirit is working repentance in our heart is when we come to

---

5   While it has taken on different meanings in modern days, *evangelical* simply means *of or related to the gospel*. We get our English "good news" from the Greek word *evangelion*.

realize repentance will entail a *lifelong* and *pervasive* forsaking of sin and turning to God.

"humbles himself for it, with godly sorrow, detestation of it, and self-abhorrence..."

From this new place of humility, we forsake sin. Having been lowered by the sense of our vile, wretched and despicable state, we are desperate for change. The deep realization of the reality of our sin casts down all high thoughts of ourselves, all self-righteousness and all judgmentalism. We first experience a godly sorrow which drives us forward in repentance. Then we grow in hatred for the sins we have committed. We hate the things that are now shameful in our eyes. We hate the foolish decisions, the unloving actions and the proud feelings. We are ready to say God could justly damn us for the least sin we have committed. But our humility does not stop there. We are repulsed with ourselves. We are disgusted by our very persons. The old man, the man who's mind, will and affections were slave to sin, is now the object of our greatest detestation. We are ready to nail him to the cross; we are ready to cast him into hell forever.

"with a purpose and endeavour to walk before God so as to please him in all things."

Forsaking sin is not all repentance entails. Hating our sin and abhorring ourselves does not run the full course of true repentance. The Holy Spirit leads us, with the kindness of God in the gospel in view, toward a new direction. The patience, the grace and the love of God in Christ Jesus, invite us toward a *new orientation*. We are given new energy to run after God. We forsake sin and we turn to God. The power of true and effective repentance is a new view of God. The truly repentant person is not like Pharaoh, seeking to get something from God by forsaking sin. The truly repentant person is convinced God is most lovely, most wise and most gracious. That person sets out on a new course to please God because he believes God loves him and knows what is best for him. The grace of repentance is this: through repentance we get to go where God is; we get to live our lives under his warm smile.

MISCONCEPTIONS

It just so happens the great misconceptions with regard to repentance are simply the opposite of the categories we considered in our introduction. So, the first misconception deals with the *cause* of repentance. This misconception is believing the cause of repentance is self. Strangely enough, if we set out to forsake sin in the power of self, all we have done is dug our hole deeper. The essence of sin is self. If we attempt to turn from sin in our own power, we will find ourselves sinning all the more. This, in fact, is typical of those who are self-righteous and judgmental of others. If we turn from sin on our own, then we begin to feel proud of our accomplishment and we begin to wonder why more people can't forsake sin and turn to God like we have.

The second misconception deals with the *nature* of repentance. The misconception is the idea that repentance is *transactional*. Rather than a return to God, we see it as a deposit into an account. If sin leaves us in a debt to God, then repentance is how we pay God back. We get really sorry, we pay our dues and we accept our lashes so that God will forgive us. That is not repentance. That is penance, but it is not true repentance.

The third misconception deals with the *outcome* of repentance. This misconception is believing repentance is merely purging the bad. We emphasize forsaking sin. We emphasize sorrow for sin. We emphasize hatred of sin. We emphasize self-detestation. But in all our purging, we forget to turn to God. We sit in sorrow and deteriorate in despair. We become like the person in Matthew 12 who has had the unclean spirit driven out, but has not replaced it with any good thing to occupy the space—our present condition becomes worse than the first. Repentance is no less than forsaking sin, but it is so much more! It sets us on a new Godward course. It replaces the bad with the best—Jesus Christ himself.

The fourth misconception deals with the *extent* of repentance. This misconception is tricky, but it is so important because it teaches that the surface area of repentance is simply some of our worst actions. It focuses on the big sins, the outward sins and the known sins. As we have seen, in true repentance, the Spirit of God makes us aware of the manifold evil of sin. Whatever big sins there are, there exists a root from which it flowed. Whatever outward sins there are, there exists some inward motive. Whatever known sins there are, there are a thousand more unknown. We are masters at justifying a thousand little sins because we have found one big ugly sin to turn from—this is not the heart of true repentance. True repentance takes every sin just as seriously, and it knows each sin is involved in an interconnected web encompassing the whole person. True repentance deals with the *state* of sin just as forcefully as the *acts* of sin.

The fifth misconception deals with the *place* of repentance. This misconception is believing repentance is the cause of regeneration. It puts the power for new life in Christ in the hands of sinners, rather than in the hands of the Spirit of Christ. As we have looked at before, if the mind, will and affections were held captive by sin, then how could a person forsake sin unless they were first loosed from sin's captivity? The true character of repentance necessitates a quickened life. Repentance is a gift because regeneration is a gift, and repentance is not able to be enjoyed by us until we have been brought from death to life. Dead people don't repent.

The final misconception deals with the *context* of repentance. This misconception puts repentance under the umbrella of works rather than the gospel. It treats repentance like a side show or an add on to the gospel. This view drives a wedge between the work of Christ and the work of the Spirit. Their works are inseparable. We don't forsake sin so God will love us—in Christ, God has already demonstrated his love for us. We don't forsake sin so Christ will welcome us—Christ has already welcomed us through his outstretched arms on the cross. We don't forsake sin so God will justify us—only the righteousness of Jesus can or will justify anyone. Repentance is a grace, a fruit and a benefit, applied through the gospel. God's love leads us to repentance. Christ's welcome humbles our hearts toward repentance. And, the justifying righteousness of Jesus frees us to repent in heartfelt and loving earnest, without constantly questioning if we have repented enough, if we have been sorry enough or feeling like the force of our salvation actually rests on our shoulders.

APPLICATION

Article IX: Repentance

Repentance is an evangelical grace, wherein a person being by the Holy Spirit, made sensible of the manifold evil of his sin, humbles himself for it, with godly sorrow, detestation of it, and self-abhorrence, with a purpose and endeavour to walk before God so as to please him in all things.

Repentance is one of the appropriate *responses* to the preaching of the gospel. But, before we end by challenging ourselves to actually repent, it is important to clarify our understanding of true repentance.

1. ***We should view the Christian life as perpetual repentance.***
We never get to a place when repentance is not an aspect of our Christian life. There will always be sin to forsake, and there will always be a new endeavour to set our face toward. If we attempt to sum up the whole of the Christian life, one way we could say it is: The whole of the Christian life is Holy Spirit empowered evangelical repentance—forsaking sin and turning to God.

2. ***We should see brokenness as a good thing.***
We live in a day when everything is trivialized. We are beckoned toward a life of ease. True repentance, however, will break a person. We must believe it is good to boast in our weaknesses, "Blessed are the poor in spirit, for theirs is the kingdom of heaven"[6] and Christians are called to work out their salvation with fear and trembling.[7] We must not allow the world, the flesh or the devil to trick us into believing that brokenness, weakness and godly sorrow are bad things.

---

6 Matthew 5:3.
7 Philippians 2:12.

3. We should always remember repentance is a grace of God.

Repentance is something God grants. We are at his mercy if we are to forsake sin and turn to him. This makes us completely dependent on the front end. Turning from sin without God is just a new form of sin. But it also means he deserves all the glory on the back end. When we slay our sin and when we succeed in new endeavours which are pleasing to God, we should fall down on our face and worship him. We don't deserve a sin-free life. We don't deserve to walk in the newness of a life lived to God. And whenever God gives us what we don't deserve, it completes the gift when we express gratitude to him for it. Praising God for our progress will keep us humble and hopeful in the painful joy of repentance.

4. We should wholeheartedly embrace the reality that only the kindness of God leads us to repentance.

Whether we are trying to help someone else in repentance or we are trying to fan the flames of repentance in our own lives, the ultimate motivator for forsaking sin and turning to God is the kindness of God in Christ. He wins our hearts to him with his love. The fear of God and the justice of God are helpful motivators alongside, but it is the kindness of God that seals true repentance.

5. Let us repent and live a life of repentance!

Let's forsake sin and run to God! It is one thing to understand it, it is another thing to do it. It is one thing to understand humility, it is another thing to humble ourselves. Pray to God for repentance, follow through with repentance and praise God for his grace as you wrestle with true repentance.

X

Faith

Saving faith is the belief, on God's authority, of whatsoever is revealed in his Word concerning Christ; accepting and resting upon him alone for justification and eternal life. It is wrought in the heart by the Holy Spirit, and is accompanied by all other saving graces, and leads to a life of holiness.

Faith

INTRO + OVERVIEW

The role of faith in the Christian experience has created controversy from the very beginning. It is hard for us to imagine how offensive it must have been for Jesus to proclaim the necessity and exclusivity of faith in himself. There is a barrage of evidence proving Jesus meant to proclaim himself as the watershed of history. He clearly made belief in himself the litmus test for eternal life or eternal death. Observe a handful of these straightforward proclamations in the Gospel of John:

> "For God so loved the world, that He gave His only Son, so that everyone who believes in Him will not perish, but have eternal life. For God did not send the Son into the world to judge the world, but so that the world might be saved through Him. The one who believes in Him is not judged; the one who does not believe has been judged already, because he has not believed in the name of the only Son of God" (John 3:16–18).

> "The one who believes in the Son has eternal life; but the one who does not obey the Son will not see life, but the wrath of God remains on him" (John 3:36).

> "Truly, truly, I say to you, the one who hears My word, and believes Him who sent Me, has eternal life, and does not come into judgment, but has passed out of death into life" (John 5:24).

> "Do not work for the food that perishes, but for the food that lasts for eternal life, which the Son of Man will give you, for on Him the Father, God, has set His seal." Therefore they said to Him, "What are we to do, so that we may accomplish the works of God?" Jesus

answered and said to them, "This is the work of God, that you believe in Him whom He has sent" (John 6:27-29).

Now on the last day, the great *day* of the feast, Jesus stood and cried out, saying, "If anyone is thirsty, let him come to Me and drink. The one who believes in Me, as the Scripture said, 'From his innermost being will flow rivers of living water'" (John 7:37-38).

And He was saying to them, "You are from below, I am from above; you are of this world, I am not of this world. Therefore I said to you that you will die in your sins; for unless you believe that I am, you will die in your sins" (John 8:23-24).

So then, many other signs Jesus also performed in the presence of the disciples, which are not written in this book; but these have been written so that you may believe that Jesus is the Christ, the Son of God; and that by believing you may have life in His name (John 20:30-31).

This is just a sample of passages from one book of the Bible, which make a clear and compelling case for the vital importance of faith. This kind of evidence should make believing in Jesus for salvation simple and clear right? Well, not exactly. Even before the canon of Scripture was closed,[1] there was intense debate about faith and its role in the lifeblood of Christianity. *How did faith relate to keeping the law? Who is invited to believe?* And, most controversial of all: *What was the relationship between faith and works?*

To try and answer these questions, we will look to six helpful categories,[2] which will aid us in understanding the true character of saving faith.

1. The cause of saving faith

The *cause* of saving faith is the the Spirit of God and the Word of God. Now, while regeneration is wholly an act of God, both repentance and

---

1   For help on understanding the *canon* (or rule) of Scripture, see Article I: The Scriptures, note 16.

2   Some categories are shared with repentance and some are unique to faith.

faith require an individual to be involved. It is God who regenerates, it is an individual who repents. Likewise, it is an individual who believes. But, the *cause* of faith is the Spirit and the Word. Faith is something we *do*, but it is something we do *by the grace of God*. There is no saving faith without the Word of God, and there is no saving faith without the Spirit of God. We could say it in this way: faith is the *act* of an individual, but it is a *work* of God. We ourselves really do believe, and God himself really causes us to believe.

2. The nature of saving faith

The *nature* of saving faith is trust. It is a resting and a resigning. John Murray, in his classic *Redemption Accomplished and Applied*, says it so helpfully this way, "Faith is knowledge passing into conviction, and it is conviction passing into confidence."[3] Here, Murray helps us understand why the conversation about faith is controversial. Faith does include knowledge. But faith doesn't stop there. Faith also includes conviction. It means to know something in a way we know it to be true. Conviction is to be convinced of that thing of which you know. But faith doesn't even stop there. Yet, for many of us that is where faith stops. We think once something has become a conviction, we believe it. But see, there is a difference between believing it and believing *in* it. There is a difference between being *convinced* of something and *trusting* something. The nature of saving faith is trusting. Faith must pass beyond knowledge and conviction if it is to be saving faith. It must take the final step of resting and resigning.

3. The object of saving faith

The *object* of saving faith is Jesus Christ. It is him. We must stop at Jesus *himself*. The object of faith is not assurance of salvation, faith itself or the work of the Holy Spirit in our lives. The object of faith is *Jesus Christ*. Faith is saving when it trusts in Jesus. He is the foundation upon which our faith must rest.

4. The subject of saving faith

The *subject* of saving faith is whoever will believe. Male, female, slave,

---

3 John Murray, *Redemption Accomplished and Applied* (1955; Grand Rapids: Eerdmans, 2015), 116 (Kindle version).

free, Jew, Gentile, sinner, righteous—all are invited, called and commanded to believe on the Lord Jesus Christ. We tend to listen to the
"whosoever will" passages with different ears than those who lived at
the dawn of Christianity. We underestimate the social structures at
play surrounding the initial preaching of the gospel. When Jesus told
Nicodemus, "God so loved the world," Nicodemus would have gasped.
God loves *the world? The dirty, grimy, pagan, idolatrous, sinful, shameful
world?* God loved *the Jews!* God had set up Jewish society to separate
out from the world! *Right?!* This *universal* proclamation of the gospel
was revolutionary! The gospel of Jesus Christ cuts through every class,
every social structure, every ethnic divide and every religious stereo-
type. There is no one on earth excluded from the invitation to become
the subject of saving faith.

5. The place of saving faith

The *place* of saving faith means faith is the instrument by which we
receive Christ. An instrument is a tool. An instrument is secondary.
Here is an intentionally contentious thought: faith doesn't save any-
body. We must keep that straight. Jesus *alone* saves, and faith—and
faith alone—is the instrument by which we receive and rest in Jesus.
We must be careful not to insinuate it is faith *itself* that saves. Faith is
what brings us into contact with our Saviour. That is why the *size* of
faith makes no difference with regard to salvation. Faith the size of a
mustard seed[4] will get the job done because faith is merely the conduit.
As long as there is a mustard seed sized instrument, Christ saves.

6. The outcome of saving faith

The *outcome* of saving faith is God-glorifying works. True faith *produces
fruit.* If there are no God-honouring works in the life of a professing
Christian, we can assume their faith has stopped short of trust. They
may have the knowledge, maybe even the conviction, but they have
fallen short of *confidence.* When our confidence is in God and when
our trust is in Jesus, it will change the way we act. The Holy Spirit
works in our hearts so all of our God-glorifying actions are done in
dependence on him and according to faith in Jesus.

---

4 Matthew 17:20.

SCRIPTURAL FOUNDATIONS

▬▬▬▬▬▬▬

Genesis 15:1-6

After these things the word of the LORD came to Abram in a vision, saying,

> "Do not fear, Abram,
> I am a shield to you;
> Your reward shall be very great."

But Abram said, "Lord GOD, what will You give me, since I am childless, and the heir of my house is Eliezer of Damascus?" Abram also said, "Since You have given me no son, one who has been born in my house is my heir." Then behold, the word of the LORD came to him, saying, "This man will not be your heir; but one who will come from your own body shall be your heir." And He took him outside and said, "Now look toward the heavens and count the stars, if you are able to count them." And He said to him, "So shall your descendants be." Then he believed in the Lord; and He credited it to him as righteousness.

The story of Abram/Abraham is a beautiful illustration of faith. Abraham was not a perfect man. In fact, there were times when he was a bad man. But, he believed in the Lord, and God credited him righteousness as a gift. The idea of reckon or credit is a term of calculation. God calculated Abraham as righteous when Abraham believed in God.

Now, notice carefully it doesn't just say he believed *what* the Lord said. It says he believed *in* the Lord. It wasn't just that Abraham believed *what God said* was true, he believed *God himself* was true. He put his faith in God. Saving faith includes trust in God himself.

Psalm 25:1-3

> To You, LORD, I lift up my soul.
> My God, in You I trust,

Do not let me be ashamed;
Do not let my enemies rejoice over me.
Indeed, none of those who wait for You will be ashamed;
Those who deal treacherously without cause will be ashamed.

In Psalm 25, we observe God's Word to us through David's prayer to God. This is faith in action. Faith and prayer are very connected because prayer is one of the active forms of faith. When we go to God in prayer, it shows we trust him.

There are three powerful things we learn about faith in these few short verses. First, faith is *an offering up of our soul to God*. True faith seeks its protection in God. The thing that is most vulnerable to us, our very soul, is placed in his hands through faith. Jesus offered up his spirit to God before his last breath on the cross.[5] As he was feeling the curse and wrath of God beat him down, this was his ultimate act of faith. When it seemed as though God had abandoned him, and when all of his closest friends had left him, he cast the anchor of his soul into the hands of God. This is faith: we commit our spirit to God, when all else is crashing around us.

Second, faith is *trust*. It is opening ourselves up to be put to shame if God does not vindicate us. It is positioning our lives so that if God were to fail us, we would utterly fail. It is locating our existence where we would crash unless God continued to hold us up.

Third, many times faith means *waiting*. Waiting is the opposite of scurrying. Waiting is the opposite of moving forward. Waiting is the opposite of striving. Faith has an element of patience because God is the One who must win the battle for us. When we try to go ahead without him, it betrays our lack of trust. Sometimes the greatest act of faith is to wait on God, trusting the promise, "none of those who wait for You will be ashamed." Waiting on God is trusting our trust in a trustworthy God.

Habakkuk 2:1-4

I will stand at my guard post
And station myself on the watchtower;

---

5 Matthew 27:50.

And I will keep watch to see what He will say to me,
And how I may reply when I am reprimanded.
Then the LORD answered me and said,
"Write down the vision
And inscribe *it* clearly on tablets,
So that one who reads it may run.
For the vision is yet for the appointed time;
It hurries toward the goal and it will not fail.
Though it delays, wait for it;
For it will certainly come, it will not delay *long*.

"Behold, as for the impudent one,
His soul is not right within him;
But the righteous one will live by his faith."

We learn from Habakkuk that waiting on God is not a *passive* waiting. It includes watching intently, like a person on guard duty. All of God's promises are "Yes" in Christ,[6] even if many of those promises are awaiting their consummation. The delay will reveal one of two things in us: it might reveal we are puffed up and self-interested—then our waiting easily turns to complaining and striving; or, the delay might reveal the kind of faith Abraham had. Faith which is accompanied by eager expectation and watchful listening is the lifeblood of those counted righteous. All of God's "Yes" promises in Christ will certainly come to pass. Our eager longing is no threat to faith. Instead, it is the proof of its genuineness.

Romans 10:8–17

But what does it say? "THE WORD IS NEAR YOU, IN YOUR MOUTH AND IN YOUR HEART"—that is, the word of faith which we are preaching, that if you confess with your mouth Jesus as Lord, and believe in your heart that God raised Him from the dead, you will be saved; for with the heart *a person* believes, resulting in righteousness, and with the mouth he confesses, resulting in salvation. For the Scripture says,

---

6 2 Corinthians 1:10.

"WHOEVER BELIEVES IN HIM WILL NOT BE PUT TO SHAME." For there is no distinction between Jew and Greek; for the same *Lord* is Lord of all, abounding in riches for all who call on Him; for "EVERYONE WHO CALLS ON THE NAME OF THE LORD WILL BE SAVED."

How then are they to call on Him in whom they have not believed? How are they to believe in Him whom they have not heard? And how are they to hear without a preacher? But how are they to preach unless they are sent? Just as it is written: "HOW BEAUTIFUL ARE THE FEET OF THOSE WHO BRING GOOD NEWS OF GOOD THINGS!"

However, they did not all heed the good news; for Isaiah says, "LORD, WHO HAS BELIEVED OUR REPORT?" So faith *comes* from hearing, and hearing by the word of Christ.

Salvation—being made right with God and being swept up into his new creation in Christ—is inextricably linked to faith. Jesus Christ is the Saviour, and if we are to be saved then we must believe in him. Herein lies the importance of our preaching, and herein lies the burden for world missions. If faith in Christ is necessary for salvation, then *gospel proclamation* is necessary for faith!

But there is even more than this to consider. Faith flattens all our petty distinctions. It doesn't matter where we are from, what our earthly customs and backgrounds are or how righteously or sinfully we have lived. What matters is whether we call on the Lord in response to hearing the Word of Christ. Many will rely on where they are from and be disappointed. Many will believe in their own customs and backgrounds and be disappointed. Many will believe in their own sense of self-righteousness and be disappointed. Whoever believes in *Jesus* will not be disappointed. In the end, whether we believe in Jesus is the only distinction that really matters.

Galatians 5:4-6

You have been severed from Christ, you who are seeking to be justified by the Law; you have fallen from grace. For we, through the Spirit, by faith, are waiting for the hope of righteousness. For in Christ Jesus neither circumcision nor uncircumcision means anything, but faith working through love.

Faith is serious business. What hangs in the balance between genuine faith and false faith is nothing short of being "severed from Christ" and "fallen from grace."[7] Faith is not what saves us, but faith is what unites us to the only One who can save us. If we aren't willing to wait to be righteous until Christ makes us righteous,[8] then we haven't actually trusted in Christ at all. We need the Spirit of God to continue the work of faith in us, so that we keep our eyes looking forward on our final destination, rather than falling into the temptation of looking backward. But when this true and genuine faith is at work in our lives, even while we wait for the hope of final and complete righteousness, we work out our faith in exercises of love. We get a taste of our future perfect righteousness, as the Spirit of God works in us even now, by faith, to love God and others with true sincerity.

Hebrews 11:1,32-40

Now faith is *the* certainty of *things* hoped for, a proof of things not seen.... And what more shall I say? For time will fail me if I tell of Gideon, Barak, Samson, Jephthah, of David and Samuel and the prophets, who by faith conquered kingdoms, performed *acts of* righteousness, obtained promises, shut the mouths of lions, quenched the power of fire, escaped the edge of the sword, from weakness were made strong, became mighty in war, put foreign armies to flight. Women received *back* their dead by resurrection; and others were tortured, not accepting their release, so that they might obtain a better resurrection; and others experienced mocking and flogging, and further, chains and imprisonment. They were stoned, they were sawn in two, they were tempted, they were put to death with the sword; they went about in sheepskins, in goatskins, being destitute, afflicted, tormented (*people* of whom the world was not worthy),

---

7   For a detailed discussion on whether someone can "lose their salvation," see Article XIII: Perseverance of the saints.

8   In Article XI: Justification and Article XII: Sanctification, we will discuss the difference between being *declared righteous* and being *made righteous*. Being declared, reckoned or credited righteous happens *instantaneously*. But, being made righteous happens *progressively* and is not completed until we die. That is why we must wait for the hope of righteousness, rather than seeking a righteousness of our own. See Romans 10:1–3.

wandering in deserts, *on* mountains, and *sheltering in* caves and holes in the ground.

And all these, having gained approval through their faith, did not receive what was promised, because God had provided something better for us, so that apart from us they would not be made perfect.

Hebrews 11 is a famous chapter about faith. At the beginning, we get a helpful definition of faith, and then the author provides numerous examples of how faith worked itself out in the lives of God's people. Hebrews 11 is about faith at work.

The definition of faith teaches us at least two things. First, faith deals with things that are in the future and things that are invisible. Faith takes things promised in the future and bends them backward into the present. It allows God's people to live with the future in mind. This looking-forward faith is what we call *hope*. But faith also takes invisible things and gives clarity and sight for those who trust in God. One day, the future will become the present and the invisible will become sight. But for now, living by faith means banking our lives on those realities, even when they are not yet here and not yet seen. We hope for what is not yet here and we see what is not yet visible, when we place our faith in the God who is the beginning and the end, and the substance of all reality.

EXPLANATION

"Saving faith is the belief, on God's authority…"

While it is impossible to deal with saving faith without dealing with Christian faith in general, it is important for us to approach this article from the more narrow sense of "saving faith," since that is what it deals with. We aren't talking about simply trusting God. We are aiming at the belief which leads to salvation.

This article expresses that saving faith must first approach God as God. It is impossible to believe in a saving way until we know this is God's world, we belong to him and he has the authority to command whatever he will from us. However God has chosen to relate to his people and save his people, it is his prerogative. We are bound to submit to his authority. But this is not just demanding and threatening. When we believe in God's authority, it is also comforting. When we are tempted to ask, "Just believe? That's all? But how can I be sure?" We hear the reply, "Yes. Just believe." We think, "Says who?" The Word of God replies, "On God's authority!" We haven't concocted this salvation out of our own imagination. If it were up to us, *faith alone* would not be our choice. Faith alone is so offensive to our pride, even after we are convinced of it, we must be reminded this instrument for receiving salvation was established on nothing less than God's authority.

"of whatsoever is revealed in his Word concerning Christ…"

It is not just God's authority which we must believe in for salvation. Our saving faith is believing what God has revealed in his Word about Jesus Christ. God has made Jesus Christ the central and overwhelming theme of his Word. We are compelled to believe *all* God has revealed about him. We must take great pains to make sure we have believed in the correct Jesus. Of course, there is not really more than one Jesus, but many people have construed a Jesus who they want him to be. We typically get Jesus wrong when we attempt to pick and choose from the Word of God what suits our ideas of Christ. Saving faith, on the other hand, demands a belief in everything revealed about Jesus in God's Word. It is the Jesus Christ of the Scriptures who saves. He imposes his salvation upon us. There is no more important situation in life where it is true that beggars cannot be choosers. Jesus is who he is, and he and no one else will do.

"accepting and resting upon him alone for justification and eternal life…."

Now, it is extremely important that this article places Jesus himself as the *object* of saving faith. There is an easy mistake many make, which spoils the validity of their faith and gives them much grief in their walk with God. Instead of, "accepting and resting upon him alone for justification and eternal life," we sometimes believe saving faith is, "accepting and resting upon *justification* for eternal life."[9] There may be no more vital doctrine in the life of the believer—and to the health

---

9 See Article XI: Justification.

of the church—than justification by faith. But, we sometimes run the risk of replacing Jesus himself with the doctrine. We must be careful to remember justification is one of the *benefits* of faith in Jesus, *not* the object of faith itself. The Bible never tells people to place their faith in justification for eternal life—it tells people to place their faith in Jesus for justification and eternal life. When we rightly emphasize Jesus as the object of our faith, we mitigate the pitfall of misunderstanding the relationship between Jesus as Lord and Jesus as Saviour[10] *and* we correctly join repentance and faith as two sides of the same coin.[11]

"It is wrought in the heart by the Holy Spirit..."

Faith, like repentance, is something we do. But it is not something we would or could do without the Holy Spirit. That is why faith and repentance *follow* regeneration. Faith obviously flows out of the mind, will and affections, but these have been corrupted by sin. Therefore, for our mind, will and affections to move us to trust God, the Holy Spirit must work faith into our hearts. Certainly, it is we who believe, not the Spirit, but we would not believe without his work. Faith is a *gift* from God—something we do for which we should thank God.

"and is accompanied by all other saving graces..."

All of the things at work in the heart of a saved person—like faith, joy, hope and love—come as a package deal. It is not as though we believe and then a few years later we love God. Or, it is not as though we find joy in Christ and then a few months later we believe in him. The graces of a Christian are all wrought in the heart by the Spirit of God *together*. It is true all of these graces can increase and decrease, even faith itself. But in a true believer, they can never be extinguished. We might impair the grace of love in ourselves, but the grace of love cannot be squashed completely, because it is a grace wrought in the heart by the Spirit. A

---

10 Many people talk about accepting Jesus as their Saviour but not as their Lord. Growing up as a self-righteous Pharisee-type, I myself have thought I accepted Jesus as my Lord but not as my Saviour. But in all reality, this is a false dichotomy. Jesus is *Jesus*. He is not a buffet. We either accept and rest in him—*all of him*—or we have not accepted and rested in any of him. Emphasizing Jesus *himself* as the object of faith can minimize this type of thinking and believing.

11 How can someone turn from their sin without believing in Jesus? How can someone believe in Jesus without turning from their sin?

Christian might shrink back in their faith, but the grace of faith will not shrink to the point of not accepting or resting on Jesus. The saving graces of the Spirit of God come to all believers at conversion. They do not come in stages, and they can never die off completely.

"and leads to a life of holiness."

All those who have placed their faith in Jesus will possess a holiness which those who have not placed their faith in Jesus do not possess. While believers are reckoned holy, that is not what we are talking about here. This is referring to real and personal holiness. Saving faith does not only bring the *ability* for holiness, it carries in it a *virtue* of holiness. Faith, like repentance, is a benefit of our salvation, as much as it is an instrument of receiving our salvation. True faith in Christ will create real holiness in us. This does not mean every Christian will be as holy as they could be, but it does mean every Christian is holier than every non-Christian. This holiness is a work of the Spirit in them by faith.

MISCONCEPTIONS

We opened this chapter by talking about the controversy over faith. While there have been minor disputes over the different categories of faith, there is no more difficult question with regard to this article than *the relationship between faith and works*. And the reason this is so difficult is the biblical data does not make it obvious for us. As we will see, there initially appears to be a discrepancy over the relationship between faith and works. This is the biggest misconception related to faith, so we need to dive in.

We must remember we are committed to the fact the Holy Spirit is the author of the Scriptures. We received the Bible by inspiration of God. And we are committed to the fact the Holy Spirit spoke through real men—their words, their personalities and their situations. So, as we look at what two different authors wrote about faith, we must remember that the same Holy Spirit worked through these two men as they wrote the very words of God. These authors cannot be

contradicting each other because God cannot contradict himself.[12]
So what appears to be a discrepancy is actually complementary.

First, let's take a look at Paul. In his letter to the church in Rome,
he sounds forth the clear and sharp message of the gospel. He makes
a point to prove that all people are shut up under the guilt of their sin.
All those who will be saved must be saved in Jesus Christ alone. This
salvation is a complete work of free grace alone, and it is received from
God through faith alone. Faith is the *only instrument* whereby we can
receive the *only salvation* which is *found in Christ alone*. Establishing
this, Paul turns to ask a pointed question of application:

> Where then is boasting? It has been excluded. By what kind of law?
> Of works? No, but by a law of faith. For we maintain that a person is
> justified by faith apart from works of the Law (Romans 3:27–28).

Paul's whole point is we cannot take any credit for our salvation
because it is entirely a gift of God. We cannot elevate ourselves over
anyone else, since we are what we are by grace alone. And in case we
are tempted to believe our faith must be accompanied by good works—
these works themselves completing what is "lacking" in Christ or
making up any part of our right standing before God—Paul states the
case clearly: salvation must exclude works, if it is to honour Christ and
find its true rest in him. If works accompanied our faith in salvation
as a *basis* for righteousness, then we would have something to boast
about! And Paul—and the Holy Spirit—will have none of it.

Having looked at Paul, we now turn to look at James. James is a very
practical book. It is what we might call doctrine-practical. The book
of James grounds the nitty gritty of our daily lives in foundational
doctrines of the Christian faith. Like Paul, James sees faith as a central
and vital aspect of Christianity, and not something we can afford to
get wrong. And like Paul, James asserts the object of our faith is Jesus
Christ. He clearly states,

> My brothers *and sisters*, do not hold your faith in our glorious Lord
> Jesus Christ with *an attitude* of personal favoritism (James 2:1).

---

12 Numbers 23:19.

While both Paul and James are clear on the object of saving faith, Paul was mainly focusing in Romans 3 on the *subject* and *place* of saving faith and here James is focused on the *nature* and *outcome* of saving faith.[13] It is extremely important to understand faith is faith and salvation is salvation, but there are different aspects of both faith and salvation. We need to keep in mind what each of the writers is trying to emphasize.

James writes,

> But someone may *well* say, "You have faith and I have works; show me your faith without the works, and I will show you my faith by my works." You believe that God is one. You do well; the demons also believe, and shudder. But are you willing to acknowledge, you foolish person, that faith without works is useless? Was our father Abraham not justified by works when he offered up his son Isaac on the altar? You see that faith was working with his works, and as a result of the works, faith was perfected; and the Scripture was fulfilled which says, "AND ABRAHAM BELIEVED GOD, AND IT WAS CREDITED TO HIM AS RIGHTEOUSNESS," and he was called a friend of God. You see that a person is justified by works and not by faith alone. In the same way, was Rahab the prostitute not justified by works also when she received the messengers and sent them out by another way? For just as the body without *the* spirit is dead, so also faith without works is dead (James 2:18–26).

First, we see James is interested in the *outcome* of saving faith because he brings up the idea of *showing* our faith. In other words, he wants to discuss what saving faith produces. How can you see faith? You see faith by the works it produces. Second, James is articulating the *nature* of saving faith. Saving faith includes knowledge, but it is more than knowledge. That is the point of saying a person does well for believing God is one—James acknowledges this. Furthermore, saving faith includes conviction, but it is more than conviction. That is the point of bringing up demons. Even they are affected by their belief in God. Their belief in God changes their existence, but having knowledge and conviction do not make things better for them. The demons don't trust

---

13 Earlier in this chapter, I explain the nuance of these categories.

God, love God, enjoy God or know God, even though they believe and shudder. *Saving faith* must pass from knowledge, to conviction, and finally from conviction, to confidence. Abraham clearly had saving faith because he displayed confidence in God. Rahab clearly had saving faith because she displayed confidence in God. This is what James means when he says, "faith was perfected." In other words, it was the right type of faith. The kind of faith which saves is the kind that actually lovingly trusts God, not what James calls "faith alone" which we would define as faith-knowledge or even faith-conviction. He ends with this slam dunk point about the nature of saving faith: faith in the form of *knowledge* and faith in the form of *conviction* are dead without faith in the form of *confidence*. Like a body without a spirit, faith without confidence belongs to a different class than saving faith—and saving faith always produces works.

So, in Romans, when Paul argues for faith alone, he means faith is the only instrument by which we may receive and rest on Jesus Christ for salvation. All people will either be saved by Jesus Christ alone, or they will not be saved at all. James would agree—this is the place of saving faith. And when James urges faith must not be alone, he means there is a kind of faith which will not save because it stops at knowledge and conviction, but does not move to confidence. Paul would agree—this is the nature of saving faith. Remember, Paul himself said in Galatians 5:6, "For in Christ Jesus neither circumcision nor uncircumcision means anything, but faith working through love." It is not as though James is saying, "As a result of your works, your salvation is perfected," he is saying, "As a result of your works, faith was perfected." For Paul, faith alone is about *highlighting the sufficiency of the object of our faith*. For James, faith with works is about emphasizing *the genuineness of our faith in the object*. Paul is pressing us to acknowledge not one ounce of our self has contributed to our salvation, and James is pressing us to acknowledge if we don't see faith at work in our lives then we haven't really believed in Jesus—at least not in a saving way. Paul and James are our friends leading us to understand real and genuine salvation.

APPLICATION

Article X: Faith

Saving faith is the belief, on God's authority, of whatsoever is revealed in his Word concerning Christ; accepting and resting upon him alone for justification and eternal life. It is wrought in the heart by the Holy Spirit, and is accompanied by all other saving graces, and leads to a life of holiness.

---

1. *Faith is not just generic belief or trust—it is belief and trust in particular things.*

This trust begins with God's authority—to walk in faith is to submit to God. This trust also includes God's Word—to walk in faith is to listen to God. This trust includes God's Messiah—to walk in faith is to confess Jesus Christ as Lord. This trust includes God's righteousness—to walk in faith means to receive the gift of Jesus Christ as our right standing before God. This trust includes God's Spirit—to walk in faith is to walk in the Spirit. And this trust includes God's holiness—to walk in faith is to bear out God's very character in our lives.

If we are to be true men and women of faith, it won't be that we were *generically* spiritual or religious, it will mean we put our belief and trust in God and in everything revealed to us by God—especially what has been revealed about his Son Jesus Christ.

2. *Faith in Christ, while it is passive in what it receives, is active in how it works.*

Faith is an empty hand receiving from the God of grace. But, because of the gift received, true faith will inevitably be *active*. Christianity adamantly proclaims a *passive* faith for salvation—by faith we receive Christ, who has done everything for us. But Christianity also adamantly proclaims an *active* faith for Christian living, because the Christ we receive has commanded us to work out our salvation. If we trust Christ for all of our life and salvation, then our life will display him, and we will genuinely live and love in the same ways he did.

XI

Justification

Justification is God's gracious and full acquittal of sinners, who believe in Christ, from all sin, through the satisfaction that Christ has made; not for anything wrought in them or done by them; but on account of the obedience and satisfaction of Christ, they receiving and resting on him and his righteousness by faith.

Justification

INTRO + OVERVIEW

While the roots of Reformation theology may stem from an earlier date, the fruit came to the forefront in the sixteenth century. In the very first article on the Scriptures, we looked at the *material* and *formal* principles of Reformation theology. We saw that the formal principle of Reformation theology was that the ultimate source of authority from God is the Scriptures of the Old and New Testaments. This was a major shift back to pure and undefiled Christianity. Reformation theology did not throw out the great history of the church, with its councils and its creeds, but it put those things in their place—*underneath* the authority of God's Word. So, in the early 1500s when Martin Luther made a personal shift toward reading and interpreting Scripture as God's ultimate authority, it was inevitable his interpretations would be at odds with the church of his day. It is just a basic principle of life that if you put different ingredients in, then you are going to get something different out. The material principle of Reformation theology is what came out.

The formal and the material principles are closely linked even though they ask different questions. If the formal principle asks the question, "Where is God's authority?" then the material principle asks, "How can sinners be made right with God?" How one answers the second question must absolutely be affected by how one answers the first question. So, if the formal principle teaches us God's authority is in his Word, then the material principle must seek to answer, *What do the Scriptures actually teach about how a person can be righteous in God's sight?*

As a young man, though Luther had many things wrong in his view of Christianity, there is one thing he got right: God is unbendingly righteous. Luther knew himself to be a sinner and he was terrified that God's law is merciless. If God is just, and according to his nature he must be, then we *all* should be very afraid. This unwillingness to bend God's justice, and his stark honesty about his own lawlessness, drove Luther mad. The system which the church of his day had created for dealing with the problem of sin was not able to cleanse Luther's conscience. It was like Luther found himself back under the Mosaic Covenant:[1]

> For the Law, since it has *only* a shadow of the good things to come and not the form of those things itself, can never, by the same sacrifices which they offer continually every year, make those who approach perfect. Otherwise, would they not have ceased to be offered, because the worshipers, having once been cleansed, would no longer have had consciousness of sins? But in those *sacrifices* there is a reminder of sins every year. For it is impossible for the blood of bulls and goats to take away sins (Hebrews 10:1-4).

Through the Roman Catholic process of absolution,[2] Luther was only reminded more and more of how sinful he was, more and more how holy God is and more and more how unable he was to make himself right before God.

The righteousness of God

So, in 1515, as Luther prepared to begin lecturing through the book of Romans, he ran across a phrase that haunted him, but which would eventually set him free: *the righteousness of God*. Romans 1:16–17 says,

> For I am not ashamed of the gospel, for it is the power of God for salvation to everyone who believes, to the Jew first and also to the Greek. For in it *the* righteousness of God is revealed from faith to faith; as it is written: "BUT THE RIGHTEOUS *ONE* WILL LIVE BY FAITH."

---

1 The Mosaic Covenant was the formal relationship God graciously established with Israel through the mediation of Moses. The book of Exodus, in particular, teaches us about the the foundation of this covenant.

2 These two words, *process* and *absolution*, are extremely important to this discussion. *Absolution* is what we need if we are to be right with God, but when we turn absolution into a *process* we take salvation out of God's hands and place it in our own. Any *process* of absolution should drive any honest God-fearer mad. It is a hopeless endeavour, which is why we all desperately need Jesus.

At first it seemed Luther was just being haunted even further. Everywhere he turned, he was reminded of God's righteousness. Except this time, by God's grace, it struck him differently. This is how it happened in his own words,

> Then finally God had mercy on me, and I began to understand that the righteousness of God is a gift of God by which a righteous man lives, namely faith, and that sentence: The righteousness of God is revealed in the Gospel, is passive, indicating that the merciful God justifies us by faith, as it is written: "The righteous shall live by faith." Now I felt as though I had been reborn altogether and had entered Paradise. In the same moment the face of the whole of Scripture became apparent to me. My mind ran through the Scriptures, as far as I was able to recollect them, seeking analogies in other phrases, such as the work of God, by which He makes us strong, the wisdom of God, by which He makes us wise, the strength of God, the salvation of God, the glory of God. Just as intensely as I had now hated the expression "the righteousness of God," I now lovingly praised this most pleasant word. This passage from Paul became to me the very gate to Paradise.[3]

When Luther uses the word *passive*, he means not only is our right standing before God not something we *do*, it is not even something God *does* in us. Our right standing before God is altogether outside of us. It is *God's righteousness*, in Christ, *given* to us as a gift. That is the heart of justification, and justification is at the heart of the gospel.

Now, before we caricature Roman Catholicism, or the Pharisees for that matter, we need to understand that most of the time a works-based salvation doesn't present itself that way. It is not like a person would be welcomed with open arms if they were walking around in the sixteenth century saying, "I am excited to earn my way to heaven!" But that is what makes the doctrine of justification so important, since it only takes a little bit of leaven to rise the dough. We don't have to be saying, "I am trying to earn my way to heaven!" to spoil the gift of God.

---

3   Martin Luther, *D. Martin Luthers Werke*, vol. 54 (1543/46; Weimar: Weimarer Ausgabe, 1883–2009), 183–185. Cited in https://lutheranreformation.org/theology/luthers-breakthrough-romans/.

Apparently, refusing God's grace is as "innocent" as accepting circumcision as a necessary requirement for union to Christ. Could Paul say this any more emphatically,

> And I testify again to every man who has himself circumcised, that he is obligated to keep the whole Law. You have been severed from Christ, you who are seeking to be justified by the Law; you have fallen from grace (Galatians 5:3-4).

Even if we are reading Paul through our own modern lens as some have suggested,[4] and even if Rome has made some adjustments as others have argued,[5] justification is so close to the heart of the gospel, we cannot afford any compromise. Any system, whether on paper or in our hearts, which treats our right standing before God as an *active* process in which we must participate, nullifies the grace of God and cancels out the cross.

Maybe the point isn't whether or not we are intentionally trying to climb our way to God. Maybe the point is God's righteousness is inflexible, and all of us will struggle with the idea of passive righteousness because it totally and finally demolishes our pride. In God's eyes, sincerity doesn't justify us:

> For I testify about them that they have a zeal for God, but not in accordance with knowledge. For not knowing about God's righteousness and seeking to establish their own, they did not subject themselves to the righteousness of God (Romans 10:2-3).

There are a million ways to sincerely seek to establish a righteousness of our own—they all still leave us guilty before God. Justification—which rests on passive righteousness—must be at the heart of the gospel because justification simultaneously humbles and exalts us in a way only the gospel of Christ could. This humble exaltation is

---

4 See these two helpful resources for interaction with the New Perspective on Paul: https://www.ligonier.org/learn/articles/nt-wright-and-new-perspective-paul/; https://www.thegospelcoalition.org/essay/justification-new-perspective-paul/.

5 See Mark Noll's analysis and conclusion in Mark A. Noll, *Is the Reformation Over?: An Evangelical Assessment of Contemporary Roman Catholicism* (Grand Rapids: Baker Academic, 2008).

simultaneous, which is the foundation of Luther's famous Latin formulation, *simul justus et peccator*—meaning we are simultaneously righteous and sinners. And this mirrors who God is in our salvation— simultaneously just and gracious. That is why the reaction to God's gracious justification of sinners is always the same,

> But *it is* due to Him *that* you are in Christ Jesus, who became to us wisdom from God, and righteousness and sanctification, and redemption, so that, just as it is written: "LET THE ONE WHO BOASTS, BOAST IN THE LORD" (1 Corinthians 1:30–31.).

When justification (our right standing before God) is experienced by grace alone, through faith alone and in Christ alone, then our salvation is unto to *God's glory* alone.[6] United to Christ, justification means God declares us righteous because he credits the righteousness of Jesus to us. This is to us, like Luther, "the very gate to Paradise." Glory be to God forever!

SCRIPTURAL FOUNDATIONS

Psalm 32:1–5

> How blessed is he whose wrongdoing is forgiven,
> Whose sin is covered!
> How blessed is a person whose guilt the LORD does not take into
>   account,
> And in whose spirit there is no deceit!
>
> When I kept silent *about my sin*, my body wasted away
> Through my groaning all day long.
> For day and night Your hand was heavy upon me;
> My vitality failed as with the dry heat of summer. *Selah*

---

6   These, together with *Scripture alone*, comprise the five Latin phrases which summarize the formal and material principles of the Reformation. They are called the "five solas": *sola Scriptura, sola gratia, sola fide, solus Christus* and *soli Deo gloria.*

I acknowledged my sin to You,
And I did not hide my guilt;
I said, "I will confess my wrongdoings to the LORD";
And You forgave the guilt of my sin. *Selah*

Here in Psalm 32, David tells us about one of the greatest blessings of life: for God to not impute iniquity. Imputation means to regard, to account or to attribute something to someone. In other words, through faith, God does not relate to a sinner as a sinner, because he does not attribute their sin to them. This is one way to talk about forgiveness, and it speaks to the negative side of justification. Through justification by faith, God no longer regard, accounts or attributes sin, to those who are sinners.

But where do we see faith here? David's faith was exercised in that, "in his spirit there is no deceit." David is not saying, "God did not impute sin to me because I was so squeaky clean and full of integrity that there was no sin to impute." He is saying, "God did not impute sin to me because in faith I trusted his forgiving love enough to confess my sins in total openness and honesty before him." It was when David kept silent that he was carrying the burden of his own sin, but through confession he exercised faith. Here we learn one side of justification: God doesn't hold our sins against us. The true guilt of our sin is forgiven. We *are* sinners, but it is the height of all blessings that through justification God doesn't hold our sin against us—our sin is removed from our account.

Luke 18:9-14

Now He also told this parable to some people who trusted in themselves that they were righteous, and viewed others with contempt: "Two men went up into the temple to pray, one a Pharisee and the other a tax collector. The Pharisee stood and *began* praying this in regard to himself: 'God, I thank You that I am not like other people: swindlers, crooked, adulterers, or even like this tax collector. I fast twice a week; I pay tithes of all that I get.' But the tax collector, standing some distance away, was even unwilling to raise his eyes toward heaven, but was beating his chest, saying, 'God, be merciful to me, the sinner!' I tell you, this man went to his house justified rather than the other one; for everyone who exalts himself will be humbled, but the one who humbles himself will be exalted."

Many times, when Jesus tells a parable, the key to understanding the parable comes from *who* his audience is. In this instance, before we enter into the parable itself, we learn the audience before him were those who trusted in themselves and believed themselves to be righteous. They believed they were in right relationship with God because of how they had lived their lives. This sense of self-righteousness led them to look down on other people who they did not think were righteous like they were. It is at this point where we begin to see that while justification is important to our relationship with God, how we relate to God impacts our relationships with others. Because the desire to be "right" runs deep into the core of our identity, justification possesses more than just a vertical dimension. We can't afford to relegate justification to an ivory tower doctrinal debate. While justification presses the question, "How can sinners be made right with God?" it is inevitable our *unrighteousness* in relation to God makes us *unrighteous* in relation to the world around us. Our souls, made to flourish in the light of God's approval, become twisted by pride. Our false sense of self-righteousness and our deep desire to achieve righteousness before God by our own efforts, distorts our relationships with others.

Jesus paints this picture for us, using two radically different characters. A Pharisee was a conservative, devout and religious man. A tax collector was a selfish, loose and lawless man. The Pharisee would have looked on the tax collector as someone to be avoided. The tax collector would have looked on the Pharisee as someone who was morally superior. When Jesus tells us the tax collector was justified before God and the Pharisee was not, he is teaching there are *two* paths by which we can *attempt* to be right before God, but *only one* whereby we can actually be right before God. There is *active righteousness*, a right standing before God that comes from what we do, and there is *passive righteousness*, a right standing before God that comes as a gift of mercy. Only those who cry out to God for the mercy of passive righteousness will be justified before him. Justification is good news for bad people. We know we have embraced passive righteousness, when we no longer feel the need to exalt ourselves above others and compare ourselves to them. When we give up on our self-righteousness and accept the gift-righteousness of God in Christ, we stop seeing bad people as those to be avoided—we humbly acknowledge *we* are the bad people. We can't rest in our sense of moral superiority, while we are crying out to God for mercy. Trusting God's gift-righteousness and trusting our own righteousness stand at complete odds with one another. The path we choose has sweeping implications for how we relate to God, how we understand ourselves and how we view everyone around us.

Romans 3:21-28

But now apart from the Law *the* righteousness of God has been revealed, being witnessed by the Law and the Prophets, but *it is* the righteousness of God through faith in Jesus Christ for all those who believe; for there is no distinction, for all have sinned and fall short of the glory of God, being justified as a gift by His grace through the redemption which is in Christ Jesus, whom God displayed publicly as a propitiation in His blood through faith. *This was* to demonstrate His righteousness, because in God's *merciful* restraint He let the sins previously committed go unpunished; for the demonstration, *that is*, of His righteousness at the present time, so that He would be just and the justifier of the one who has faith in Jesus.

Where then is boasting? It has been excluded. By what kind of law? Of works? No, but by a law of faith. For we maintain that a person is justified by faith apart from works of the Law.

In Psalm 32, we observed God did not impute sin to someone who had indeed sinned. This non-imputation is the negative side of justification. In Luke 18, we observed God giving passive righteousness to someone who had given up on their own ability to be righteous before God. This gift-righteousness is the positive side of justification. But this brings us to the great dilemma of justification. How can God be righteous if he doesn't count men's sins against them *and* he goes around declaring people righteous who, in fact, are not righteous? Is God just in the free justification of sinners? Romans 3 was written to justify God in the justification of sinners, by relating justification to the cross of Jesus Christ.

First, Romans 3 tells us why we all need to be justified by passive righteousness instead of active righteousness. We all need gift-righteousness because no matter where we were born, what religion our family claims or how much of a bent toward morality we maintain, every single one of us has sinned. Sin cuts through all typical distinctions—male/female, religious/irreligious, law-abiding/lawless, conservative/liberal, majority/minority, good/bad—and puts us all in one sweeping category: fallen. God and his glory is the standard and goal of humanity and every single human being has fallen short of this.

Second, Romans 3 tells us the good news is God declares sinners righteous *as a gift of grace*. Grace means getting something good we didn't earn or deserve. God justifies sinners, and he does it for free.

Third, Romans 3 tells us the way God does this is in Christ Jesus. God's justice demands sinners be punished for their sin. Any good judge applies a punishment commensurate with the crime. Sin is a crime against an eternal God. The punishment commensurate with that crime is nothing short of God's full and unbridled wrath poured out upon the sinner, forever. That is what all humans deserve. When Jesus died on the cross, he was not dying for his own sake. He was not dying to be a mere example. He was not dying as a martyr. In his body, Jesus was receiving the just penalty all sinners deserve—the full and unbridled wrath of God. By willingly sacrificing himself in this way, Jesus was satisfying the just demands of God. All God's righteous fury toward rebels like us was fully poured out on Jesus Christ.

Fourth, Romans 3 shows us how the death of Jesus satisfies the dilemma of justification. The reason God cannot count our sins against us is because he did count our sins against Jesus. The reason we can receive the blessing of justification is because Jesus bore the curse of our sins. And the reason God can offer us passive righteousness is because Jesus was fully obedient to God, even unto death. His perfect, righteous life isn't just an *example*, it is the *substance* of our gift-righteousness before God. Justification is only possible in Jesus Christ, because only in Jesus Christ is God both the just and the justifier of sinners. God can righteously count us righteous because, through union with Christ, we receive a righteousness we did not earn *and* the punishment for our sins has been satisfied by God in Jesus.

Finally, Romans 3 tells us that if this is true, then we have absolutely nothing to boast about except the cross of Jesus Christ. There is no room for self-righteousness. Putting confidence in our own righteousness before God renders the gift of Christ's righteousness null and void. The dilemma of justification is the glory of justification. All of God's glorious perfections—his justice, his love, his grace, his wisdom, etc.—all scream forth, in perfect harmony, his free and gracious justification of sinners. In the face of justification, all boasting in self is excluded; boasting only in God is demanded.

Romans 4:22–5:1

> Therefore it was ALSO CREDITED TO HIM AS RIGHTEOUSNESS. Now not for his sake only was it written that it was credited to him, but for our sake also, to whom it will be credited, to *us* who believe in Him who raised Jesus our Lord from the dead, *He* who was delivered over because of our wrongdoings, and was raised because of our justification.
>
> Therefore, having been justified by faith, we have peace with God through our Lord Jesus Christ

It is easy to focus on the *cross* of Jesus when we talk about justification, but we must also see how the whole existence of the God-man grounds the good news of justification. At the end of Romans 4, Paul shows it wasn't just the death of Jesus involved in our justification, but Jesus' resurrection was vital as well. It may seem odd to think in these terms, but Jesus *himself* was justified in the resurrection. In other words, God publicly declared him to be righteous by raising him from the dead. Jesus is the only human who was justified before God based on active righteousness. Jesus didn't fall short, but instead met the standard and goal of the glory of God. The gift of justification we receive comes to us because the justification of Jesus was earned. The resurrection was the declaration that in God's courtroom, Jesus was pronounced righteous. This relates to our justification because in our union with him we are pronounced righteous through his resurrection. All those united by faith to the resurrected Christ, visibly witness their justification in him as God raised him from the dead.

Furthermore, this right standing before God establishes *peace* with God. The hostility of sin, the anxiety of seeking approval and the wrath of God, are turned into peace through Jesus Christ. God's deepest heart of grace and mercy gets through to us through justification by faith. In Christ, we experience the peace of God *and* we enter a new relation of peace with God. In sin, there is genuine enmity between God and men and women—and our self-justifying attempts at self-produced active righteousness only aggravate his displeasure. In Christ, there is genuine peace between God and men and women—and all we must do to enter his pleasure is to embrace Jesus as Lord.

2 Corinthians 5:18–21

> Now all these things are from God, who reconciled us to Himself through Christ and gave us the ministry of reconciliation, namely, that God was in Christ reconciling the world to Himself, not counting their wrongdoings against them, and He has committed to us the word of reconciliation.
>
> Therefore, we are ambassadors for Christ, as though God were making an appeal through us; we beg you on behalf of Christ, be reconciled to God. He made Him who knew no sin *to be* sin in our behalf, so that we might become the righteousness of God in Him.

We can think of the peace of God we receive in justification as reconciliation with him. Though we were enemies of God, through Christ, God has made us his friends. That is what reconciliation means. And because God was the offended party, only he could enact true reconciliation. As the offender, we were at his mercy. The way God pushed through our rebellion and toward renewed friendship was by not counting our trespasses against us. God takes enemies, restores them to friendship with himself through forgiveness and then unleashes them as his very ambassadors.

Justification shows God going way beyond just tolerating sinners. Sinners, when united to Christ, are so unalterably declared righteous and approved of, they become worthy to speak on behalf of God. God, in his wisdom and grace, uses reconciled enemies to make his appeal for reconciliation to the world. But, what gives us the right to do this? What makes us worthy mouthpieces for God? In ourselves, we have no right because we are not righteous. At this point, Paul grounds the whole operation in the doctrine of justification. Those who have received gift-righteousness are the perfect candidates to declare gift-righteousness. This is justification in its most distilled form: *Jesus took all that is not right about us and he gave us all that is right about him.* The sinless Jesus took on our sin, so unrighteous ones could take on his righteousness. Jesus is the only hope for a right standing with God because he is the only One who stood right before God.

Galatians 2:15–21

[Paul, speaking to Peter] "We *are* Jews by nature and not sinners from the Gentiles; nevertheless, knowing that a person is not justified by works of the Law but through faith in Christ Jesus, even we have believed in Christ Jesus, so that we may be justified by faith in Christ and not by works of the Law; since by works of the Law no flesh will be justified. But if, while seeking to be justified in Christ, we ourselves have also been found sinners, is Christ then a servant of sin? Far from it! For if I rebuild what I have *once* destroyed, I prove myself to be a wrongdoer. For through the Law I died to the Law, so that I might live for God. I have been crucified with Christ; and it is no longer I who live, but Christ lives in me; and the *life* which I now live in the flesh I live by faith in the Son of God, who loved me and gave Himself up for me. I do not nullify the grace of God, for if righteousness *comes* through the Law, then Christ died needlessly."

Justification by grace alone, through faith alone and in Christ alone, is offensive to our pride. That makes it difficult to embrace, and even more difficult to continue in, for those who have much to be proud of in this life. This is why Peter, when his pride was on the line, struggled with the doctrine of justification. The Jews had so much to be proud of—they were, after all, God's chosen people! But Paul addressed Peter with the all-or-nothing clarity justification requires. Even God's chosen people were not made right before God because of their heritage or their relation to the law of God. Paul reminds Peter that all justified sinners have abandoned all personal righteousness—including Jew-ishness and law-keeping—for faith in Christ. Paul reminds Peter that Jesus is so pure and righteous that even if our own reputation and personal identity is diminished by aligning ourselves with Christ, this in no way diminishes the reputation of Christ. It is not Christ who needs sinners, but sinners who need Christ.

This brings up an important question for Paul: *Does justification by faith in Christ alone make the law of no value?* In fact, Paul reminds Peter of the great value of the law—it was the law of God itself which proved to both Paul and Peter they must die to righteousness according to the law. The only way to come alive to God in righteousness before him is to die with Christ, to die to all things except Christ. Justification by grace alone, through faith alone, in Christ alone, is nothing short of a public execution of our own active righteousness. The justified sinner can say with joy, "I have been crucified with Christ." And this is why it is all or nothing: the death of Jesus makes absolutely no sense, and the grace of God is cancelled out, when we attempt to be righteous before God on our own merit. Justification by grace through faith is the glory of the cross. We honour the cross when we trust in Christ. We honour the grace of Christ when we die to our pride.

EXPLANATION

"Justification is God's gracious and full acquittal of sinners..."
Justification is gracious because it is not deserved. There is nothing in us which moves God to declare us righteous before him. We bring nothing to our justification except our sin, for which the wrath of God fell upon Christ. Grace ceases to be grace when it is deserved, which is why justification must be a free gift from God. This grace from God comes by way of a full acquittal. Justification is more than a pardon. It is more than simply being set free from having to pay the penalty we owe. A *pardoned* person is declared *guilty*, but set free from the penalty. An acquitted person is declared *not guilty*. In Christ, we cannot be charged for our sins because the guilt of those sins has been removed. Acquittal goes deeper than pardon. In pardon, the guilt of sin remains, but the consequence of sin is removed. Justification, as a gracious and full acquittal removes both the consequence *and* the guilt of sin. In Christ, the records aren't just sealed, they are unsealed, brought forward, only to be openly displayed as spotlessly righteous before the eternal Judge. By justification, real guilty sinners become really not guilty.

"who believe in Christ..."
The objects of God's justifying grace are those who believe in Christ. Only those who believe in Christ are acquitted of sin, and only those who believe in Christ *alone* are acquitted of sin. We must believe in Christ, and we must *only* believe in Christ. The only appropriate response to God's gift-righteousness is to put our faith in Jesus. Everyone who does not believe in Christ stands guilty and condemned before God.

"from all sin..."
When God justifies a sinner, he acquits that person of all their sin. This acquittal includes all sins past, present and future. Justification is not a state or mode a person can oscillate in or out of. Because justification is a full acquittal, it cannot be demerited by past sin. Because justification is a gift, it cannot be demerited by future sin. The present state of every believer in Christ—in any and all times, places and circumstances—is right standing before God.

"through the satisfaction that Christ has made..."
Those who are justified before God are not acquitted on their own account. The grounds for their acquittal is the life, death and resurrection of Jesus. Jesus paid the ransom due for our sins. Jesus received the punishment rightly due to traitors against an infinitely holy God. This satisfaction objectively happened in the past, and it was a one time, non-repeatable, full satisfaction of the justice of God. The justified sinner owes God nothing for their sins. God cannot, and happily does not, hold them responsible for their rebellion against him, since Christ has freely and fully represented them at the cross.

"not for anything wrought in them or done by them..."
The only person who stands before God in righteousness based on their own merit is Jesus Christ. No one else is righteous in God's sight, in and of themselves. There is nothing a sinner can do to be acquitted of their sin. Their basis for free and full justification is not even something God does in them. God does not make us justifiable—he justifies us. In other words, justification is not that God brings us up to speed so that we are actually righteous. Justification is not God making us better. Justification is not God making us more lovable. Our grounds

for justification is completely and totally outside of ourselves. It is alien righteousness.[7]

"but on account of the obedience and satisfaction of Christ..."

When God declares a sinner to be righteous in his sight, it is on account of that person being united with Christ. As our representative, *his* obedience becomes *our* obedience. *His* perfect record becomes *our* perfect record. This is the *positive* side of justification: when God declares us righteous, he is declaring Christ righteous; when God declares Christ righteous, he is declaring us righteous in him. As our representative, his satisfaction for sins becomes our satisfaction for sins. He stood in our place and died the death we deserved. And this is the *negative* side of justification: when God does't count our sins against us, it is because he counted them against Christ. When Jesus was condemned on the cross, our sins were condemned forever in his body.

"they receiving and resting on him and his righteousness by faith."

Jesus himself is the object of our faith. It is through our faith-union with him we receive all that he is. When it comes to justification, it is important to emphasize that by placing our faith in Jesus Christ the person, we are receiving and resting in his righteousness and not our own. When we embrace Jesus as Lord, we receive his righteousness as our own. When we declare trust in him, we rest on his righteousness as all we need for a right standing before the eternal Judge. To trust in Jesus is to rest on his righteousness, so to rest on our own righteousness is to deny trust in Jesus. Justification is a gift of grace, and it is a particular grace which has its location in the righteousness of Christ. Jesus himself is the free gift we do not deserve, and through which God acquits us of all our sin and welcomes us into his family.

---

7   This phrase is from Luther: *justitia alien*, an *alien righteousness*.

MISCONCEPTIONS

One of the most common misconceptions related to justification is the conflation of justification and sanctification. Because justification and sanctification both deal with righteousness (or in the case of sanctification, more specifically *holiness*), it is easy to mix the two together.[8] The way we can misunderstand justification is by thinking it involves *empowered* righteousness. It is easy to do because empowered righteousness can be "by grace." But, even though empowered righteousness is a wonderful and great gift of God which comes to us through regeneration and sanctification, it is in no way the *basis* for our justification before God. The technical mistake is made in grounding our right standing and approval before God in our *own* righteousness—even if that righteousness is empowered by God. The doctrine of justification says our approval before God is *Christ's righteousness alone*. God doesn't acquit us by changing us, he acquits us because we are *in Christ* and Christ is perfect. The mistake is made in believing God must change us to love us. God justifies sinners *because* God loves sinners, he doesn't love sinners because he has changed us into something lovable.

Another common error we can make is believing it is *our faith* which justifies us, or our faith is our righteousness. When we say, using shorthand,[9] "We are justified by faith," it is easy to get confused. It is not as though God comes to us and says, "Wow. You believed in me. That counts as your righteousness." If this were the case, then the death and resurrection of Christ would not be necessary for our justification. What counts as our righteousness is the righteousness of Jesus. We can

---

8   The next article deals with sanctification. In the overview section there is a more detailed explanation of the difference between justification and sanctification and the dangers of conflating them.

9   In Romans 3:28, when Paul says, "For we maintain that a person is justified by faith apart from works of the Law," he clearly has in mind we are justified by Christ, and we receive Christ by faith. The whole reason Paul argued for justification in this way was to magnify the righteousness of God, "so that He would be just and the justifier of the one who has faith in Jesus" (verse 26). It is faith in Jesus that justifies us because it is Jesus who is the grounds for our justification.

say we are justified by faith because faith is the instrument through which we come to receive and rest on Christ, not because faith itself absolves us of our sin. That is why, when it comes to justification, it is not the *amount* of faith which makes us right before God—it is the *object* of our faith—Jesus—who makes us right before God.

A final misconception relates to how we view the *heart* of God in relation to the dilemma of justification. In Article III: The Trinity, we talked about the error of *dualism*. This error becomes most hideous when it comes in contact with the doctrine of justification. When we treat justification in a dualistic way, we portray God the Father like he is an angry, blood-thirsty tribal deity who must be told to simmer down by his loving and gracious son. This is not God's heart in justification! God sent his Son into the world to save sinners because he loved them! The triune God, Father, Son and Holy Spirit, graciously and lovingly works together on behalf of sinners to justify them. The Son is no less naturally repulsed by sin than the Father. The Father and Spirit are no less involved in the justifying of sinners than the Son. Justification certainly has the Son as its figurehead, but this is because the triune God—together—chose to put Jesus forth as a public display of God's righteousness in the justification of sinners. It is their righteousness which was vindicated at the cross, a righteousness eternally shared in infinite perfection by the Father, Son and Holy Spirit. It is true, in one sense, God in his love was saving us from his own just condemnation. However, this denigrates into dualism if we believe the Son was somehow saving us *from* the Father. God's deepest heart toward us, which is seen most vividly in justification, is that he loves us. He went to the greatest lengths, in all the harmony of his wisdom, grace and justice, to prove his great and eternal love.

APPLICATION

Article XI: Justification

Justification is God's gracious and full acquittal of sinners, who believe in Christ, from all sin, through the satisfaction that Christ has made; not for anything wrought in them or done by them; but on account of the obedience and satisfaction of Christ, they receiving and resting on him and his righteousness by faith.

----

1. *Justification is the grounds of our new identity in Christ.*
   Justification is closely related to adoption. In justification, we are legally declared righteous, and in adoption, we are legally declared sons and daughters. Those who are justified can truly know that the banner which hangs over their lives is "Loved." Justified sinners are no longer on the outside, at enmity with God; they are at *peace* with God. And, even more amazing, they are *children* of God.

2. *Our identity as justified children leads to a new posture toward God and toward others.*
   Those who are justified have nothing to prove before God, no need of constant self-defense before him and are relieved of the burden of vindication and validation before the eyes of the world. When justification is internalized, rest is sure to follow. The anxieties and worries of winning the approval of God and of others slowly begins to dissipate as we learn to embrace what it means to be affirmed by God.

3. *Since God himself justified us in Christ, he alone deserves the praise for it.*
   Knowledge of our justification is constant fuel for our worship. When we come to grips with the fact that Jesus has done everything for us, and God upheld his righteousness while declaring us righteous, we are led to worship. We have no boast except the cross.

4. If we cannot boast before God, then we cannot boast before people either.

Partiality and judgmentalism have no place in the family of God. To judge someone else, is to make a declaration about their righteousness. Knowing God justified us *while* we were sinners, cuts through any judgmentalism we might be tempted to have. If, as a justified sinner, we judge someone else, we are not walking worthy of the gospel. Justification, like total depravity, completely levels the field, so that no one can boast and no one can judge.

5. Justification means we are qualified ambassadors.

Every person who proclaims the gospel could be labelled as a hypocrite if it weren't for justification. No one stands right before God based on their own merits, which means no one is worthy to represent Jesus Christ to the world. But, in an amazing twist, God now uses those whom he has reconciled to himself through Jesus to proclaim the gospel of reconciliation. It is those whom God has justified freely, whom he sends to declare the gospel of justification. No one is qualified to be an ambassador of Jesus, which simultaneously means no one is unqualified to be an ambassador of Jesus. The gospel message is carried *by* sinners *to* sinners!

XII

Sanctification

Those who have been regenerated are also sanctified by God's Word and Spirit dwelling in them. This sanctification is progressive through the supply of divine strength, which all saints seek to obtain, pressing after a heavenly life in cordial obedience to all of Christ's commands.

Sanctification

INTRO + OVERVIEW

There are so many wonderful benefits that flow from being united to Christ. As we have seen with justification, one of these benefits is that God *declares us righteous* before him. This righteousness is not our own righteousness, but is the righteousness of Jesus counted to us as a free gift. While we began to explain in the last chapter why justification and sanctification should not be mashed together,[1] we do not want to diminish the wonderful and gracious reality of sanctification. Sanctification is just as precious a gift as justification. Sanctification is God's promise to bring to completion what he began through regeneration. Through sanctification, God graciously transforms us to be like him.

One of the best ways to explain and clarify sanctification is to set it side by side with justification. To sanctify something means *to set it apart*. This is why it specifically relates to holiness. God is holy, which means he is set apart. In sanctification, God sets us apart just as he is set apart. But, while sanctification technically deals more with holiness, when contrasting it with justification, we can also speak of sanctification in terms of righteousness. The Bible does talk about sanctification in different ways, but for the sake of the clarity we will define sanctification as *God's transformative power in our lives by which he forms himself in us.*

Distinguishing between justification and sanctification
The first distinction between justification and sanctification is that in justification we are *declared* righteous but through sanctification we are actually *made* righteous. Our right standing before God is based on the fact that in Christ we are justified before him. He accepts us without making one change to us. However, salvation includes more

---

1   See Misconceptions in Article XI: Justification.

than just our position before God. God is committed to making us, in reality, what he declares us, in Christ, to be. Sanctification means all Christians will actually grow in moral righteousness. This growth in righteousness does not add, in any sense, to their justification before God, but it does serve as one proof of their being justified.

The second distinction between justification and sanctification is in justification we receive *imputed* righteousness, while in sanctification we receive *imparted* righteousness. Imputed righteousness is the perfect record of Jesus attributed to us. Imparted righteousness is the fruit of the Spirit worked in us. Both imputed and imparted righteousness are gifts of God's grace. Imputed righteousness surrounds us with the life and death of Christ, so we are hidden in him before the judgment seat of God. Imparted righteousness is planted in us by the Spirit of God, so that from the inside out we begin to live differently. Imputed righteousness makes no visible change in us, but imparted righteousness makes a visible change in us.

The third distinction between justification and sanctification is that justification is an *instantaneous act*, while sanctification is a *progressive work*. God justifies a sinner in an instant—he declares them righteous. At the moment of union with Christ, a Christian has peace with God and is acquitted of all their sin. Sanctification, however, is a transformation that happens over the course of a lifetime—from the moment of regeneration until death and glory. The progressive nature of sanctification means God works it in us as we walk with him, and it also means there is progress over time.

The fourth distinction is justification mainly deals with the *condemnation* incurred by sin, while sanctification mainly deals with the *corruption* caused by sin. In the Fall, sin has wreaked destruction on us. Because it is rebellion against God, sin makes us guilty and deserving of wrath. But, sin also corrupted the very *nature* of Adam, and therefore the nature of all of those born in him. Justification means we are no longer under the wrath of God because our guilt has been removed. Sanctification is a reformation of the mind, will, affections and actions. Through regeneration, we become a new creation, and through sanctification that new creational life begins to overcome what remains of the old creation—until it is finally perfected in us, when we are glorified and resurrected.

The final distinction we will explore is that in justification we are *passive*, while in sanctification we are *active*. We add nothing to our justification, and we are not justified on the basis of anything in us or done by us. While we are commanded not to work for our justification, we are commanded to work for our sanctification. This work is a faith-engaged work, and it is a grace-empowered work, but it is our activity nonetheless. God calls Christians to be engaged in the process, and he gives them new desires to want to be involved in the process. A love for Jesus, an excitement about his righteousness and the thrill of becoming more like him captivate our energy.

Before moving on to the Scriptures, we must look at why this is all so important. This may seem like technical precision which isn't relevant to the Christian life, but nothing could be further from the truth. Many of our problems in the Christian life come because we do not understand the significance of justification and sanctification. We all tend to sink into one of the following categories and this has ramifications for our walk with God.

Danger of legalism

One easy mistake we make is divorcing justification from sanctification. This puts our own righteousness in the wrong category, and we fall into *legalism*.[2] Legalism treats our right standing before God as connected to our keeping of his law. God's law is good, but it cannot justify sinners. When we divorce justification from sanctification, we begin to believe God's declaration over our lives is dependent on our activity. Christians work *from* justification, not *for* justification. Trying to get God to declare us righteous by making ourselves righteous, strips God of his graciousness and typically leads to a hypocritical and judgmental spirit.

Danger of antinomianism

Another easy mistake we make is divorcing sanctification from justification. This treats God's gift of righteousness in Christ so lightly that we fall into *antinomianism*.[3] Antinomianism treats our freedom in

---

2 When you hear *legal*, think law.

3 *Antinomianism* comes from the Greek word *nomos*, which means *law*. So this is a technical word for someone who is against the law. There are some people who are antinomian because they feel convinced by the Scriptures that a Christian is not called

Christ as an excuse to sin. Christians aren't just freed from the *condemnation* of sin, they are also freed from the *power* of sin. God's grace deals with both our guilt *and* our corruption. Rather than justification being an *excuse* to sin, justification is the *fuel* for righteous living.

Confusing justification and sanctification

While divorcing justification and sanctification comes with its problems, confusing them brings its own set of deadly challenges. When *we confuse justification for sanctification*, we treat sanctification with the categories of justification, especially as it relates to the timeline. In doing this, we can believe sanctification is immediate. Just as we are justified by an instantaneous act, we are also sanctified by an instantaneous act.[4] This is a type of *perfectionism*, where we believe all Christians should automatically behave in certain ways and be certain types of people as soon as they believe. This can lead to extreme discouragement or a blind overlooking of indwelling sin in our own lives, and it leads to judgmentalism toward other Christians who can't seem "to get their act together." When we confuse justification for sanctification, we create an environment where we constantly question other people's salvation.

Finally, *when we confuse sanctification for justification*, we treat justification with the categories of sanctification. When we make this error, we treat justification as though it were a process. We drag out the declarative verdict of God into *subjective* experience, rather than seeing it in the *objective* gospel. Underneath this process view of justification is disbelief that God is gracious enough to love sinners. When we doubt his grace, we begin to believe he will only love us once he has changed us. But, herein lies the fatal error, how much change is enough? How much repentance is enough? And what if old sins keep popping up again? When justification is treated like sanctification, we can never be certain we have peace with God. Process justification

---

to observe the moral law of God. Others are antinomian because they abuse the grace of God. The latter is mainly in view in this discussion.

4   For clarity's sake, it is helpful to mention that sometimes the Bible does speak of a *positional* sanctification, which tracks with the categories of justification. But, even if we have this positional sanctification in view, we still must distinguish it from *progressive* sanctification. Positional sanctification means, "In Christ, I am holy." Progressive sanctification means, "In Christ, I am being made holy."

destorys assurance of salvation. This is the self-deprecating side of a works-based salvation.

Justification and sanctification come together like a package deal, through union with Christ. Both are wonderfully gracious realities, given to us as gifts, and applied by the Spirit of God. Many of our problems in the Christian life—legalism, antinomianism, perfectionism and lack of assurance—come because we divorce one from the other or we confuse one with the other. Clearing up the distinction allows us to praise God equally, as we rest in the gift of Christ's righteousness and as we passionately pursue our own righteousness. God has declared us righteous, and he has committed to make us in reality what he has declared us to be, not so he can love us, but because he already loves us so much.

SCRIPTURAL FOUNDATIONS

Leviticus 22:31–33

So you shall keep My commandments, and do them; I am the LORD.

"And you shall not profane My holy name, but I will be sanctified among the sons of Israel; I am the LORD who sanctifies you, who brought you out from the land of Egypt, to be your God; I am the LORD."

Holiness is a major theme in the Old Testament, especially in the Pentateuch.[5] Here, in the book of Leviticus, God declares his holiness and anyone related to him in a positive way must be holy as well. What we see in Leviticus (and throughout the Bible) is that God himself is sanctified—he himself is *set apart*. And he, as the sanctified One, sanctifies his people. This passage represents, in a typological way, the realities of justification and sanctification. God didn't give the Israelites the law and tell them to set themselves apart so he would bring them out of Egypt. He claimed them as his people, and then gave them

---

5   The *Pentateuch* refers to the first five books of the Old Testament: Genesis, Exodus, Leviticus, Numbers and Deuteronomy.

his holy law.[6] They already belong to him, and he is going to work in them to make them holy like he is.

John 17:13–19

[Jesus speaking] "But now I am coming to You; and these things I speak in the world so that they may have My joy made full in themselves. I have given them Your word; and the world has hated them because they are not of the world, just as I am not of the world. I am not asking You to take them out of the world, but to keep them away from the evil one. They are not of the world, just as I am not of the world. Sanctify them in the truth; Your word is truth. Just as You sent Me into the world, I also sent them into the world. And for their sakes I sanctify Myself, so that they themselves also may be sanctified in truth."

It is easy for us to think of sanctification in terms of ridding ourselves of the world. In one sense, this is true. The process of sanctification is a call to come out from living, thinking and loving like those who do not know Jesus. However, in this last prayer with his disciples before he is abducted and crucified, Jesus takes an interesting approach to the world. He does not pray for God to take them out of the world, but Jesus does ask God to sanctify them. This pushes us in at least two directions. One direction is toward seeing that our main problem is not *outside* of us, but *inside* us. The *subject* of sanctification is ourselves. We are corrupt, and not because we find ourselves in a corrupt environment. Jesus wants his disciples to experience transformation from the inside out. But another direction this pushes us is toward those in the world. Jesus wants his sanctified ones to live out their sanctified life in the world, for others to see. The tension of sanctification is this: we live out the process of being set apart to God in an unsanctified environment. In fact, Jesus wants it this way, in order for us to be set apart not just in morality and integrity, but also in purpose and mission. We are set apart to God as *holy priests* who offer up worship to him, as *holy soldiers* who choose not to engage in civilian affairs,

---

6 We must remember types are not the same thing as their fulfilment. They represent, in a mysterious way, something greater and more profound.

and as *holy ambassadors* who have been chosen to declare his message of reconciliation to an unsanctified world. While God sanctifies us with his Word, he sends us with his Word to sanctify his world.

Romans 6:15-23

What then? Are we to sin because we are not under the Law but under grace? Far from it! Do you not know that *the one* to whom you present yourselves *as* slaves for obedience, you are slaves of *that same* one whom you obey, either of sin resulting in death, or of obedience resulting in righteousness? But thanks be to God that though you were slaves of sin, you became obedient from the heart to *that* form of teaching to which you were entrusted, and after being freed from sin, you became slaves to righteousness. I am speaking in human terms because of the weakness of your flesh. For just as you presented the parts of your body as slaves to impurity and to lawlessness, resulting in *further* lawlessness, so now present your body's parts as slaves to righteousness, resulting in sanctification.

For when you were slaves of sin, you were free in relation to righteousness. Therefore what benefit were you then deriving from the things of which you are now ashamed? For the outcome of those things is death. But now having been freed from sin and enslaved to God, you derive your benefit, resulting in sanctification, and the outcome, eternal life. For the wages of sin is death, but the gracious gift of God is eternal life in Christ Jesus our Lord.

One common concern about keeping justification and sanctification clear and distinct is it can seem like we are going overboard on grace. When free justification is preached, won't people inevitably take advantage of grace and abuse it? Paul responds emphatically to this concern in Romans 6. Not only does grace not give us a license to sin, but when it is received rightly, it catapults us toward sanctification. When we were slaves to sin, we gladly obeyed our slave master and produced lawlessness. But now that we are slaves to righteousness, we get to gladly obey our new master, which results in our sanctification. One of the reasons we put our trust in Jesus in the first place was because the sin which once enslaved us only led us to shame and death. When we trust in Jesus and he frees us from sin, we now follow a new path toward a clean conscience and true life. Sanctification is one of the great benefits of the free gift of eternal life. We know what we deserve, but God gives us, in Christ, this free and gracious gift. What more motivation do we need to pursue the holiness of God in our lives?

Galatians 3:1-5

> You foolish Galatians, who has bewitched you, before whose eyes Jesus Christ was publicly portrayed as crucified? This is the only thing I want to find out from you: did you receive the Spirit by works of the Law, or by hearing with faith? Are you so foolish? Having begun by the Spirit, are you now being perfected by the flesh? Did you suffer so many things in vain—if indeed it was in vain? So then, does He who provides you with the Spirit and works miracles among you, do it by works of the Law, or by hearing with faith?

Galatians is typically thought of as mainly dealing with the doctrine of justification. However, Paul deals with both justification and sanctification in very detailed and meticulous ways. In chapter 3, Paul calls the Galatians fools for believing God would have started the process of salvation in them only to leave it up to their own flesh to complete. This is the threshold between justification and sanctification: while the two are distinct, they both come to pass in our lives "by hearing with faith." The same Spirit of God who justified us is the One who brings the work he began in us to completion. Seeking to be perfected by the flesh—a faulty perspective of sanctification—is actually a denial of justification. This is so helpful for us to see because it teaches us that when we misunderstand either sanctification or justification, and their respective roles in our lives, then it inevitably spoils the other.

Galatians 4:12-20

> I beg of you, brothers *and sisters*, become as I *am*, for I also *have become* as you are. You have done me no wrong; but you know that it was because of a bodily illness that I preached the gospel to you the first time; and you did not despise that which was a trial to you in my bodily condition, nor express contempt, but you received me as an angel of God, as Christ Jesus *Himself*. Where then is that sense

of blessing you had? For I testify about you that, if possible, you would have torn out your eyes and given them to me. So have I become your enemy by telling you the truth? They eagerly seek you, not in a commendable way, but they want to shut you out so that you will seek them. But it is good always to be eagerly sought in a commendable way, and not only when I am present with you. My children, with whom I am again in labor until Christ is formed in you— but I could wish to be present with you now and to change my *tone of* voice, for I am at a loss about you!

As we continue in Galatians, we see the importance of the relationship between justification and sanctification. Paul feels the Galatian Church has abandoned the gospel, even though they had initially received it with gladness. But here is the key: Paul knows the reason the church's sanctification is being spoiled is because they do not have a clear and decisive view of free and gracious justification. Paul envisions himself as a mother who has had to go back into labour for the same child. His labour is to reclaim the gospel of free grace, and the desired outcome is Christ formed in them. This is the target of every believer's and every church's sanctification—for Christ to be formed in them. The way God makes us like himself is by making us like Jesus. In one sense, all human beings are made in the image of God, but in another sense, since the Fall the image of God in humanity has been marred. Sanctification, then, is a remaking of humans into the image of God, by forming us into the image of Christ, who is himself the image of the invisible God. Jesus, the last Adam, is the final goal of our transformative process. We are most like God when we are most like Jesus.

Galatians 5:13-25

For you were called to freedom, brothers *and sisters*; only *do* not *turn* your freedom into an opportunity for the flesh, but serve one another through love. For the whole Law is fulfilled in one word, in the *statement*, "YOU SHALL LOVE YOUR NEIGHBOR AS YOURSELF." But if you bite and devour one another, take care that you are not consumed by one another.

But I say, walk by the Spirit, and you will not carry out the desire of the flesh. For the desire of the flesh is against the Spirit, and the Spirit against the flesh; for these are in opposition to one another, in order to keep you from doing whatever you want. But if you are led by the Spirit, you are not under the Law. Now the deeds of the flesh are evident, which are: sexual immorality, impurity, indecent behavior, idolatry, witchcraft, hostilities, strife, jealousy, outbursts of anger, selfish ambition, dissensions, factions, envy, drunkenness, carousing, and things like these, of which I forewarn you, just as I have fore-warned you, that those who practice such things will not inherit the kingdom of God. But the fruit of the Spirit is love, joy, peace, patience, kindness, goodness, faithfulness, gentleness, self-control; against such things there is no law. Now those who belong to Christ Jesus crucified the flesh with its passions and desires.

If we live by the Spirit, let's follow the Spirit as well.

Throughout the book of Galatians, Paul goes to great lengths to show that justification is full and free. He proves that the beautiful and glorious end of justification is total reconciliation with God. This reconciliation goes even further than friendship. God actually adopts justified sinners into his family. They become his very sons and daughters. So what are we to do with all this freedom? How are we to express our newfound relationship with God as free sons and daughters? God gives us his Spirit, so as the life of Christ is formed in us, the communicable attributes[7] of God shine through us. The reason sanctification is a process is because we live out the war between the old flesh and the Spirit of God. The Spirit and the flesh are at odds with each other. As the Spirit of God gains ground, we begin more and more to walk by the Spirit. Sanctification is the joyous and gruelling process of killing the flesh in the power of the Spirit, until the life of Christ is formed in us. The Holy Spirit in us is our only hope for sanctification.

---

7   See Article II for more on communicable and non-communicable attributes.

EXPLANATION

"Those who have been regenerated are also sanctified..."

There is a direct link between regeneration and sanctification. In Article VIII we learned that regeneration is the first, fundamental and decisive change by which the Holy Spirit makes a person a new creation in Christ. Sanctification, then, is the process by which the Holy Spirit's regenerative life in us is brought to completion. It is impossible for someone to be regenerated and not also be sanctified. Because regeneration is decisive, sanctification is inevitable. It is a key and vital point that regeneration must precede sanctification. We are not transformed by the Spirit from the outside in, but rather from the inside out.

"by God's Word..."

If the Fall corrupted our minds, wills, affections and actions, then sanctification must deal with transformation in each of these areas. God uses his Word to inform us and to challenge our assumptions. God uses his Word to change what we want and what we long for. God uses his Word to create in us new loves, both for himself and for the things he loves. And as God transforms us by his Word, the activities of our life are new and different. The fruit of the Spirit is the life of God coming through us as the Word of God transforms us.

"and Spirit dwelling in them...."

The Word of God itself is not enough to sanctify us. The Word of God is wielded by the Spirit of God who illumines and animates his Word in us. While we are active in our sanctification, it is not activity which is empowered by our own strength. Only when we walk in the Spirit, can we be transformed. It is the Holy Spirit alone who makes us holy.

"This sanctification is progressive through the supply of divine strength..."

As God works in the life of a believer, they are progressively formed into the image of Jesus. Any progress toward real righteousness is a gift from God. This progressive transformation is key to understanding one of the major aims of our walk with God.

"which all saints seek to obtain…"
To be a *saint* simply means to be *a holy one*. All those who have been declared holy through faith in Jesus are true saints. All true saints pursue sanctification. When God the Spirit regenerates us, he gives us a new delight for holiness. This seeking is a process, but it is a true reality in all true believers.

"pressing after a heavenly life…"
One way to think about sanctification is to begin pursuing heaven while on earth. In other words, one of the benefits of being united to Christ is we get to start living now like we are going to live forever. When we feel weak in pursuing holiness, this reality can energize us toward transformation. It is such a wonderful gift that God allows us to enjoy our ultimate future, even now. Knowing it is our promised future, who wouldn't want to press after delighting in the new creational life of God?

"in cordial obedience to all of Christ's commands."
Christians, though free, are not against commands. The Christian, who has believed in the good news that Jesus Christ is Lord, wants nothing more than to obey him. We enter the sanctification process knowing we need an outside source who can speak new paths of wisdom and righteousness into our heart. Part of the equation of growing in sanctification is acknowledging we are still in process. We all need the commands of Jesus to conform us to the life of Jesus. When we buck against the commands of Jesus, we stall in our Christian growth. When we come to grips with the fact that Christ's commands are his life in law form, then the same law that condemned us becomes the law which delights us. Having been set free from the curse of the law, we can willingly and happily submit to the law of Christ.

MISCONCEPTIONS

There are various misconceptions related to sanctification that we must deal with if we are to enjoy life with God. The first misconception is the idea sanctification means *moving on* from the gospel. Many people treat faith in Jesus—his perfect life, death and resurrection—as only the starting point of walking with God. They see growing as a Christian as moving on from Jesus to "deeper" things. This, as we have seen in the Galatian Church, is a fatal error. The gospel is not just for unbelievers—it is the controlling factor in the ongoing life of the church. Our sanctification, because of our union with Christ, mirrors the gospel, and is fueled by the message of the cross.

Another misconception is the idea we can become perfect *in this life*. It is true, if we are in Christ, we will be perfected by God, but this perfection will not take place in this life. The war between the Spirit and the flesh will exist in us until we die or until Jesus returns. We will never grow out of the need for repentance. In some ways, because we see God more clearly as we are progressively sanctified, we will actually see ourselves as more sinful the longer we walk with God. Contrasted with the holiness of God, even the slightest blemish appears woefully inadequate.

A third misconception is the idea that sanctification means we separate ourselves from the world. Many people approach sanctification from the outside in. It is so easy to see the transformation project from the standpoint of merely changing our environment. It is true, we are influenced by our environment and bad company corrupts good morals,[8] but this approach to sanctification misses an important fact. The reason we need to be sanctified is we are sinners. The thing that needs reform is us. So, while our environment matters, and while sanctification does indeed take place within the church, we cannot be sanctified simply by removing ourselves from the world. Because we are called to pursue both sanctification and living "on mission," we must pursue sanctification in the context of living in the world. It takes wisdom (and we will fail) but the commission we have been given by Jesus to make disciples of all nations[9] demands we press after a heavenly life. God wants to use our progressive transformation as one proof to a lost and dying world that the gospel is the power to save. This tension of living out our faith *in* the world but not *of* the world will look different for everyone, but it is a tension we must strive to uphold.

8　1 Corinthians 15:33.

9　Matthew 28:19–20.

A final misconception, which initially seems counterintuitive, is sanctification takes constant self-focus. Self-awareness is important insofar as we accurately acknowledge who we are before God. However, sanctified people will think less and less about themselves as God and his glory take up more and more focus. Sanctification is not self-deprecation. Sanctification is Christ exaltation.

APPLICATION

Article XII: Sanctification

Those who have been regenerated are also sanctified by God's Word and Spirit dwelling in them. This sanctification is progressive through the supply of divine strength, which all saints seek to obtain, pressing after a heavenly life in cordial obedience to all of Christ's commands.

In a way, our sanctification mirrors the death and resurrection of Jesus. Through the sanctification process, certain things are put to death and other things are brought to life. We call the putting to death, *mortification*, and the bringing to life, *vivification*. While the Spirit is the person of power at work in our sanctification, we are active participants in both mortification and vivification.

1. Mortification

Sometimes mortification looks like God, by his sovereign power, setting us free from strongholds. These might be addictions, habits or ways of believing that have power over us. Many times there are demonic forces at work which God himself must cast away by the authority of Jesus. It could also look like learning something new in the Bible that contradicts our current pattern of behaviour. As God's Word teaches us new and wise ways of living, we obey—and thereby put to death our old way of life. Mortification can also be catalyzed in our life by suffering or other difficult life circumstances. Many times God rips idols out of our hearts, as we come to sense their emptiness in the midst of a trial. One of the reasons mortification happens best within the church is that God uses faithful brothers and sisters who help prod us toward repentance. Through their wise counsel and loving rebuke, we are called to say no to certain harmful and sinful attitudes and behaviours. Finally, mortification looks like genuine repentance. When we looked at repentance, we saw that there was a negative side to it—a turning from sin. Repentance is a humble and sorrowful turning from sin. We actively participate in mortification as we regularly hate our sin and turn from it. In all these ways, we experience mortification because through them God is putting something to death.

2. Vivification

Sometimes vivification looks like God, by his sovereign power, giving us new desires. Through prayer, God grants us a heart for righteousness, holiness and love. As these things grow in us, we can only thank God. And just like mortification, the Bible plays an invaluable role in vivification. Sometimes the Bible's role is to teach us to start certain behaviours. The Bible calls us to bring things to life like praise, thanksgiving and gentleness. God also uses suffering to bring new things to life in us. The best example is how God grows our faith through difficult circumstances. In fact, in a few places in the Bible we are told to rejoice in suffering because of the good things it produces in us by the power of God.[10] Also, our vivification happens best in the context of a local church, as other members of the body build up and encourage us. Here we grow in our sanctification in ways not possible without others. Our sanctification is a community project. Finally, vivification also looks like genuine repentance. Repentance doesn't just have a negative side, it also has a positive side—a turning to God. Repentance is our endeavour to walk before God and be pleasing to him. We actively participate in vivification, as we regularly turn to God and pursue him. In all of these ways, we experience vivification because through them God is bringing us to life.

3. Discipleship

A final thought about sanctification is this: when we talk about discipleship, we should have sanctification in mind. The goal of our own personal discipleship is to have Christ formed in us. We ought to be passionately seeking ways to become more like him. And our goal in discipling others should be to see Christ formed in them. We can and should take the posture of the apostle Paul who saw himself as a woman in labour for her child. Discipleship is hard work, but God supplies divine strength for the task. Only in the power of the Spirit

---

10 See Romans 5:3–5; James 1:2–4.

can our discipleship efforts actually produce progressive sanctification. The mission of the church is to see, by the power of the Holy Spirit, more and more people come to reflect the image of Christ to the glory of God.

ARTICLE

XIII

—

Perseverance of the Saints

Those whom God has accepted in the Beloved, and sanctified by his Spirit, will never totally nor finally fall away from the state of grace, but shall certainly persevere to the end; and though they may fall through neglect and temptation, into sin, whereby they grieve the Spirit, impair their graces and comforts, bring reproach on the Church, and temporal judgments on themselves, yet they shall be renewed again unto repentance, and be kept by the power of God through faith unto salvation.

Perseverance of the Saints

INTRO + OVERVIEW

We opened Article VIII: Regeneration considering the distinction between the *history* of salvation and the *order* of salvation. As we have moved through the order of salvation, which is the Holy Spirit applying in us the history of salvation Jesus accomplished for us, we have observed some glorious benefits of being united to Christ. The life, death and resurrection of Christ become the blueprint for the Christian life as the Holy Spirit sanctifies us. As the apostle Paul says,

> Or do you not know that all of us who have been baptized into Christ Jesus have been baptized into His death? Therefore we have been buried with Him through baptism into death, so that, just as Christ was raised from the dead through the glory of the Father, so we too may walk in newness of life (Romans 6:3-4).

We undergo a death and resurrection with Christ because we have been united to him. But this brings up some important questions: *Can a person who has been united to Christ turn back and fall away? Can a Christian sin so badly God disowns them? Is it possible to fall short of completing our sanctification process?* To answer these questions, we are going to circle back and briefly look at a few previous articles.

Election
We believe God chose us in Christ before the foundation of the world, and his choice was not based on foreseen merit but on mercy in Christ. This is the wonderful grace of election. Election means God set his love on us before we had ever done one good or righteous thing. His initial love for us was not dependent on our loveliness, but only on his great love. If God chose us while we were sinners, is there anything we could do to make him turn his love away from us?

Regeneration

We also believe God has brought us from death to life, causing us to be born again by his Spirit. This is the wonderful grace of regeneration. Regeneration means we are a new creation in Christ Jesus. Our second birth was a birth into Christ Jesus, who is the head of a new humanity. We belong to this new humanity, whose citizens are indwelt by God's very Spirit. Through regeneration, we weren't just given a second chance, we were given a *new heart*. If God has graciously renewed our nature and given us the new birth, prior to our having either the desire or ability to pursue him, is there any way this could be reversed?

Justification

We wholeheartedly believe God has freely and fully acquitted us from all sin, past, present and future, in Christ Jesus. This is the wonderful grace of justification. Justification means we have peace with God. It means God himself, the judge of the universe, has declared us righteous in his sight. Our justification is not based on anything we did or anything God did in us, it is based on the life, death and resurrection of Jesus. If God has accepted us and made us friends and adopted us as children on the basis of Christ's obedience alone, could our future unrighteousness nullify his perfect righteousness on our behalf?

Sanctification

We also believe God has promised to make us in reality what he has declared us to be on the basis of Christ. This is the wonderful grace of sanctification. Sanctification means the Holy Spirit is forming Christ in us, and displaying God's attributes through us. By his own design, this transformation is a process meant to be lived out in the context of the world and over our entire Christian life. If God himself continues to work in us, forming his very life in us, even while sin remains and our very flesh wages war against his Spirit, is it conceivable God would allow this process to fail?

God's faithfulness

We have been chosen by God. We have been born of the Spirit. We have been declared righteous. We have been, and are being, set apart as those who reflect God. In view of these great gifts of grace, we must conclude it is God's purpose and intention to carry us to the very end.

If our election, regeneration, justification and sanctification were hanging on *our* faithfulness to God, we would have fallen long ago. But, since these are gracious gifts from God to us, we can trust in his absolute faithfulness.

Covenant of grace

Throughout the Bible, there are different covenants. Each covenant, which is between God and people, is a gracious covenant. But even in view of the graciousness of all covenants, there are two very different types of covenants. One type is a covenant of works, and the other type is a covenant of grace. Again, while both types are gracious because they involve God's goodwill toward men and women, they differ with regard to how their promises and punishments come to pass. A covenant of works sets up certain promises and punishments, which come about on the basis of obedience or disobedience to the covenant. A covenant of grace offers certain promises, which come about whether the covenant is obeyed or disobeyed.

The gospel is a covenant of grace. That means those who have been united to Christ enter into a relationship with God where the promises and benefits come into their lives whether they obey or disobey. The reason a Christian can be so certain of God's faithfulness is because this covenant of grace is grounded in a covenant of works. Our gracious relationship with God is based on Christ fully obeying God on every point, and he was rewarded accordingly. Therefore, all those who belong to Christ enter this gracious relationship with God, immovably anchored on the perfect obedience of Jesus. We can know for certain God will be faithful to bring us to completion because our salvation is all of grace. If our relationship with God was rooted in a covenant of works, we would fail—in fact, in Adam, we did. But since our relationship with God is rooted in grace, we cannot fail—in fact, in Jesus, we are seen as perfectly obedient. The order of salvation applied to us is the demonstration of God's faithfulness to the covenant of grace. The Spirit's work in applying salvation to us cannot fall short because Jesus' work in accomplishing salvation for us did not fall short.

The reason a Christian can be certain they will persevere to the very end is each member of the Trinity is actively involved in bringing us to our final destination. The Father's purpose and calling cannot be revoked. The Son's merit cannot be rendered void. And the Holy

Spirit's seal cannot be removed. God is faithful. Salvation cannot be lost for those to whom it has been graciously given.

SCRIPTURAL FOUNDATIONS

Genesis 15:7–17

> And He said to him, "I am the LORD who brought you out of Ur of the Chaldeans, to give you this land to possess it." But he said, "Lord GOD, how may I know that I will possess it?" So He said to him, "Bring Me a three-year-old heifer, a three-year-old female goat, a three-year-old ram, a turtledove, and a young pigeon." Then he brought all these to Him and cut them in two, and laid each half opposite the other; but he did not cut the birds. And birds of prey came down upon the carcasses, and Abram drove them away.
>
> Now when the sun was going down, a deep sleep fell upon Abram; and behold, terror *and* great darkness fell upon him. Then *God* said to Abram, "Know for certain that your descendants will be strangers in a land that is not theirs, where they will be enslaved and oppressed for four hundred years. But I will also judge the nation whom they will serve, and afterward they will come out with many possessions. As for you, you shall go to your fathers in peace; you will be buried at a good old age. Then in the fourth generation they will return here, for the wrongdoing of the Amorite is not yet complete."
>
> Now it came about, when the sun had set, that it was very dark, and behold, a smoking oven and a flaming torch *appeared* which passed between these pieces.

Genesis 15 is not about personal salvation. Genesis 15 is about a gracious promise God makes to Abram, in the form of a covenant of grace. Genesis 15 gives us a picture of how a covenant of grace works. Abram has been promised an amazing inheritance. And he asks for proof, not out of mistrust but simply from a desire for something to hold on to, as his trust in God is stretched. God graciously formalizes a covenant with Abram. The animals represent death, which is the penalty for breaking the covenant. If this had been a covenant of works, then Abram would have been the one to walk between the pieces, signifying his necessity to hold up his end of the coveant. God dealt graciously with Abram and wanted him to know for certain God's promises would come true, and his faithfulness wasn't based on anything Abram would or would not do. In this odd scene, *God himself* is envisioned as passing between the animals, as if to say, "I will sooner die, than not keep this promise." This is a covenant of grace and God wants us to have this kind of certainty about his faithfulness toward us in the gospel.

John 6:35-40

> Jesus said to them, "I am the bread of life; the one who comes to Me will not be hungry, and the one who believes in Me will never be thirsty. But I said to you that you have indeed seen Me, and *yet* you do not believe. Everything that the Father gives Me will come to Me, and the one who comes to Me I certainly will not cast out. For I have come down from heaven, not to do My own will, but the will of Him who sent Me. And this is the will of Him who sent Me, that of everything that He has given Me I will lose nothing, but will raise it up on the last day. For this is the will of My Father, that everyone who sees the Son and believes in Him will have eternal life, and I Myself will raise him up on the last day."

Here we see how Jesus relates election to perseverance. It is only by the Father's choice anyone comes to Jesus. And those who come to Jesus will not be cast out. This is God's will and it will not be thwarted. Jesus won't let anyone slip or slide through the cracks. All those chosen of the Father and saved by the Son, will be raised to life on the day of resurrection. Eternal life is not a future reality for believers, it is a present reality.

John 10:24-30

> The Jews then surrounded Him and *began* saying to Him, "How long will You keep us in suspense? If You are the Christ, tell us plainly." Jesus answered them, "I told you, and you do not believe; the works that I do in My Father's name, these testify of Me. But you do not

believe, because you are not of My sheep. My sheep listen to My voice, and I know them, and they follow Me; and I give them eternal life, and they will never perish; and no one will snatch them out of My hand. My Father, who has given *them* to Me, is greater than all; and no one is able to snatch *them* out of the Father's hand. I and the Father are one."

In John 10, Jesus makes the most amazing assertion about himself. He calls himself the *Good Shepherd*. Throughout this chapter, he explores different angles of the shepherd/sheep relationship. One of the key components of this relationship is sheep *hear* the shepherds voice. Here, Jesus relates his effectual calling to perseverance.[1] Strikingly, Jesus proclaims the reason many of them do not have faith is because they don't belong to him. Conversely, those who do belong to him are effectually called by him. They will hear and know and follow Jesus, because the Father has given them to Jesus. Jesus then explains how those who are given eternal life will never perish. Their hope for enduring in the Christian life is not found in their *own* goodness or strength, but in the knowledge that Jesus won't let anything or anyone take them out of his hand. And, if that isn't enough, Jesus doubles down on this promise by saying not only can his sheep not be snatched out of his hand, they cannot be snatched out of his Father's hand either. This union with his Father only further proves our salvation is sealed in the hands of the eternally triune God.

Romans 8:35-39

Who will separate us from the love of Christ? *Will* tribulation, or trouble, or persecution, or famine, or nakedness, or danger, or sword? Just as it is written:

"FOR YOUR SAKE WE ARE KILLED ALL DAY LONG;
WE WERE REGARDED AS SHEEP TO BE SLAUGHTERED."

---

1   See the Explanation section of Article V: Election for further clarity on effectual calling.

> But in all these things we overwhelmingly conquer through Him who loved us. For I am convinced that neither death, nor life, nor angels, nor principalities, nor things present, nor things to come, nor powers, nor height, nor depth, nor any other created thing will be able to separate us from the love of God that is in Christ Jesus our Lord.

Romans 8 gives us special insight into both providence and election. Paul has shown earlier in this chapter how God is working all things according to his purpose. And he has connected the dots between predestination, calling, justification and glorification. These wonderful truths form an unbreakable chain in salvation. But, there is one final question Paul wants to address: Can anything separate those in Christ from Christ? Notice how each of these is some of the harshest of human experiences. If these things were to take place in our lives, people would consider us accursed. But instead of drawing that conclusion, Paul says it is actually in those things we overwhelmingly conquer. Those who have been united to Christ cannot be separated from Christ by *anything*. Our conquering rests securely in his love.

1 Corinthians 1:4-9

> I thank my God always concerning you for the grace of God which was given you in Christ Jesus, that in everything you were enriched in Him, in all speech and all knowledge, just as the testimony concerning Christ was confirmed in you, so that you are not lacking in any gift, as you eagerly await the revelation of our Lord Jesus Christ, who will also confirm you to the end, blameless on the day of our Lord Jesus Christ. God is faithful, through whom you were called into fellowship with His Son, Jesus Christ our Lord.

This passage in 1 Corinthians seems pretty straightforward at first. As you begin reading this letter from Paul to the church at Corinth, it is easy to slowly drift into the boggy mire of sin you encounter, while forgetting about these foundational verses in the letter. You would think with an opening to a letter like this, Paul would be writing to "saints."[2] But it quickly becomes clear there is rampant disorder and misconduct in the church. So with that in mind, how can Paul be so confident they will be confirmed to the end? How can he be so confident they will be blameless on the day of Christ? There is only one foundation to Paul's confidence that this fleshly, immature and splintered flock will make it to the end: God is faithful. God's faithfulness is the foundation of our perseverance. If he called us into fellowship with his Son, then he will bring us into glory.

Ephesians 1:13-14

> In Him, you also, after listening to the message of truth, the gospel of your salvation—having also believed, you were sealed in Him with the Holy Spirit of the promise, who is a first installment of our inheritance, in regard to the redemption of God's own possession, to the praise of His glory.

One of the reasons we must maintain those who are truly saved cannot lose their salvation is that salvation means the indwelling of the Holy Spirit and regeneration. When a person believes in Jesus and receives the truth of the gospel, God the Spirit seals them in Christ. His coming to take up residence in them is like a downpayment of all God has promised to those who love him. Perseverance is certain because God the Father, God the Son and God the Spirit are unified in bringing about the full and final salvation of the elect, to the praise of his glorious grace.

Ephesians 4:30

> Do not grieve the Holy Spirit of God, by whom you were sealed for the day of redemption.

While it is true believers are sealed with the Holy Spirit of promise so they will persevere to the end, it is also true believers can grieve the

---

2 The irony here is Paul actually does address the Corinthian Church as *saints* in 1 Corinthians 1:2, even though they were far from what we would identify as *saintly*, "To the church of God which is in Corinth, to those who have been sanctified in Christ Jesus, saints by calling...."

Holy Spirit living in them. When a believer falls into temptation or persists in unrepentant sin, they do bring on themselves God's displeasure. This does not mean they are *un*justified or disinherited. That is not possible. It does mean, however, God disciplines his children out of love for them. His discipline is one of the means he uses to bring about his children's perseverance.

EXPLANATION

"Those whom God has accepted in the Beloved, and sanctified by his Spirit..."
The fruit of justification in Christ is acceptance by God. This acceptance is a one time, never to be repeated, experience for those who place their faith in Jesus and are born again. While the angle from which we looked at sanctification in Article XII was mainly the *progressive* angle, there is also a *positional* angle. Those who are being sanctified are those who *have been* sanctified. Perseverance of the saints relates to saints. Saints are those who have been set apart by God's Spirit both positionally and progressively. Those who can claim the promises of perseverance are those who are accepted and sanctified by God.

"will never totally nor finally fall away from the state of grace, but shall certainly persevere to the end..."
If it is true a person is accepted by God on the basis of the merit of Jesus, and they are set apart as a saint by the Holy Spirit, then it is guaranteed they will persevere to the end. There may be partial fallings, but not a total fall. There may be temporary fallings, but not a final fall. Saints of God have entered the state of grace. One cannot fall *out* of a state of grace if salvation is by grace not works. No one gets into the state of grace because they deserved it. No one gets into the state of grace because they cleaned up their act. No one gets into the state of grace because there was anything in them to make God want to be gracious to them. A relationship with God through Jesus Christ is not deserved, so then it cannot be undeserved. The relationship starts as undeserved and remains that way forever. Those who belong to Christ swim in a sea of bottomless grace.

"and though they may fall through neglect and temptation, into sin..."

While it is true a believer will not totally or finally fall away from the state of grace, it is also true they may suffer very bad falls in their walk with God. Although their sins have been paid for by Jesus on the cross, the sanctification process is still a war within them. Defeating sin is an arduous process and believers must be vigilant to fight against sin. In that sense, it is very appropriate to call this article, perseverance of the saints. Perseverance is determination despite difficulty. It is continuing to move forward despite serious and troubling obstacles. There are two ways believers are called to persevere. First, they are called to persevere in the *means of grace* God has appointed and, second, they are called to persevere in the *battle* against temptation. When a believer neglects God's means of grace—like reading the Bible, prayer or gathering regularly with God's people on the Lord's Day[3]—they can expect to fall into sin. Believers must not be naive to the constant temptations, from both inside and outside of themselves. Perseverance suggests temptation is constant and relentless. In this sense, faith and repentance are lifelong projects for the persevering saint.

"whereby they grieve the Spirit..."

Grieving the Spirit is an extremely important category for those who misunderstand the freeness of grace in Christ. It is true that those who are *in Christ* are justified and therefore accepted and in a right standing with God. They are set apart as saints, and nothing is able to separate them from the love of God in Christ Jesus. However, this does not remove the ebb and flow of natural relationship with God. God, as the wonderful Father he is, lovingly disciplines his children. A Christian's justification and acceptance by God in love does not exempt them from grieving or quenching the Holy Spirit in them. When believers fall into sin, remain unrepentant or become hard-hearted, it negatively affects their relationship with God. This in no way means they are not justified, become disinherited or are unloved by God, but it does mean they will not enjoy the fullness of all they have been given in Christ.

---

3   The *Lord's Day* is the first day of the week, Sunday. See Article XVII: The Lord's Day.

"impair their graces and comforts..."

One of the things which happens when a Christian falls into sin or walks in unrepentance, is their graces, like love, joy, peace, faith, etc., are impaired. Scripture commands us, "Walk by the Spirit."[4] When we grieve the Spirit, we are feeding the flesh rather than bearing the fruit of the Spirit. But not only are our *graces* impaired—those good and wonderful things borne out in us by the Spirit—but our gospel *comfort* is impaired. The fellowship of the Spirit, the assurance of the blood of Jesus and the fatherly pleasure of God, which are ours in Christ, are experientially weakened when we walk in unrepentant sin. The graces and comforts of a true believer can never totally or finally be snuffed out, but the enjoyment of them in this life may be greatly hindered.

"bring reproach on the Church..."

Another thing which happens when a Christian falls into sin and walks in unrepentance is that we put obstacles in the way of the witness of the church. Jesus has commissioned his church to be his witnesses, through the power of the Spirit. The reputation of the church is already strained in the world because of the offense of the gospel,[5] but when believers fall into temptation they add unnecessary offense.

"and temporal judgments on themselves..."

It bears repeating that a believer is loved by God at all times and in all circumstances. A Christian cannot fall from grace, since the *whole* of the Christian life is of grace. This does not mean, though, God does not discipline his children or his church. A believer can be sure that even when they are being disciplined by God, the strokes of the rod are strokes of love. This does not, however, remove the pain of those strokes. Not every suffering in the life of a Christian is a temporal judgment from God for their correction, but because God loves his children and has promised to form Christ in them, it should bring them great encouragement to know he will stop at nothing to accomplish his will in our lives. God knows our happiness is bound up in our holiness, so he will gladly and lovingly take those things that steal our happiness from us. This is a painful but gracious process.

---

4 Galatians 5:16.

5 1 Peter 2:8.

"yet they shall be renewed again unto repentance, and be kept by the power of God through faith unto salvation." Because a Christian is justified in Christ and sealed in the Spirit, even when they fall into temptation and grieve the Spirit, God will renew them and lead them to repentance. God's very power has underwritten the safe-keeping of every one of his chosen ones. The experiential impediments of graces and comforts, and the temporary divine judgments some believers bring on themselves, cannot and will not spoil God's power in fully and finally saving them. Every believer has entered the New Covenant of grace, which means their obedience is not the foundation of whether or not they will receive the promises of God in the covenant. Even when they are under God's discipline, they remain under the banner of the covenant. The gospel is the power of God unto salvation,[6] and this salvation cannot be rescinded once it has been given as a free gift in Christ.

MISCONCEPTIONS

There are two common misconceptions about perseverance, representing two opposite perspectives. The first takes the position that when someone makes a profession of faith in Jesus, they are eternally secure. This article does not say everyone who makes a *profession* of faith is in fact saved. This article argues everyone who *actually* believes in Christ is saved and cannot be lost. The Bible clearly says there are those who make false professions. To glibly offer assurance to anyone and everyone who makes any sort of profession of faith in Jesus is not the heart of this article, nor is it consistent with the Scriptures.

Second, an opposite perspective takes the position that a true believer could in fact lose their salvation. There are serious warning passages in the Bible which should cause all true believers to examine the validity of their own profession; but, these warning passages do not teach that true believers can lose their justification or be disinherited by God. One of the more famous of these warnings comes in Hebrews 6:4–6:

---

6 Romans 1:16.

> For it is impossible, in the case of those who have once been enlight-
> ened and have tasted of the heavenly gift and have been made par-
> takers of the Holy Spirit, and have tasted the good word of God and
> the powers of the age to come, and *then* have fallen away, to restore
> them again to repentance, since they again crucify to themselves the
> Son of God and put Him to open shame.

Let this passage stand as a warning! It is a sobering passage. But, there
are a number of reasons to believe this passage is not teaching a *true
believer* can fall from grace.[7] Probably the best reason comes from
reading further in the text. Notice how just a few verses later, we are
guarded from making a wrong conclusion when the Scripture says,

> But, beloved, we are convinced of better things regarding you, and
> things that accompany salvation, even though we are speaking in
> this way.[8]

What was being said in verses 4–6, can't be applied to these beloved
believers of whom the author is sure of better things.

A third misconception is the belief that if we emphasize how God
keeps us secure in our salvation, it will lead people to take advantage
of it. The idea is security in our salvation breeds complacency.
Biblically, however, this is not the case. Some of the most challenging passages calling us to *do* something, are also undergirded by the

---

7   See this article by Ardel Caneday for one examination of the purpose of this
important passage: https://www.thegospelcoalition.org/article/does-hebrews-6-teach-
you-can-lose-your-salvation/. There is diversity of opinion, however, even among those
who do not believe this passage teaches a Christian can lose their salvation. For
example, Jonathan Edwards wrote in his work *Religious Affections*, "Persons may have
those impressions on their minds, which may not be of their own producing, nor from
an evil spirit, but from the Spirit of God, and yet not be from any saving, but a common
influence of the Spirit of God; and the subjects of such impressions may be of the
number of those we read of, Heb. 6:4, 5, 'that are once enlightened, and taste of the
heavenly gift, and are made partakers of the Holy Ghost, and taste the good word of
God, and the power of the world to come;' and yet may be wholly unacquainted with
those 'better things that accompany salvation' spoken of in ver. 9" (IV). For Edwards,
verses 4–6 and verse 9 represent two different groups entirely.

8   Hebrews 6:9.

fact God's *power* is at work underneath our doing. For example, in 1 Corinthians 15:10, Paul connects his own hard work with God's undergirding grace:

> But by the grace of God I am what I am, and His grace toward me did not prove vain; but I labored even more than all of them, yet not I, but the grace of God with me.

And in 2 Peter 1:10–11, Peter calls us to diligent confirmation of our election, while reminding us salvation is given as a gift:

> Therefore, brothers *and sisters*, be all the more diligent to make certain about His calling and choice of you; for as long as you practice these things, you will never stumble; for in this way the entrance into the eternal kingdom of our Lord and Savior Jesus Christ will be abundantly supplied to you.

And probably the most clear description of this reality comes in Philippians 2:12–13, where Paul commands us to work out our salvation, all the while underwriting the whole experience with God's working in us:

> So then, my beloved, just as you have always obeyed, not as in my presence only, but now much more in my absence, work out your own salvation with fear and trembling; for it is God who is at work in you, both to desire and to work for *His* good pleasure.

We work because God is at work in us. We labour, but every drop of sweat is a drop of grace. *Perseverance* is such a good word because it is those who are in Christ who must persevere, but it is God who makes sure we persevere.

APPLICATION

Article XIII: Perseverance of the Saints

Those whom God has accepted in the Beloved, and sanctified by his Spirit, will never totally nor finally fall away from the state of grace, but shall certainly persevere to the end; and though they may fall through neglect and temptation, into sin, whereby they grieve the Spirit, impair their graces and comforts, bring reproach on the Church, and temporal judgments on themselves, yet they shall be renewed again unto repentance, and be kept by the power of God through faith unto salvation.

---

1. We can be comforted in the assurance of salvation.

It isn't just knowing we are saved, it is the assurance God will never forsake us—that is assurance built on the doctrines of justification and sanctification. We have been declared righteous and we are being made righteous, not because of anything we are or have done. If it wasn't our doing to begin with, then it's not up to us to persevere to the end. God began this work in us, and he will see it to its final conclusion.

2. Another great comfort is God's fatherly discipline.

We will at times in our walk with God experience his displeasure and discipline. But, this does not mean God has ceased to love us. In fact, it is just the opposite. When we feel the holy displeasure and discipline of God, it is precisely *because* he loves us. God has promised to conform us to the image of his Son and one of the important ways he is doing that is through loving discipline.

3. A final comfort is knowing we are kept by God's power and not our own power.

Since we feel our constant weakness, both physically and spiritually, this is a wonderful comfort. But knowing we are upheld by God's power doesn't mean we sleepwalk through life. Instead, knowing it is God's power which will keep us to the end, forces us to live prayerful lives. When we sin against God, we pray for him to forgive us, unwilling to presume on his grace. When we feel temptation coming against us, we pray for God to keep us, unwilling to fight temptation on our own. When we see our idols and sense our worldly hearts, we pray for God to sanctify us, unwilling to lose our witness for Christ in this world. And when we sense our coldness toward God and others, we pray for God to discipline us, unwilling to allow our comfort to keep us from love. Perseverance is just that—perseverance. God calls us to seek his power according to his means, knowing he won't let us go because he has set his saving love on us.

XIV

The Church

The Lord Jesus is the head of the Church, which is composed of all his true disciples, and in him is invested supremely all power for its government. According to his commandment, Christians are to associate themselves into particular societies or churches; and to each of these churches he has given needful authority for administering that order, discipline and worship which he has appointed. The regular officers of a church are pastors and servant leaders.

The Church

INTRO + OVERVIEW

This article marks another shift for us. While in some sense we are moving out of the realm of redemption accomplished and applied, the same Spirit who applies redemption also unifies, nourishes and empowers the church in labouring toward the mission Christ has given her. And, things pertaining to the church are no less related to Jesus than redemption itself. The church isn't just something we belong to, it is something we are called to believe in. As the Apostles' Creed puts it, "I believe in the Holy Spirit, the holy catholic church, the communion of saints...."[1] And to believe in the church in the right way, we must understand how it is related to God, and specifically Jesus. So, before we look at any formal definition of the church, we are going to see how the Bible connects the church to Jesus in an inseparable way. The Scriptures paint a picture for us using many different images.

A body
The first image worth considering is that of a body. The Bible refers to the church as a body in a number of different places.[2] This body imagery is supposed to help us understand our interdependence. Just like a body has many members, so the church has many members. And just like the body needs its different members to perform different functions, so the church needs its different members to perform different functions. Therefore, the body represents the need for *unity* and *interdependence*.

---

1   The Apostles' Creed, like the Nicene Creed and the Chalcedon Definition, has served as an invaluable tool for maintaining the bounds of faith for every generation since the early centuries of the church.

2   For example, see 1 Corinthians 12.

But the image of the church as a body does not stand alone. The Scriptures also teach that if the church is a body, then Jesus is the *head* of the body.[3] He gives the body life. He sends the body messages. He governs how each member functions. A body can lose fingers. It can survive without an ear or a leg. But if a body loses its head, it will die. In the same way, Jesus is the ultimate life source of the church. He alone is indispensable, and every member is connected together through him.

A house

Another image of the church is that of a house. While the Bible is not speaking of a physical building or place the church inhabits, it does invoke the picture of construction. Rather than this construction project being of a physical place, it is the church *itself*—both individual members and the whole church together—which is being built by God. The Bible says the church is God's workmanship and he is building the church up as a house for himself to live in.[4] But the image of the church as God's house is not complete until we see Jesus is the cornerstone of the construction project.[5] Jesus is the *first, central* and the *vital* piece of the house. Jesus, as the cornerstone, is first because the rest of the house needs to fit around him. He is central because each piece of the house in some way or another is held up by his support. And Jesus is vital to the house because without Him the house would fall down, leak or crack.

A temple

The third image we see for the church is of a temple. The temple image is different from the house because the focus is not on the construction and building of the structure. The temple image points us to the *holiness* of the church. The church—the people of God—are made holy by God's presence with them. The temple is a sacred space where sacred worship is offered to God. In a few different places, the Bible challenges the church to pursue holy living as they remember God's very Spirit

---

3   See Ephesians 1:22–23.

4   See Ephesians 2.

5   Ephesians 2:20.

dwells in them as a temple.[6] But we also know every temple has a priest. And so the temple imagery of the church is not complete until we see that Jesus is the High Priest of this temple. Of all the books in the Bible, the book of Hebrews paints this picture best for us. Jesus is our High Priest who has offered up the final sacrifice for sins, who mediates between God and man and who ministers in the temple as an all-approachable helper and interceder.

A priesthood

Interestingly enough, while it is true that the church is a temple and Jesus is the priest of this temple, it is also true the Bible envisions the church itself as a priesthood. With Jesus as our High Priest, the church together forms a priesthood. This means the church has direct access to God through Jesus Christ. There is no hierarchy in the church with regard to hearing from, speaking to or worshipping God. As a priesthood, we join together to offer sacrifices to God. These sacrifices are not physical, but rather *spiritual* sacrifices. The church offers up sacrifices of praise, prayer and good deeds. These sacrifices are in no way atonement or cleansing, but they are real sacrifices pleasing to God. The reason these sacrifices are pleasing to God is not because the church itself is blameless or sinless in her own right. Rather, Jesus is the altar upon which we offer our sacrifices. Hebrews 13 paints this picture for us, teaching us that Jesus sanctifies our offerings so they are acceptable to God. Jesus cleanses what is impure and adds what is lacking in our offerings. It is as we worship through Jesus, pray in Jesus name and live out our good works on behalf of Jesus, that our offerings rise as a sweet aroma to God.

A wife

One of the most powerful and memorable images the Scriptures use for the church is of a wife. Wives are loved and chosen. Wives are protected and cherished. Wives are honoured and led. Wives are connected to their husband both legally, practically and affectionately. And wives, out of deep devotion and respect, submit to their husbands. For a wife to be a wife, she needs a husband. So if the Bible portrays the church as a wife, then it portrays Jesus as a husband. In

---

6   For example, see 1 Corinthians 3.

Ephesians 5, Paul opens up this great mystery—the earthly institution of marriage is a sign of the greater reality of the marital union between Christ and his church. The church is *legally* united to Christ so all he has belongs to her. The church is *practically* united to Jesus so she lives with him and they operate with joint accounts. And the church is *affectionately* united with Christ so there is mutual love flowing back and forth, as the church glorifies Jesus and Jesus in turn glorifies the church.[7] The way we see most clearly how Christ and the church are husband and wife is in observing how Jesus loves the church so much he laid down his life for her, and how the church respects Jesus so much she submits to him.

A flock of sheep

Another prominent image of the church is of a flock of sheep. The church alone can claim the realities of Psalm 23, where they are comforted, filled with contentment, led by streams of flowing water, cared for, restored back to health, guided in right paths and able to pass through the valley of the shadow of death without fear. The image of the church as a flock is made most clear by the reality that Jesus is the Good Shepherd. Jesus is not a hired hand who runs at the first sight of trouble. As John 10:11 puts it, "The good shepherd lays down His life for the sheep." The one true flock of God, the church, hears the voice of Jesus. They *know* their shepherd, but more importantly they are *known* by their shepherd. He loves them and chases after them.

Inseparable from Jesus

There are many other images for the church we could examine, but in and through all these images, the biggest thing we need to remember is *Jesus and the church are inseparably connected.* The church's whole self-identify is wrapped up in Jesus Christ. We understand who we are more and more, as we understand who Jesus is more and more. The church is what it is because of what Jesus is. There is no church without Jesus, and by virtue of his great grace, the church is united to Jesus forever.

So, we might say the church is: the people of God, who are called to serve the Son of God, by the power of the Spirit of God, according

---

7   See Paul's prayer in 2 Thessalonians 1:11–12 for more on this profound reality.

to the Word of God. In all times and places, the members of the church are those who belong to God. These members serve the Son of God, both in their worship of him and their obedience to him—including in their faithfulness to one another and their focus on Christ's mission to make and multiply disciples. These members serve the Son, in the power of the Spirit, who has caused them to be born again and who has gifted them in unique ways through his grace and power. And these members join themselves to one another, submitting their lives together underneath the rule of God's Word, as the church rightly preaches the Scriptures, rightly administers the ordinances and rightly orders itself in leadership, worship and discipline.

SCRIPTURAL FOUNDATIONS

Matthew 16:13–19

Now when Jesus came into the region of Caesarea Philippi, He was asking His disciples, "Who do people say that the Son of Man is?" And they said, "Some *say* John the Baptist; and others, Elijah; and *still* others, Jeremiah, or one of the *other* prophets." He said to them, "But who do you yourselves say that I am?" Simon Peter answered, "You are the Christ, the Son of the living God." And Jesus said to him, "Blessed are you, Simon Barjona, because flesh and blood did not reveal *this* to you, but My Father who is in heaven. And I also say to you that you are Peter, and upon this rock I will build My church; and the gates of Hades will not overpower it. I will give you the keys of the kingdom of heaven; and whatever you bind on earth shall have been bound in heaven, and whatever you loose on earth shall have been loosed in heaven."

Until this point in Matthew, Jesus had been teaching and healing with authority. Along the way, he had called disciples to himself and specifically marked out twelve of them as his closest followers. Jesus knew there was controversy swirling as he and his disciples continued to engage in ministry in the surrounding areas. There was talk about who he was and what he was doing. So he asked his disciples what they thought. After getting close to him and observing all he had done and said, who did *they* think he was? Peter spoke up, confessing Jesus as both God's Messiah and the Son of God.

In response to Peter's confession, Jesus teaches us at least five important things about the church. First, Jesus tells us the church is built on this confession of Peter's: Jesus is the Christ, the Son of the living God. Second, Jesus tells us all those who belong to this church of common confession did not come to this confession by their own intuition, will or intellect. Rather, it has been *revealed* to them by God. Third, Jesus tells us *he* is the one who builds the church. It is his church and he has promised to build it. Fourth, Jesus tells us the church will not be overpowered. Not even death itself is able to overcome the church of Christ. And finally, Jesus teaches us something extraordinary about the role of the apostles in the church. The twelve disciples whom Jesus had called out from the larger group were given a unique and outstanding authority. Because Jesus gave the apostles the authority of the kingdom of heaven, the true church must be an apostolic church—that is, a church which submits itself to the apostolic witness, handed down and delivered to the saints in the Scriptures.

Acts 2:37–47

Now when they heard *this*, they were pierced to the heart, and said to Peter and the rest of the apostles, "Brothers, what are we to do?" Peter *said* to them, "Repent, and each of you be baptized in the name of Jesus Christ for the forgiveness of your sins; and you will receive the gift of the Holy Spirit. For the promise is for you and your children and for all who are far away, as many as the Lord our God will call to Himself." And with many other words he solemnly testified and kept on urging them, saying, "Be saved from this perverse generation!" So then, those who had received his word were baptized; and that day there were added about three thousand souls. They were continually devoting themselves to the apostles' teaching and to fellowship, to the breaking of bread and to prayer.

Everyone kept feeling a sense of awe; and many wonders and signs were taking place through the apostles. And all the believers were together and had all things in common; and they would sell their property and possessions and share them with all, to the extent that anyone had need. Day by day continuing with one mind in the temple, and breaking bread from house to house, they were taking their meals together with gladness and sincerity of heart, praising God and having favor with all the people. And the Lord was adding to their number day by day those who were being saved.

Here in Acts 2, we see the launch of something amazing. The Holy Spirit had come down on a small group of believers whom Jesus had instructed before his ascension. The Spirit empowered the church to witness to Jesus. When this large crowed of people heard the good news of Jesus, it struck them and they wanted to know how they could respond appropriately to what they had just heard. When the apostle Peter responds, we learn the church is made up of all those who have repented and turned to Christ, been forgiven of their sins, received the gift of the Holy Spirit and been baptized. And we learn the invitation to join is both for those who are near to those who are far off. In other words, *anyone* willing to trust Christ is invited. Then something amazing happened: 3,000 people received Peter's words and were baptized! And what did those 3,000 do next? They committed themselves *to each other*, and devoted themselves to the apostles' teaching. They met regularly to eat meals and to pray. They took care of one another's needs. And most importantly, they kept on praising God. So, what did God do? He poured out his power and called many to himself. This is what the Christian church can look like in the world, when the Spirit of God comes down in power. The church is a place of joy, love, sincerity, praise, truth and awe.

Ephesians 4:1–16

Therefore I, the prisoner of the Lord, urge you to walk in a manner worthy of the calling with which you have been called, with all humility and gentleness, with patience, bearing with one another in love, being diligent to keep the unity of the Spirit in the bond of peace. *There is* one body and one Spirit, just as you also were called in one hope of your calling; one Lord, one faith, one baptism, one God and Father of all who is over all and through all and in all.

But to each one of us grace was given according to the measure of Christ's gift. Therefore it says,

"WHEN HE ASCENDED ON HIGH,
HE LED CAPTIVE *THE* CAPTIVES,
AND HE GAVE GIFTS TO PEOPLE."

(Now this *expression*, "He ascended," what does it mean except that He also had descended into the lower parts of the earth? He who descended is Himself also He who ascended far above all the heavens, so that He might fill all things.) And He gave some *as* apostles, some *as* prophets, some *as* evangelists, some *as* pastors and teachers, for the equipping of the saints for the work of ministry, for the building up of the body of Christ; until we all attain to the unity of the faith, and of the knowledge of the Son of God, to a mature man, to the measure of the stature which belongs to the fullness of Christ. As a result, we are no longer to be children, tossed here and there by waves and carried about by every wind of doctrine, by the trickery of people, by craftiness in deceitful scheming; but speaking the truth in love, we are to grow up in all *aspects* into Him who is the head, *that is*, Christ, from whom the whole body, being fitted and held together by what every joint supplies, according to the proper working of each individual part, causes the growth of the body for the building up of itself in love.

If we just stopped at Acts 2 in the story of the church, we might think everything was smooth sailing. But by Acts 6 we start to see some conflict. And then, if one reads the Pauline epistles,[8] it becomes very clear the story of the church includes great struggles alongside great triumphs. The great challenge of the church is to live up to her calling. The church is supposed to be this place where the holistic fruit of the Spirit permeates the collective community of God, in all its beauty and glory. Peace, love and patience, for example, are to be evident markers of the Spirit's work in the life of a church. Peace reigns over strife, love reigns over selfishness and patience reigns over pushiness. It is the unity of the grace of God in individual believers which unifies an individual with the church. Each believer is a member of the one body. Each believer is indwelt by the one Spirit. Each believer submits to the

---

8   Specifically Paul's letters to the churches at Rome, Corinth, Galatia, Ephesus, Philippi, Collosea and Thessalonica.

one Lord. Because each believer has the same graces and hope, we are called to persevere with diligence in maintaining the bond of peace. There is individuality in the church. Each member is unique and has been given unique gifts by the Spirit through Jesus. But this individuality is not meant to eclipse unity. Rather, it is meant to increase unity. The church is unified by its interdependence and it is edified by its genuineness. The only way for the church to become a mature body is for each member to receive life from the head and to strive to build up its other members. We receive both our unity in Christ and our diversity in Christ, so that as we grow, Christ becomes all in all.

1 Timothy 3:1–16

It is a trustworthy statement: if any man aspires to the office of overseer, *it is* a fine work he desires to do. An overseer, then, must be above reproach, the husband of one wife, temperate, self-controlled, respectable, hospitable, skillful in teaching, not overindulging in wine, not a bully, but gentle, not contentious, free from the love of money. *He must* be one who manages his own household well, keeping his children under control with all dignity (but if a man does not know how to manage his own household, how will he take care of the church of God?), *and* not a new convert, so that he will not become conceited and fall into condemnation incurred by the devil. And he must have a good reputation with those outside *the church*, so that he will not fall into disgrace and the snare of the devil.

Deacons likewise *must be* men of dignity, not insincere, not prone to *drink* much wine, not greedy for money, *but* holding to the mystery of the faith with a clear conscience. These men must also first be tested; then have them serve as deacons if they are beyond reproach. Women *must* likewise *be* dignified, not malicious gossips, but temperate, faithful in all things. Deacons must be husbands of one wife, and good managers of *their* children and their own households. For those who have served well as deacons obtain for themselves a high standing and great confidence in the faith that is in Christ Jesus.

I am writing these things to you, hoping to come to you before long; but in case I am delayed, *I write* so that you will know how one should act in the household of God, which is the church of the living

God, the pillar and support of the truth. Beyond question, great is the mystery of godliness:

> He who was revealed in the flesh,
> Was vindicated in the Spirit,
> Seen by angels,
> Proclaimed among the nations,
> Believed on in the world,
> Taken up in glory.

While there may be things from culture to culture, and from local church to local church, which will be different, some marks and boundaries are universally true for every church in every place. One of these things is *leadership*. The Bible is clear about the roles and characteristics of those called to lead the church. The overwhelming concern is for those who are called by God to lead in the church to exhibit the *character* of Christ. The Bible clearly emphasizes the fruit of the Spirit as the most important evidence of qualification for leadership in the church.

Beyond the high standard of character, the Bible also highlights two different leadership *offices* which are to be established in each local church. The prototype for these two offices is Jesus Christ himself. Jesus is both the prototypical overseer and the prototypical deacon.

An *overseer* in a church is a man called by God and affirmed by the church to be a pastor. The words *overseer, elder* and *pastor* are not identical in the Bible, but they are three different words used to describe different functions of the same person. Jesus is the perfect pastor who shepherds every member of his flock. He is also the perfect example to pastors of local churches as to how they should shepherd the flocks they have been entrusted. Jesus is the prototype for those called to be overseers in teaching, disciplining, ruling, commanding, protecting, caring for, praying, discipling, encouraging, equipping. Jesus does these things perfectly and effectively. It is wise and biblical for each local church to call out multiple, qualified and gifted men to serve and lead the church as overseers.

A deacon in a church is a person called by God and affirmed by the church to be a lead servant. The word *deacon* simply means, *servant*. Many men and women are distinguished as deacons throughout the

New Testament. They are people who lead without authority. They manage ministry without ruling. Their leadership is of a different kind—rather than being vocal and visible, it is quiet and tangible. Through humility, skill and faithfulness, deacons lead the church forward more by what they do than by what they say. Jesus is the perfect deacon who quietly and humbly offered himself on the cross in the greatest act of leadership the world has ever seen. Each local church should call out lead servants who are qualified and gifted to carry out the vision and ministry of the church.

Paul gives these clear instructions so we can get a sense for what the shape and character of each local church should be. There will be variety from culture to culture, but all true churches everywhere together make up the one household of God. This is the assembly of the living God, which is his outpost in the world for the truth of the gospel. The church is bound together by a common confession, and it is constrained to uphold the integrity of that confession. The standard and call for leadership in the church is no small matter. These offices, with their qualifications and duties, are God's plan for maintaining the stability of the church and the purity of its confession. As faithful overseers and deacons live out their ministries in word and deed, the mystery of godliness—Christ himself—is made known for all to see.

EXPLANATION

"The Lord Jesus is the head of the Church..."

When the resurrected and ascended Lord Jesus poured out his Spirit on the day of Pentecost, the visible church was born. Christ Jesus is in charge of the church, the vital life source throughout the church and the unifying factor in the church. As head, Jesus makes the decisions. As head, Jesus pours his life into the body. As head, Jesus causes the members of the body to work together in harmony for his purposes. No pastor, priest or family member is head of the church. Jesus alone is its indispensable head.

"which is composed of all his true disciples..."

Those who belong to the true church of Jesus Christ, throughout all times and in all places, are true disciples of Jesus. To be a disciple of Jesus means to follow Jesus. Those who follow Jesus have been brought into resurrecting union by faith in Jesus. They are indwelt by the sanctifying Spirit of Jesus. They are those who have turned from self and sin and turned to Jesus for life and righteousness. A true disciple of Jesus has been called out from the world and set apart for service to God. They worship Jesus and witness to Jesus. His life has become their life. His truth has become their truth. His mission has become their mission.

"and in him is invested supremely all power for its government...."

Jesus Christ does not share his headship over the church. He alone represents the church. He alone orders the church. He alone lays down the law in the church. The buck stops with him.

"According to his commandment, Christians are to associate themselves into particular societies or churches..."

There is a difference between the universal church and the local church. All people everywhere who possess and are possessed by the Spirit of God belong to the universal church. However, since one of the most basic identities of the church is God's assembly, the local church is a local congregation we are called to unite ourselves to so we can be faithful to Jesus. Every disciple of Jesus is called to gather together with other disciples of Jesus, submitting their lives together under the rule of God's Word. It is in the local church where God works by his Spirit to sanctify his people and call lost sinners into saving fellowship with his Son Jesus Christ. Each local church should never forget the fellowship of the Spirit far exceeds its own small society. Every Christian is called as a member of the church universal and the church local. To neglect the local church or to forget the universal church is to fall into pride and undermine the very heart of Christ.

"and to each of these churches he has given needful authority..."

While it is true Jesus alone possesses all the power for the government of the church, he does bestow his authority on others for the sake of carrying out his plan for order in the church. We must never forget it is his authority and belongs to no human, even when Jesus empowers someone to lead and serve with his authority. For example, the apostles were given the authority of Jesus, as the foundation of the church universal. As the Holy Spirit used these men to bear witness to Jesus, they were given unique authority to deliver, once for all, the message of the Christian faith. This message, what we call the New Testament, is the authoritative apostolic witness to the gospel of Jesus Christ. But it is not as though authority resided in these men themselves. It was a *derived* authority. The authority always and ever belongs to Jesus, and at times Jesus sees fit to bestow his authority on men to carry out his orders. In the same way, each local church exercises a derived authority. No member of the church possesses authority, except what has been given to them by Jesus Christ to steward under his lordship. If the apostles themselves did not have an authority of their own, then no member of any church has the right to claim it either. Those who do exercise authority in the church, and they must, will only exercise it appropriately under the lordship of Jesus Christ.

"for administering that order and worship which he has appointed...."

The derived authority which Jesus gives to leaders in local churches is to administer order and worship. By order is meant things are carried out according to the Word of God. Ordinances are correctly administered. Saints are faithfully equipped. Members are graciously disciplined. And the ministry and mission of the church is defined and focused so that the church faithfully bears witness to the gospel. By worship is meant the gathering of the saints on the Lord's Day to sing, pray, see one another and preach the Word. There is a standard for what a church does and how a church is formed, and Jesus calls leaders in the church to administer his ways in the power of his authority.

"The regular officers of a church are pastors and servant leaders."

Each local church must call and affirm pastors and servant leaders to bear the burden of leadership in the church. *Pastors*, which are sometimes referred to in the Scriptures as *elders* or *overseers*, are those men called to steward the authority of Jesus in the church. They are called by Jesus and given gifts from Jesus to administer the order and worship in the church which he has appointed. Pastors are the public leaders of the local church who shepherd the flock of God as they give themselves to the ministry of the Word and prayer. They are not called to do all the ministry in the church, instead they are called to equip the members of the church to do the work of the ministry. *Servant leaders*, which is simply a translation of the word *deacon*, are those gifted and called by Jesus to bear the responsibility of carrying out the ministry and mission of the church. They rarely lead in public ways and specialize in caring for people and stewarding the resources of the church with care. Because every local church is different and different in size, there is no set number of pastors or servant leaders for each church. It does seem both wise and biblical, for each local church to have multiple pastors and multiple servant leaders. There is clear evidence not all pastors or servant leaders perform the same functions at the same rate or level.[9] But most congregations will be large enough that the shared responsibility is healthy both for the church and the leaders themselves. Shared leadership gives opportunities for accountability and personal health; it creates an environment of genuine member care; and creates pathways for discipleship and multiplication.

MISCONCEPTIONS

There are too many misconceptions about the church to articulate them all, but there are a handful that are important for us to unearth. The first misconception is the belief that all that matters in the church is loving God. While this initially sounds nice, it is both *naive* and *dismissive*. The reason it is naive is if it was as easy as just loving God, then we would already be doing it. Everyone has a different definition of love and everyone has a different idea of what it means to love God. For some, loving God means defending truth. For others, loving God means lots of singing and praising. For others, loving God means loving people. When we say all that matters is loving God, what we

---

9   1 Timothy 5:17.

really mean is, "Can't we all just do what I think is important?" This is why this kind of mentality actually breeds disunity rather than unity. But this is also a misconception because it is dismissive. The Bible actually does have a lot to say about the church and about the order of local churches. Most, if not all, of the New Testament letters were written to their original audience to inform the doctrine, life and practice of particular local churches. These letters get very specific, with instructions about preaching, prayer, care, gender roles, authority and leadership, money and stewardship, ordinances, singing, conflict and many other specific situations and details. To disregard what God has said, under the guise of "just loving God," is actually not to love God at all.

Another misconception is that the mission of the church is to help people. First, this is a misconception because it misses the primary goal of the church and of life: to give glory to God. Many people who want to make the mission of the church about helping people, do so because they are embarrassed by what the Bible has to say about Jesus. God is the primary focus in the church and to take the focus off him does not help people, no matter how good our intentions might be. But also, Jesus has clearly defined the mission of the church as bearing witness to him and making disciples of him. The church ought to love helping people, and usually most local churches do help lots of people. But, there are many great and good organizations who help people. The unique mission of the church is to bear witness to the resurrection of Christ and to make disciples of Jesus by the power of his Spirit.

A third misconception is that being a member of a church is *optional*. In the Bible, there is no such thing as a solo Christian. All disciples of Jesus are called to gather together to worship on the Lord's Day, engage in the Lord's mission and care for the Lord's people. There ought to be little time between a person confessing Christ as Lord and entering fellowship with a local church through baptism. A Christian who is not an active and committed member of a local church is living in disobedience. In fact, they are a walking contradiction. It is impossible to be connected to Jesus as the head and not be connected to his body.

A final misconception has to do with worship. This is a difficult one because there are two different directions this mistake is regularly made. One misconception is that worship is what you do Monday to Saturday and therefore not what you do on Sunday. The other is that worship is what you do on Sunday and therefore not what you do Monday to Saturday. The way we clear up this misconception is by distinguishing between *personal* worship and *gathered* worship. It is true every believer is invited to worship God in everything they do every day of their lives. The way we do our work can be an act of worship. The way we love our families can be an act of worship. The way we think, feel and talk can be acts of worship we perform all day long. Christians are called to personal worship as a way of life. However, personal worship does not take the place of gathered worship. From the days of Pentecost, believers have gathered together on the Lord's Day to worship in a unique and special way. Gathered worship does not take the place of personal worship, but it is a vital aspect of a faithful Christian life. Those who neglect gathering to worship with God's people (who aren't hindered by illness or unique circumstances), are living in disobedience. As Christians, we ought to embrace personal *and* gathered worship, and enjoy the way they fuel one another. Personal worship makes our gathered worship sweeter, and gathered worship unites us to the larger reality of God's global and eternal glory and grace.

APPLICATION

Article XIV: The Church

The Lord Jesus is the head of the Church, which is composed of all his true disciples, and in him is invested supremely all power for its government. According to his commandment, Christians are to associate themselves into particular societies or churches; and to each of these churches he has given needful authority for administering that order, discipline and worship which he has appointed. The regular officers of a church are pastors and servant leaders.

---

1. *As the family of God, we are called to belong.*
Every Christian is called to participate in the family of God, to love and support one another. This will look like what most families look like—messy but loyal.

2. *As the body of Christ, we are called to complement one another.*
Each body part serves the other. Each member is treated with care, respect and honour because each member of the body is needed. The picture of the body of Christ is extremely functional because the church is to come together for ministry, rather than exist in isolation. Different gifts should be developed and utilized so that as the parts work together, there is genuine health in the body.

3. *As the assembly of God, we are called to gather.*
Christians join together to worship God. We listen to the Word read and preached, we sing the Word out loud together and to one another, we pray the Word back to God and we observe the Word made visible through baptism and the Lord's Supper. When the church gathers, Christ is there—ministering his grace to his church by the power of his Spirit.

4. As disciples of Christ, we are called to grow in Christ and help others grow.

Our maturity in the body of Christ is not an individual enterprise. We learn together, grow together, change together, repent together and become conformed to the image of Christ together. As disciples we make disciples, baptizing them and teaching them to follow Jesus.

5. As ambassadors of Christ, we are called to join together on the mission of making the gospel known to the ends of the earth.

We give, we go and we pray for mission efforts around the world. We share our faith with others. We serve and love our communities. We plant other churches, train and develop leaders and make personal sacrifices, all so the message of Jesus Christ can be heard around the world. The church is God's plan to accomplish his mission in the world—the mission of witnessing to the resurrected Christ and making disciples for him from all nations.

XV

—

Baptism

Baptism is an ordinance of the Lord Jesus, obligatory upon every believer, wherein they are immersed in water in the name of the Father, and of the Son, and of the Holy Spirit, as a sign of their fellowship with the death and resurrection of Christ, of remission of sins, and of giving themselves up to God, to live and walk in newness of life. It is prerequisite to church membership, and to participation in the Lord's Supper.

Baptism

INTRO + OVERVIEW

B
ecause the church is the people of God who are called to serve the Son of God by the power of the Spirit of God according to the Word of God, we must pay close attention to what it means to serve the Son of God according to the Word of God. We are not at liberty to minimize the things Jesus has emphasized. We must do our best to carry out the ordinances Jesus has given the church in the most biblical manner possible. The two ordinances Jesus has given to his church, to receive and observe until he returns, are baptism and the Lord's Supper. Most of the different views about what the church believes about the ordinances and how they are practiced comes from different interpretations of the Bible. Bible believing, Jesus loving Christians, who agree on all the gospel essentials, disagree on the who, what, when and why of these ordinances. And particularly with baptism, these different views affect the life of the church because the ordinances are something to be regularly practiced.

What baptism is
All traditions agree that baptism includes water. The word *baptism* literally means *to immerse*. In baptism, a new member of the community of faith is put under the waters. This ritual is performed in the presence of the community. The triune name of God is spoken over them.[1] This is a celebration, but it is also solemn and sacred.

What baptism means
The most important reason baptism is an ordinance in the life of the church is it represents *union with Christ*. This has two different aspects

---

1   See the scriptural foundations section in Article III: The Trinity, for a discussion of the triune name in Matthew 28.

to it. First, going down and coming out of the water symbolizes the life, death and resurrection of Jesus. Baptism proclaims the *history* of salvation. But second, going down and coming out of the water is a symbol of our own death and resurrection with Christ. We died with Christ and we live with Christ. In this sense, baptism proclaims the *order* of salvation—we are washed, we are sanctified and we are made new. Baptism itself doesn't make us new, but it proclaims the reality of what the Spirit of God has done in our hearts by virtue of our union with Christ.

But union with Christ is not all baptism represents. Baptism is also an *initiation*. It is the first right of induction into God's family. The church is the family of the baptized. Just as there is one faith, one Lord, and one Spirit, so there is one baptism.[2] In that sense, baptism precedes church membership, but it is also organically connected to church membership. But baptism isn't just an initiation ceremony, it also declares to the assembled congregation that we have put our faith in Christ and experienced regenerating grace. We especially see the grace of God in baptism because the one being baptized is passive. Baptisms are reminders God still brings life from death, and are an opportunity to tell individual and unique stories of how God saves sinners.

Why baptism matters

We may be tempted to think baptism isn't a big deal. After all, baptism doesn't carry any specific *moral* significance in and of itself. However, being baptized sets a believer on a trajectory of obedience. Obedience isn't just about being good or righteous, it is about honouring God. Under each covenant in the Bible, there are different *neutral* commands which do not carry *moral* significance in them. However, by virtue of God's command, they demand obedience. We are foolish to take these neutral commands lightly, if for no other reason than it was a neutral command which brought about the Fall of humanity and the curse of the earth in the Garden of Eden.[3] Baptism is almost a more

---

2 See Ephesians 4:4–6.

3 Another prominent neutral command under the Old Covenant was circumcision. Circumcision itself holds no moral significance, but as can be seen in Exodus 4:24, God holds disobedience to neutral commands just as worthy of death as natural commands.

important act of obedience because *it is* in the form of a neutral command. Because baptism doesn't carry moral significance, it is only because of God's command in his Word that we would, in obedience, take the sign on ourselves.

Related to obedience is the importance of *discipleship*. Discipleship is the process of following Jesus and becoming like him. Baptism matters because Jesus himself was baptized. Baptism is one thing in a long line of important things by which Jesus leads his people forward. One of the most striking realities of the baptism of Jesus[4] is the way Jesus exhibited extreme humility. Baptism is a humbling experience for anyone. But for Jesus, it was an extreme act of humility. The eternal Son of God, the Lord of history, the perfect man, allowed another man to put his hands on him and plunge him under the water. When a person is baptized, it is not only an act of obedience, it is a participation in the humility of Christ.

Baptism isn't just important from our end. Baptism, like reading the Bible, prayer and gathering with God's people on the Lord's Day, is a *means of grace*. Means of grace are not mystical and they are not operative void of faith in Christ. Means of grace are the ordinary and usual channels through which God blesses and sanctifies his people. God is not bound to these means, but we are. If we expect God's gracious blessing in our lives, and if we expect to grow in our walk with Christ, then baptism—alongside the other means of grace— should be welcomed with humility and obedience. Baptism doesn't save us, but it is one important way God blesses us.

Who should be baptized?

Finally, we need to consider who should be baptized. This centres on the question of how a person becomes a new member of the community of faith. There is both a biblical and a theological response. The *biblical* response is baptism is for those who have been born again, placed their faith in Jesus Christ and repented of their sin. Every person who is baptized as a new member of the Christian church is baptized as a response to faith in Christ.

There is also an important *theological* response to be addressed. It is no secret that for centuries many different traditions of the church

---

4 See Matthew 3 and Mark 1.

have baptized children by virtue of relation to their parents who are themselves members of the community of faith. Each tradition has its own nuance and rationale for why and how this works, but generally speaking, the thought process goes in one of two ways. One is driven by the belief of what baptism accomplishes. For some traditions, because baptism *itself* possesses saving significance, to baptize an infant or a child is to begin the process of salvation in their lives. For other traditions, because baptism is theologically linked to circumcision, it is then practiced in the New Covenant under the same method as circumcision was practiced in the Old Covenant.

Those who hold to a belief in believer's baptism and regenerate church membership[5] will be greatly helped by reflecting on the theological response to infant baptism. First, baptism cannot possess saving significance without diminishing the once-for-all sacrifice of Jesus Christ. To add baptism as a salvific requirement would literally be adding works to Christ's finished work. Emphasizing the importance of baptism, though in a slightly different way, is similar to emphasizing the importance of repentance. Both are a response to the Spirit of God applying the work of the Son of God in our lives. They are not, however, additions to our justification in the sight of God.

But not all church traditions which baptize infants do so under the banner of saving significance. So, second, while it is extremely important to hold forth the truth that all people who have and will be saved are saved by virtue of the New Covenant which is in Christ Jesus alone, that does not mean there is a one-to-one correlation between Old Covenant ordinances and New Covenant ordinances. While Israel does *symbolize* the church, point forward to the church and, by virtue of Jesus Christ himself, give birth to the church, *Israel is not the church.* There were members of the church who were also citizens of Israel, but *it was their union with Christ by faith*, not their citizenship in Israel, which will in the end be their confidence of justification and salvation in the sight of God. Along the same line, while circumcision does

---

5 Regenerate church membership is the belief that all those who are admitted as members into a church are those who have been regenerated by the Holy Spirit. It is impossible to know for certain whether or not someone is truly regenerate, since only God sees our hearts. So, churches who practice regenerate church membership base membership on a personal profession of faith.

symbolize baptism, point forward to baptism and, in a sense, find its culmination through Christ in baptism, *circumcision is not baptism*. Circumcision was a neutral command from God. Neutral commands, because they do not contain moral significance, do change from covenant to covenant. Just because one neutral command was a sign of a later neutral command in another covenant, does not mean the same rules and methods apply under a different covenant. To summarize, while it is true infants entered the Old Covenant community by the initiating ordinance of circumcision, it does not mean infants should enter the New Covenant community by the initiating ordinance of baptism. These two neutral commands are different in *substance* (one is a cutting of flesh, while the other is immersing in water), different in *recipients* (one was instituted for Abraham's physical male offspring, while the other was instituted for those united to Jesus by faith—both male and female) and they belong to different *covenants* (one was a neutral command of the Old Covenant, while the other is a neutral command of the New Covenant). The covenants are not one, but two covenants, and the ordinances are not one, but two different neutral commands.[6] While the Old Covenant was a *shadow* of the New Covenant, it was not itself the *substance* of the New. In the same way, while circumcision was a *shadow* of baptism, it was not itself the *substance* of baptism.

Putting all these elements together then, baptism is an immersion into water in the triune name of God. It is a symbol of union with Christ, faith in Christ and cleansing regeneration. It is an act of humble obedience and a means of God's grace, which initiates a person into the church. Baptism is an ordinance of the New Covenant, which is to be passively received by all those who profess faith in Christ and repent of their sin.

---

6 It is true that those under the Old Covenant partook of the grace of Jesus Christ, but not by virtue of the Old. They partook of the grace of Jesus Christ by virtue of the New Covenant, as it was promised and foreshadowed for them through the Old. It would be shocking if Israel, circumcision, Passover, the Day of Atonement, etc., did not bear striking resemblance to substantial realities in the New Covenant, since those things were instituted as *types* and *tutors* which revealed and guided people to Jesus Christ. However, a *type* is never the same in *substance* to its fulfilment. Hence, the role of and rules of circumcision do not maintain a one-to-one correlation with baptism.

SCRIPTURAL FOUNDATIONS

Matthew 3:11-17

"As for me, I baptize you with water for repentance, but He who is coming after me is mightier than I, and I am not fit to remove His sandals; He will baptize you with the Holy Spirit and fire. His winnowing fork is in His hand, and He will thoroughly clear His threshing floor; and He will gather His wheat into the barn, but He will burn up the chaff with unquenchable fire."

Then Jesus arrived from Galilee at the Jordan, *coming* to John to be baptized by him. But John tried to prevent Him, saying, "I have *the* need to be baptized by You, and *yet* You are coming to me?" But Jesus, answering, said to him, "Allow *it* at this time; for in this way it is fitting for us to fulfill all righteousness." Then he allowed Him. After He was baptized, Jesus came up immediately from the water; and behold, the heavens were opened, and he saw the Spirit of God descending as a dove *and* settling on Him, and behold, a voice from the heavens said, "This is My beloved Son, with whom I am well pleased."

In this section of Matthew 3, we encounter some teaching on baptism from John the Baptist. While the baptism John was doing was an outward fleshy experience, the baptism Jesus was bringing was something of the heart. Baptism is clearly a sign—it reflects immersive realities. The more important baptism, the *inward* baptism of the heart, is something only Jesus can do through his Spirit. John also alludes to the judgment as a baptism of fire. Baptism by the Spirit and baptism by fire are two realities of the ministry of Jesus separated by his first and second coming. Those who identify with Jesus through baptism now, will escape the fire baptism of judgment by virtue of Christ having been judged in their place. Baptism is a symbol both of life and of death.

With John the Baptist's words fresh in our minds, the narrative turns to Jesus himself. Shockingly, Jesus himself desires to be baptized by John. We see a number of important realities in the baptism of Jesus. First, we can't help but see his humility. Even in this brief account, you can tell how uncomfortable John was. John knew Jesus was the better man and that the roles should be reversed. But Jesus was happy to allow John to plunge him under the waters in the sight of all. Second, we must assume since Jesus was not being baptized for repentance, he was being baptized for community initiation. He was endorsing John's ministry, but also submitting to it. Jesus didn't want to create a rift between himself and John because John had been sent as his forerunner. Jesus waited to launch his own ministry until he had sufficiently affirmed John's, linking the two together. Third, his baptism was a legitimate symbol of his own upcoming death and resurrection. In Luke 12, Jesus makes the connection between his death and his baptism.[7] The rite was clearly symbolic for what he knew his task to be. Fourth, the baptism was a representative act. Union with Christ is such an important aspect of baptism. The beauty of union with Christ is that before we could be united to Jesus, he became united with us. He took on flesh, to bring many sons to glory. Our baptism into him is only meaningful because he was first baptized into us. And finally, the baptism of Jesus was a means of God's blessing and grace. Jesus is one person who possess two natures, which means he clearly submitted himself to the full range of human emotions and experiences. Jesus needed encouragement, just like any human being. Jesus needed the approving voice of his Father, just like any human being needs the approving voice of their Father. And Jesus needed the anointing of the Holy Spirit, just like any of God's leaders needs the anointing of the Holy Spirit. Through baptism, Jesus received encouragement, heard God's approving voice and was anointed for ministry by the power of the Spirit.[8]

---

7   Luke 12:49–50: "I have come to cast fire upon the earth; and how I wish it were already kindled! But I have a baptism to undergo, and how distressed I am until it is accomplished!"

8   This *anointing* of the Spirit is not to be confused with the *indwelling* of the Spirit. Jesus was conceived of the Spirit and, from the moment of conception, was indwelt by the Holy Spirit. Throughout the Old Testament, God's chosen leaders received the anointing of the Spirit as a sign both of his calling in their lives and as strength to perform the task he called them to, with the gifts the Spirit would provide.

Matthew 28:16-20

> But the eleven disciples proceeded to Galilee, to the mountain which Jesus had designated to them. And when they saw Him, they worshiped Him; but some were doubtful. And Jesus came up and spoke to them, saying, "All authority in heaven and on earth has been given to Me. Go, therefore, and make disciples of all the nations, baptizing them in the name of the Father and the Son and the Holy Spirit, teaching them to follow all that I commanded you; and behold, I am with you always, to the end of the age."

Rather than the rite of baptism ending with John's ministry, Jesus infuses new value to baptism and gives it as an ordinance to the church. In these parting words before his ascension, the risen King includes baptism in his instructions to his disciples. It is those among all the nations who are made disciples of Jesus who are to be baptized into the triune name. Baptism is a first step of obedience in a lifetime of learning and observing all the commands of Jesus. Those baptized are regenerated disciples of Christ, they are marked with God's name and they are initiated into the community—the context for growing in Christ and obedience to Christ. It is in this community where a baptized disciple can expect the ongoing presence of Jesus till the end of the age.

Acts 16:25-34

> Now about midnight Paul and Silas were praying and singing hymns of praise to God, and the prisoners were listening to them; and suddenly there was a great earthquake, so that the foundations of the prison were shaken; and immediately all the doors were opened, and everyone's chains were unfastened. When the jailer awoke and saw the prison doors opened, he drew *his* sword and was about to kill himself, thinking that the prisoners had escaped. But Paul called out with a loud voice, saying, "Do not harm yourself, for we are all here!" And *the jailer* asked for lights and rushed in, and trembling with fear, he fell down before Paul and Silas; and after he brought them out, he said, "Sirs, what must I do to be saved?"
> They said, "Believe in the Lord Jesus, and you will be saved, you and your household." And they spoke the word of God to him together

with all who were in his house. And he took them that *very* hour of the night and washed their wounds, and immediately he was baptized, he and all his *household*. And he brought them into his house and set food before them, and was overjoyed, since he had become a believer in God together with his whole household.

Acts 16 is a very important passage for a few reasons. At first glance it seems to contradict some of what we have said so far. For example, is this jailer baptized with the believing community as witnesses? Does this passage prove a persons family should be baptized, including infants and children? These are important questions to answer. One thing we need to keep in mind is the setting for the book of Acts is the missionary frontier. Many times, as we trace the spread of the gospel in Acts, we get to witness the first conversions in a particular location. So, in this instance, there was no church for the jailer and his household to be baptized in front of. At the same time, we shouldn't discount that in a real sense, this jailer's house just became the first church in Philippi. God was establishing the church in front of their eyes. Now, with regard to the jailer's household, there are a number of important factors. The text never actually tells us who belongs to his household. We don't know who was included in the baptisms. However, we do know this: this passage mentions household or house four times. Paul and Silas initiate the conversation about the man's household after he asks them how he can be saved. Then we are told "they spoke the word of God to him together with all who were in his house." In other words, whoever ended up receiving baptism was also able to hear the Word of the Lord. So, when the whole household is baptized, textually speaking, they are the same "all who were in his house" who heard and responded to the preaching of the gospel. Then the last verse tells us either the whole household believed in God or it tells us the whole household rejoiced in the jailer believing in God.[9] Either way, the same people who were baptized are the same people who heard the Word of the Lord, are the same people who rejoiced in the believing of the

---

9 A number of modern English translations go in different directions with what the household is doing in verse 34. They are either said to be believing alongside the jailer or rejoicing along with the jailer that he had believed. So they themselves are either being said to believe or rejoicing about someone else's belief.

gospel. This means whoever is being referred to as receiving baptism, must be old enough and intellectually developed enough to hear the Word of the Lord and rejoice over belief in God.

Romans 6:3–7

> Or do you not know that all of us who have been baptized into Christ Jesus have been baptized into His death? Therefore we have been buried with Him through baptism into death, so that, just as Christ was raised from the dead through the glory of the Father, so we too may walk in newness of life. For if we have become united with *Him* in the likeness of His death, certainly we shall also be *in the likeness* of His resurrection, knowing this, that our old self was crucified with *Him*, in order that our body of sin might be done away with, so that we would no longer be slaves to sin; for the one who has died is freed from sin.

In Romans 6, Paul gives us the clearest connection between baptism and union with Christ. Paul shows how baptism symbolizes the narrative of gospel history *and* calls the believer to travel that same path in their subjective experience. Going under the water is envisioned as a death and burial. Spiritually, it is our old self which was killed and buried with Christ. But baptism has a raising element as well, and we are raised with Christ to newness of life. Our baptism should be something we remember, a constant memory of the new life to which we have been called. Ultimately though, union with Christ doesn't just secure spiritual realities. Jesus Christ was physically resurrected, and our union with Christ means we will be physically resurrected one day as well. The union with Christ portrayed in baptism is a reenactment of past accomplishments, a reminder of present grace and a seal of future promises.

Colossians 2:8–12

> See to it that there is no one who takes you captive through philosophy and empty deception in accordance with human tradition, in accordance with the elementary principles of the world, rather than in accordance with Christ. For in Him all the fullness of Deity dwells

in bodily form, and in Him you have been made complete, and He is the head over every ruler and authority; and in Him you were also circumcised with a circumcision performed without hands, in the removal of the body of the flesh by the circumcision of Christ, having been buried with Him in baptism, in which you were also raised with Him through faith in the working of God, who raised Him from the dead.

Colossians 2 helps us see the connection between circumcision and baptism. But we must remember the *physical* sign of circumcision pointed to a deeper *inward* reality even before the advent of Christ.[10] Circumcision was the sign of entrance into the community, but it was supposed to invoke the deeper heart reality of the cutting away of the calloused sinful heart. The circumcision Paul alludes to here is not physical circumcision but rather circumcision of the heart. Paul is reminding the church at Colossae that Jesus had given them new hearts through the regenerating, cleansing work of the Spirit.

After giving this reminder of the truth of circumcision, Paul brings in baptism. There are two important things to note. First, at times we are to envision baptism as death, and here Paul also wants us to envision circumcision as death. Circumcision, like baptism, puts the flesh to death. Here, though, baptism relates more to being buried and raised again. So circumcision is the cutting away, and baptism is the raising to newness of life. There is also a second thing to realize: this baptismal raising is a resurrection by faith. This is a *faith baptism* because it is through faith in Christ that heart circumcision and the resurrecting work of God are brought forth in our lives. Believer's baptism makes sense because what really matters is a believer's circumcision—the circumcision of the heart—not the circumcision of the flesh.[11]

Both circumcision and baptism are *outward symbols* pointing to *inward realities*. Both circumcision and baptism are initiating ordinances.

---

10 For example, see Jeremiah 4:4.

11 Romans 2:28–29: "For he is not a Jew who is one outwardly, nor is circumcision that which is outward in the flesh. But he is a Jew who is one inwardly; and circumcision is of the heart, by the Spirit, not by the letter; and his praise is not from people, but from God."

And both circumcision and baptism are passive signs which are received. But it is important to remember circumcision only relates to baptism *through Christ*. In other words, circumcision was a type whose fulfilment was Jesus himself. Jesus is the true circumcision. Baptism isn't the true circumcision. In the New Covenant of grace, baptism serves as a better sign than circumcision. Baptism, unlike circumcision, doesn't leave a permanent mark. Baptism, unlike circumcision, is received by both male and female. And baptism, unlike circumcision is received by faith. Entrance into the Old Covenant community was according to birth by design, and entrance into the New Covenant community is according to the new birth by design. Both circumcision and baptism remain helpful images for the way they teach spiritual truths. But with regard to initiation into the covenant community, baptism is a better and fuller sign of the New Covenant because it more accurately reflects what entrance into the community entails.[12]

EXPLANATION

"Baptism is an ordinance of the Lord Jesus..."

Jesus Christ instituted baptism. He gave baptism as a sign to the church as it proclaims the gospel. Baptism serves an important purpose in the ongoing life of the church, and is a means of grace for God's people. This ordinance proclaims the gospel because in it the life, death, burial and resurrection of Jesus are pictured. In this sense, the Word of God becomes visible for us through baptism. Jesus himself received this ordinance, which fills it with significance and leaves no excuse for our disobedience. It is the Lord of history, the man with all authority in heaven and on earth, who has given this gracious ordinance to his church.

---

12 And it almost goes without saying, but the same was true of circumcision with regard to the Old Covenant. Circumcision would have been a better initiating ceremony for the Old Covenant than baptism because that covenant was a covenant of the flesh, not a covenant of faith—it was a covenant of works, not a covenant of grace.

"obligatory upon every believer..."

Since Jesus, the man with all authority, graciously commanded his church to baptize all new disciples, all people who put their faith in him should be baptized. Entrance into the community of Jesus is by grace through faith. This means it is those who believe in Jesus who are commanded to be baptized.

"wherein they are immersed in water in the name of the Father, and of the Son, and of the Holy Spirit..."

The act of baptism is immersion into water. More profoundly, it is an immersion into the triune Name. There is one God who has eternally existed as three distinct persons. Those who come to faith in God through Jesus, are united to God through the one and only meditator, Jesus Christ. Baptism is a symbol of union with Christ, and through union with Christ, union with God—the one, true, living, triune God.

"as a sign of his fellowship with the death and resurrection of Christ..."

The most significant thing signalled in baptism is the death and resurrection of Christ. Any believer who receives baptism is publicly and openly accepting the objective and subjective realities of fellowship in the death and resurrection of Christ. The objective reality is the finished work of Christ on their behalf. The subjective reality is their willingness to follow Jesus in their own death and resurrection through a full and obedient surrender to his lordship over them.

"of remission of sins..."

The objective reality of the finished work of Christ is most poignantly applied to the believer through the cancellation of the debt of their sin. Water baptism drives home this image because it is a physical washing, which represents the washing of the Holy Spirit. Just as the dirt, sweat and grime is removed in bathing, baptism symbolizes the removal of sin Christ accomplished on the cross.

"and of giving themselves up to God, to live and walk in newness of life...."

The humility of baptism, to be plunged under the water by another, portrays the new believer's willingness to submit fully and completely to God himself. Baptism is a surrender of self, just as repentance toward God is a surrender of sin. Baptism is a public declaration of the desire of a believer to pursue holiness. The resurrection life of Christ is the new path for the believer. This new person of faith will need the Spirit and the church to enable them to walk in newness of life. They will stumble and fall, but their baptism will be a reminder they have died with Christ and they have been raised to a new life. Indeed, in all things, they are a new creation in Christ Jesus.

"It is prerequisite to church membership, and to participation in the Lord's Supper."

For all that baptism symbolizes, it also serves practical purposes. Baptism is an initiation into the local community of God. Jesus himself was initiated into the community of John before he launched out on his own ministry. Jesus was clearly not baptized for repentance, he was baptized to identify himself with the repentant community. All those who want to belong to the church, will gladly submit themselves to the same initiating ordinance everyone else in the church has received. Just as there is one Lord, one faith and one Spirit, so there is one baptism. While everyone in the church may have a different testimony of their subjective experience with God's saving power, in reality, every Christian is saved in the exact same way—through the finished work of Christ applied to their life by the Spirit of Christ. This means the second, ongoing and nourishing ordinance of the Lord's Supper is to be enjoyed by those who have first been baptized. Baptism comes first. It should happen to each member of the church only once. It is like the wedding day. The Lord's Supper comes after. It is received by each member every time they gather to celebrate the Lord. It is like the marriage. Both the wedding and the marriage are important, and of utmost importance is the order. Those being nourished by Christ's body should first be initiated into Christ's body.

MISCONCEPTIONS

Because baptism is a symbol, it is very easy for all of us to infuse our own meaning into it rather than allowing the Scriptures to preach the true word of baptism. With that being said, there are a number of common misconceptions about baptism. The first is one that seems easy to understand: it is the idea that baptism is a fresh start. Some people treat baptism like turning a new leaf. They see the water and think of cleansing, which is good. But they bypass faith in Christ and the regenerating work of the Spirit, and think baptism simply serves as a cleansing experience. Baptism, separated from faith in Christ, is meaningless. Needing to start over, might be a good impulse, but the gospel teaches us we need more than a do-over. What we really need is to be reborn into a new humanity. Baptism is more than a fresh start, it is fellowship with Jesus.

The second misconception runs along similar lines, but it imports some truth of the gospel into baptism which it shouldn't. It is the idea of baptismal regeneration (meaning, baptism saves us). Baptismal regeneration has a number of forms, but all the forms teach that baptism carries saving significance. This is a difficult idea to combat because on the one hand, baptism is clearly very important, it is regularly connected with the truths of the gospel and it is the first appropriate response after faith in Christ and repentance toward God. But just because something is an appropriate response to the gospel and an important act of obedience, doesn't mean it carries saving significance. If saving significance were attached to baptism, then there would be other very important commands which would also be given saving significance. And when activities we perform, or even ordinances we receive, start to be infused with saving significance, then the sufficiency of Christ is diminished. The whole of the gospel is under the Covenant of Grace. Any response to the gospel which is made to be a condition of salvation, makes grace conditional to works. And grace which is conditioned on works, even God-ordained works, is no longer grace.

A third misconception is the idea that baptism is mainly about the individual, instead of about Jesus and the church. This drives baptisms to take place in private, baptisms to take place outside of the local church and multiple baptisms of the same person. Because one aspect of baptism relates to the subjective experience, many people overemphasize the individuality of baptism to the exclusion of its corporate nature. But more importantly than balancing the individual with the corporate, is keeping Christ in our understanding of baptism. Baptism is first and foremost a proclamation of what Jesus has done—not just in this person's life, but his objective finished work on the cross. Many churches and ministries over-emphasize baptism as a declaration of a person's individual faith journey and forget baptism mainly declares a summary of the faith, the one faith we all share. The way many of us practice baptism only furthers the idea Christianity can be exclusively individualized. This damages the church, hurts the witness of Christ and is fatal for the growth of the new believer. We must hold in balance all that the ordinance of baptism offers to us—how it highlights Jesus, how it points to the subjective experience and how it initiates a person into the church.

A final misconception is the idea that requiring baptism is legalism. Legalism—the danger of believing my works add to the work of Jesus for my salvation—is deadly. But calling for obedience to Christ is not legalism. The New Covenant is an unconditional covenant, which means entrance into this covenant is *all of grace*. But every covenant, even covenants of grace, still have laws governing their participants. The only difference between a covenant of works and a covenant of grace is that in a covenant of works the laws are the conditions of the covenant, whereas in a covenant of grace the laws are the gracious paths to flourishing. When a church requires baptism for membership, they aren't doing anything Jesus himself wouldn't do. If requiring baptism is legalism, then how would we label this?

And [Jesus] was saying to *them* all, "If anyone wants to come after Me, he must deny himself, take up his cross daily, and follow Me."[13]

When Jesus requires us to do something, it is always gracious. We misconstrue the concept of legalism if we treat baptism this way, and only betray our unwillingness to submit to the lordship of Christ, the man with all authority in heaven and on earth who commands every believer to receive baptism.

---

13 Luke 9:23.

APPLICATION

Article XV: Baptism

Baptism is an ordinance of the Lord Jesus, obligatory upon every believer, wherein they are immersed in water in the name of the Father, and of the Son, and of the Holy Spirit, as a sign of their fellowship with the death and resurrection of Christ, of remission of sins, and of giving themselves up to God, to live and walk in newness of life. It is prerequisite to church membership, and to participation in the Lord's Supper.

---

1. We should practice baptism as an integral part of the life of the local church.

This means we teach on the significance of believer's baptism and regularly offer the opportunity for people to follow Jesus in this way. For baptism to be a part of the final commissioning of Jesus to his apostles displays its importance in his mind.

2. We should clearly explain what baptism is and why we do it.

Many people go through the experience of baptism and are never confronted with the reality of what they are doing. They may intentionally, or even unintentionally, fall into a misconception about what they are experiencing. It is worth taking the time to explain the significance of baptism, so those who are being baptized, and those who are witnessing the baptism, can celebrate it for all it is.

3. We should use wisdom and discretion when admitting someone to be baptized.

The Bible does not clearly define what the standard for baptism is, but no one in the Bible is baptized without expressing saving faith in Jesus Christ. Baptism can be an exciting opportunity for someone who wants to change their life around, or who has been encouraged from spending time with Christians, but in the long run it is worth making sure the person truly understands both the gospel and what baptism means.

4. Churches should use wisdom and discernment with regard to baptizing children.

The heart of the gospel is a simple message a child can understand. There are some children, though, who can repeat the truths of the Christian faith because it has been taught to them their whole life, and yet they are not born again. Usually, there will come a time when a child who grows up in the church, and professes faith, is tested for the first time. It may be wise for churches to consider delaying baptism until a child has the opportunity to test their own faith. If we are going to emphasize the importance of baptism for believers, and from our perspective baptism is not a saving ordinance, it may be wise to encourage children to wait for a season to test the genuineness of their faith. That being said, this will be for each church to decide using the knowledge of its context and the wisdom of its leadership. Baptism is a celebration of the gospel, so we should treat it with care and observe it with joy.

XVI

The Lord's Supper

The Lord's Supper is an ordinance of Jesus Christ, to be administered with the elements of bread and fruit of the vine, and to be observed by his churches till the end of the world. It is in no sense a sacrifice, but is designed to commemorate his death, to confirm the faith and other graces of Christians, and to be a bond, pledge and renewal of their communion with him, and of their church fellowship.

The Lord's Supper

INTRO + OVERVIEW

B ecause the ordinances Jesus has given to his church are regular practices and visible acts the church participates in, slight differences in perspectives on the ordinances affect the life of the church. For this reason, churches which agree on many central doctrines but disagree on the ordinances, can often work together for the sake for the gospel, even though they would have a hard time functioning as one local church. This brings up an important question: How should we categorize these doctrines? Are some doctrines the difference between orthodoxy and heresy? Do some doctrines determine church fellowship or separation? Are some doctrines in the area of personal conscience or obedience?

While there may be more than one way to dissect these categories, Gavin Ortlund offers a helpful perspective. He gives four categories for distinguishing doctrines:

> 1) Doctrines that are essential to the gospel; 2) doctrines that are urgent for the health and practice of the church, such that Christians commonly divide denominationally over them; 3) doctrines that are important for one branch of theology or another, but not such that they should lead to separation; 4) doctrines that are unimportant for gospel witness and ministry collaboration.[1]

In other words, the first are those things the Bible teaches are *at the heart of the Christian faith,* they are the difference between death and life, heaven and hell or guilt and righteousness. While churches may be in basic agreement on these central things, there may be other doctrines on which they disagree that are important enough to divide

---

1   Gavin Ortlund, *Finding the Right Hills To Die On: The Case for Theological Triage* (Wheaton: Crossway, 2020), 12.

over with charity and grace. For example, differing perspectives on the ordinances would fit into this category. Because baptism and the Lord's Supper are so connected to the regular life and practice of the church, different perspectives would cause issues in the life of one congregation.

Churches who disagree about the ordinances, yet agree about the gospel, can and should support and honour one another. The mistake many of us make is to push certain categories either up or down. We don't want to make so much of the ordinances that if we disagree on them then we disown each other. But at the same time, we don't want to make so little of the ordinances that we treat them like they aren't important. When it comes to baptism and the Lord's Supper, on the one hand, it's not a matter of life and death whether we interpret and practice these ordinances correctly; on the other hand, there are major implications from how we observe these commands. And at times, erring on these second and even third tier issues will foster problems of the first degree. For example, there are some ways of practicing baptism which could be detrimental in a person's life by giving them false assurance or by wounding their conscience. And there are some ways of practicing the Lord's Supper which short-circuit Christ's all sufficiency or offer a sense of false inclusion in the New Covenant community.

Rejecting the Trinity, the exclusivity of salvation in Jesus Christ or the necessity of regeneration are the difference between heaven and hell. These matters are of first importance. And while questions of who and how to baptize, and questions of how often and who ought to partake of the Lord's Supper, aren't of first tier importance, they still impact the church in very important ways. Every church has its impurities, which ought to produce a humility that should characterize the whole of its life and practice. And yet, humility does not necessitate avoiding all lines of division. Churches who avoid clearly defining the ordinances run the risk of deemphasizing what Jesus emphasized.

What the Lord's Supper is

The Lord's Supper is eating bread and drinking the fruit of the vine with the gathered church. Like baptism, it is a celebration and it is also solemn and sacred.

What the Lord's Supper means

The Lord's Supper has meaning that is bound up in the elements themselves. The *bread* represents the body of Jesus. The eternal Son of God was conceived of the Holy Spirit, born into the world by the virgin Mary, matured in wisdom and stature and offered up to God in a whole life of obedience. And Jesus did all this as a human being with a human body. Ultimately, Jesus offered up his body as a sacrifice, by dying on a cursed cross, and then was bodily raised to reign as King forever. The *cup* represents the blood of Jesus. Jesus was sinless and blameless before God like an unblemished lamb. His blood was atoning blood, which pacified the wrath of God toward sinners and cleansed the stain of sin.

The body and blood—the *bread* and the *cup*—have significance in three directions. They exist as an ordinance together to *remember* the past. Those who receive the bread and the cup are invited to think on all that Jesus did in saving them. He came, he lived, he died and he rose—it is finished! But the ordinance also has *present* significance because right now Jesus Christ, the real heavenly man, serves as a faithful High Priest to God on behalf of his church. His blood continues to speak and encourage his people as he ministers to their hearts and works his will in their lives. And while the bread and the cup point to the past and to the present, they also point point *forward* to the future. As the church partakes of the supper, they are reminded of that future day when they will eat another supper, the marriage supper of the Lamb,[2] with Jesus, when he comes to consummate God's kingdom and rescue his bride.

Why the Lord's Supper matters

In the Lord's Supper, we visibly *see* the gospel and we physically *taste* the gospel. The gospel is the power of God unto salvation, but it is also what washes and matures the church. Seeing and tasting the gospel, accompanied by the preaching of the gospel, sanctifies the people of God and stirs their hearts to know and love Jesus more. The supper is also a means of spiritual nourishment—a means of grace. Again, the means of grace are the natural and normal avenues whereby God ministers his grace into the lives of his people. If the Lord's Supper did not have unique spiritual nourishment for the body of Christ, then Jesus

---

2 Revelation 19:7–10.

wouldn't have instituted it. Another reason for the Lord's Supper is to foster unity in the body of Christ. This aspect is often neglected. Even in parts of the New Testament which are intended to promote the supper as an instrument of *unity*, it is easy to focus on the individual aspects of *personal* reflection and repentance. Those passages, however, always have an aim toward the unity *of the body*. There is one Lord, one faith, one Spirit, one baptism and one loaf of bread. When we approach the table, we are reminded of our common confession, our common faith and our common need of Christ. The Lord's Supper, taken together with the gathered saints, drives us to forgive one another, bear one another's burdens, seek peace with one another and humble ourselves before the Lord together. We take the supper with the church because the ordinance has been given for the sake of unity in the church.

Who should receive the Lord's Supper?

The bread and the cup are for those who have been initiated into the body of Christ through baptism. Since the supper is spiritual nourishment for the church, it is those who have been baptized into the church who receive its spiritual food. And since there is one loaf which carries with it the impulse of church unity, it is those who have been united to Christ and his church who ought to take from the one loaf. This represents the *close view* of communion.

The *open view* of the Lord's Supper invites anyone to the table who professes Christ. Typically, those who practice open communion, overemphasize the personal aspect and neglect the corporate nature of the supper.

Others see the Lord's Supper as a converting ordinance.[3]

A *closed view* of the Lord's Supper, invites only those who are members of that specific local church to participate in the supper. Oddly enough, this view undercuts the importance of the communion of the saints—not just saints of the local church, but saints of the church universal.

Close communion, therefore, takes the ordinances seriously, without offering false inclusion and without neglecting the universal communion of the saints. The Lord's Supper is for true members of

---

3 The belief that one of the *intentions* of the Lord's Supper is that it can be a means for a person to come to saving faith in Christ.

Christ's church, which means all those baptized into him are invited to the table.

SCRIPTURAL FOUNDATIONS

Exodus 12:21-28

> Then Moses called for all the elders of Israel and said to them, "Go and take for yourselves lambs according to your families, and slaughter the Passover *lamb*. And you shall take a bunch of hyssop and dip it in the blood which is in the basin, and apply some of the blood that is in the basin to the lintel and the two doorposts; and none of you shall go outside the door of his house until morning.
>
> For the LORD will pass through to strike the Egyptians; but when He sees the blood on the lintel and on the two doorposts, the LORD will pass over the door and will not allow the destroyer to come into your houses to strike you. And you shall keep this event as an ordinance for you and your children forever. When you enter the land which the LORD will give you, as He has promised, you shall keep this rite. And when your children say to you, 'What does this rite mean to you?' then you shall say, 'It is a Passover sacrifice to the LORD because He passed over the houses of the sons of Israel in Egypt when He struck the Egyptians, but spared our homes.'" And the people bowed low and worshiped.
>
> Then the sons of Israel went and did so; just as the LORD had commanded Moses and Aaron, so they did.

Just as with baptism and circumcision, the Lord's Supper has its own Old Covenant *type*, the Passover. God was redeeming his chosen people by calling them out of the land of idols and into the land he had promised them. The initial Passover was a solemn event in the life of Israel. While it was their deliverance, it came through death. On the night before God led Israel out of Egypt, either a substitutionary lamb died with its blood applied to the door of the house, or the firstborn son of that family died. Whether the son or the substitute, there was lots of death that night. The Passover sacrifice became a regular observance for all obedient generations after this great Exodus event. It served as a reminder to the people of how God had delivered them. The ordinance was intended to evoke a response. The children were eventually going to ask the meaning of this Passover ceremony, and it would give the family an opportunity to teach their children about how God saved them.

Jesus Christ is the true Lamb of God who takes away the sin of the world.[4] The communion cup represents the blood of Christ. Drinking from the cup is like marking the doorpost of our lives. For those who partake of the blood of Christ by faith, though they die, yet they will surely live, just as the true Lamb lives! As we will see, the connection between the Passover and the Lord's Supper is made explicit by Jesus himself. He came to fulfil the Passover—the true Passover—when the death penalty for sin would *pass over* those who are covered in the blood of Christ.

Just like Passover was a ceremony of remembrance, the Lord's Supper is a ceremony of remembrance. It is intended to evoke questions. As children observe their baptized parents taking part in the supper, the hope is one day they will ask, "Why do you eat the bread and drink the cup together with the church?" The Lord's Supper in this sense, may serve as a converting ordinance, not by participation but by observation. Just as there is not a one-to-one correlation between Israel and the church, or circumcision and baptism, there is not a one-to-one correlation between the Passover and the Lord's Supper. But by finding its termination in Christ, fragments of the Passover were infused with New Covenant meaning as Christ fulfilled the Passover by his own death, and instituted the Lord's Supper for the life of the church.

Luke 22:14-20

When the hour came, He reclined *at the table*, and the apostles with Him. And He said to them, "I have eagerly desired to eat this Passover with you before I suffer; for I say to you, I shall not eat it *again* until it is fulfilled in the kingdom of God." And when He had taken a cup *and* given thanks, He said, "Take this and share it among yourselves;

---

4   John 1:29.

for I say to you, I will not drink of the fruit of the vine from now on until the kingdom of God comes." And when He had taken *some* bread *and* given thanks, He broke it and gave it to them, saying, "This is My body, which is being given for you; do this in remembrance of Me." And in the same way *He took* the cup after they had eaten, saying, "This cup, which is poured out for you, is the new covenant in My blood.

In Luke 22, Jesus makes the explicit connection between the Passover and the Lord's Supper. The hour had come for him to offer his life in worshipful obedience to God and in loving sacrifice for his bride. It is no coincidence that Jesus offered up his life at the time of the Passover. Jesus had come to fulfil the law and the prophets.[5]

So Jesus took elements from the Passover ceremony, the remembrance of what God had done in saving Israel from death in Egypt, and he gave them to his apostles as a remembrance of himself. He commanded them to continue doing this in remembrance of him. The cup, Jesus told them, is the cup of the New Covenant. The New Covenant is a covenant of grace, which means it is an unconditional covenant. The New Covenant was the promise of a changed heart by the work of the Spirit, the promise of Christ's righteousness imputed to us, the promise of a new and everlasting kingdom and the promise that all of these promises could never be lost or revoked. You might say the New Covenant is the *contract* of the gospel. It is the terms and stipulations of the kingdom of Christ. Here at this Passover meal with his disciples, Jesus formally established[6] his New Covenant, which he would ratify with his own blood just a few hours later.

---

5 Luke 24:44.

6 All the Old Testament saints who belonged to God's true people and were saved and sealed by the Spirit of God, are included in God's family by virtue of the New Covenant, even though they died before its formal establishment. The visible New Covenant community is called the visible church, but the saints of old had partaken of the things to come *by faith* in the promise of what was to come. That is the sense we get from Hebrews 11:39–40: "And all these, having gained approval through their faith, did not receive what was promised, because God had provided something better for us, so that apart from us they would not be made perfect." In one sense Old Testament saints were connected to the New Covenant and received its benefits, but in another sense, they didn't partake of the New Covenant in its fullness because it had not yet been ratified by the blood of Jesus.

1 Corinthians 10:14-17

Therefore, my beloved, flee from idolatry. I speak as to wise people; you then, judge what I say. Is the cup of blessing which we bless not a sharing in the blood of Christ? Is the bread which we break not a sharing in the body of Christ? Since there is one loaf, we who are many are one body; for we all partake of the one loaf.

The book of 1 Corinthians opens up with a plea for church unity. Members of the congregation were taking sides and offering their allegiance to different leaders in their midst. Some claimed Paul, some claimed Peter, some claimed Apollos and some claimed Christ. Paul was distraught at the idea that his name would be included in a controversy like this. While he consistently affirmed his own apostleship, he adamantly opposed the idea that he or any other leader would be placed on the same plane with the Lord Jesus Christ. He clearly saw his own ministry identity as that of a steward and a servant. So one of the major themes throughout the book is the importance of unity in Christ. When Paul gets the opportunity to address the church in a positive way about the importance of unity, he points to the ordinance of the Lord's Supper.

He first starts by calling individuals in the church to renounce idolatry. He doesn't want a church full of people who are drinking from two cups. Just as Jesus had told his disciples they cannot serve two masters,[7] Paul is reminding the church they cannot drink from two fountains. Eating and drinking from Jesus should be a constant reminder to renounce seeking out or succumbing to other idolatrous cups. But Paul pushes past the individual application to the corporate application. He reminds them that just as they partake of one loaf when they enjoy the Lord's Supper together, they belong to one body—the body of Christ. The Lord's Supper does have personal implications, but it also has corporate implications. As we approach the table, we are called to forsake our natural divisions, our personal preferences and our sinful judgmentalism because there is only one body of Christ and there is only one head of the body—Jesus himself.

---

7   Matthew 6:24.

1 Corinthians 11:17–34

Now in giving this *next* instruction I do not praise you, because you come together not for the better, but for the worse. For, in the first place, when you come together as a church, I hear that divisions exist among you; and in part I believe it. For there also have to be factions among you, so that those who are approved may become evident among you. Therefore when you come together it is not to eat the Lord's Supper, for when you eat, each one takes his own supper first; and one goes hungry while another gets drunk. What! Do you not have houses in which to eat and drink? Or do you despise the church of God and shame those who have nothing? What am I to say to you? Shall I praise you? In this I do not praise you.

For I received from the Lord that which I also delivered to you, that the Lord Jesus, on the night when He was betrayed, took bread; and when He had given thanks, He broke it and said, "This is My body, which is for you; do this in remembrance of Me." In the same way *He* also *took* the cup after supper, saying, "This cup is the new covenant in My blood; do this, as often as you drink *it*, in remembrance of Me." For as often as you eat this bread and drink the cup, you proclaim the Lord's death until He comes.

Therefore whoever eats the bread or drinks the cup of the Lord in an unworthy way, shall be guilty of the body and the blood of the Lord. But a person must examine himself, and in so doing he is to eat of the bread and drink of the cup. For the one who eats and drinks, eats and drinks judgment to himself if he does not *properly* recognize the body. For this reason many among you are weak and sick, and a number are asleep. But if we judged ourselves rightly, we would not be judged. But when we are judged, we are disciplined by the Lord so that we will not be condemned along with the world.

So then, my brothers *and sisters*, when you come together to eat, wait for one another. If anyone is hungry, have him eat at home, so that you do not come together for judgment. As to the remaining matters, I will give instructions when I come.

This next chapter in 1 Corinthians takes us even deeper into understanding the Lord's Supper. There are a number of important issues which rise to the top as we examine this passage. First, we learn that it was the practice of the earliest Christian churches to come together and enjoy the Lord's Supper. Communion is one of the essential elements of gathered corporate worship. Second, we learn that while all food is from the Lord, not all food is the Lord's Supper. This supper is not a meal like other meals. This supper is not for nourishing the physical body, it is rather for nourishing the body of Christ. The Corinthian church were apparently treating the Lord's Supper as an opportunity to get full of food and wine. Paul wants the church to come together for the Lord's Supper to get full of Jesus. Third, we see that while the Lord's Supper is clearly an ordinance of remembrance, it also has ongoing present significance and ultimate future significance. Every time the church gathers to take the supper, the death of Jesus is proclaimed. It is a remembrance, but it is also an *announcement*. The supper is the Word made visible—it is the gospel made edible. But in the comment, "until He comes," we are also pointed forward. The supper works in all three directions. It fills our hearts with memories, it declares the death of Christ afresh and anew and it points us toward the future. In the supper, God's people remember forward to the certain and inevitable return of Christ and consummation of his kingdom.

Finally, for all of the rich texture found in this passage, the aspect of examination comes through in this text. Usually, this passage is taken to mean personal examination. Baptized members are called to confess and repent before approaching the table. And while this passage clearly evokes that solemnity, we need to read it carefully. Apparently for Paul, it is possible to take the supper in an unworthy manner. But we have to be very careful what move we make next. From the context, Paul has something specific in mind. The unworthy manner of taking the Lord's Supper was *the way* the church was practicing the supper. This obviously flowed from sinful hearts, but it was the way they were taking the supper that made them unworthy to take it. The supper is an announcement of grace, it is a remembrance of cleansing blood, it is the meal of the New Covenant community, it is the spiritual nourishment for the Spirit filled body of Christ and the way certain people were eating and drinking the elements of the ordinance were not worthy of its significance. Paul's charge here is more a charge of corporate examination than it is of personal examination.

Paul's idea of taking of the Lord's Supper in a worthy manner is not some sort of works-righteousness, which deems a person morally worthy to receive communion. Paul's idea of taking the supper in a worthy manner is a church who cares about union with Christ and unity in the body, they honour the significance and sacredness of the Lord's Supper with all its New Covenant significance. So while it is not wrong to emphasize personal reflection when taking the supper, that might be slightly different from what Paul had in mind. Clearly, Paul viewed the Lord's Supper as crucial for church unity, and it was his high value of grace, unity, peace, love and the gospel, that led him to deliver this message in such strong language. God cared enough about *how* this church was practicing this ordinance in a way that was inconsistent with the gospel that members of the church were getting sick and dying. The Lord's Supper calls for personal examination, yes, but more importantly it calls for corporate examination. How we embody the truth of the gospel as a body is near to the heart of Christ. It is his church, his covenant and his ordinance, so we are called to honour it with utmost respect for him and his gospel.

EXPLANATION

"The Lord's Supper is an ordinance of Jesus Christ, to be administered with the elements of bread and fruit of the vine..."

Just like baptism, the Lord's Supper belongs to and was instituted by Jesus Christ. He calls the members baptized into his church to eat bread which represents his body. Eating the bread reminds us of the incarnation: Christ's life of obedience, his death, bodily resurrection and ascension. Jesus also calls his people to drink from the cup of the New Covenant. Drinking the cup is an identification with his blood. His blood is *atoning* blood, it is *cleansing* blood and it is *ratifying* blood. His blood was poured out as a sacrifice for sins. It alone can cleanse a person's conscience before God. His blood sanctioned the New Covenant, sealing God's promises and securing every good blessing from God for Christ's people.

"and to be observed by his churches till the end of the world...."

In this present age, churches ought to continue to observe this ordinance. It is an important part of the life of the local church, and Jesus gave it both as a gift and as a command. Jesus knows what his people need. And yet, one day, there will be no more need for remembrance, gospel announcement or promise. Faith will become sight and the three directions the Lord's Supper moves will no longer be needed. The future artifact will become present reality.

"It is in no sense a sacrifice but is designed to commemorate his death..."

The Lord's Supper is not the real physical body and blood of Jesus. And it is not re-sacrificing Jesus. The sacrifice of Jesus was a one time, never repeatable, world-changing event. The supper remembers his sacrifice, proclaims his sacrifice and points to all his sacrifice accomplished, but it is in no sense a sacrifice in itself. To treat the supper as a sacrifice would be to diminish the all-sufficiency of Christ.

"to confirm the faith and other graces of Christians..."

When believers receive communion, God speaks the word of Christ into their hearts. Their adoption as sons, their justification as those declared righteous, their sanctification as those set apart, their reconciliation as friends of God, their regeneration as those made alive and their resurrection as those citizens of the new creation, are confirmed through the elements which visibly declare the gospel. The Lord's Supper is a healing balm, a welcome encouragement and a needed reminder.

"and to be a bond, pledge and renewal of their communion with him..."

Just as baptism is a declaration of the truth of union with Christ, so the Lord's Supper is a bond of the same. The Lord's Supper, like a vow renewal ceremony, is an opportunity for all humble and repentant believers to feel Christ move toward them in love, and for them to move toward him in love. It is recentring on the gospel and feeding on Christ. Union with Christ, then, includes feeding on Christ. Fellowship with God through Jesus Christ is envisioned in eating and drinking the body and blood of Jesus. In eating we are rejuvenated, but we are also sitting at a table where genuine relationship takes place. Just as through the Word of God we spiritually hear from God, in the supper we spiritually dine with God, through Jesus Christ.

"and of their church fellowship."

This same unity, fellowship and relationship with God, confirmed in the supper, is also extended to our fellowship with one another. Union with Christ is union with his body. The same vow renewal ceremony which takes place between each individual believer and Christ at the table, also takes place between members through Christ. There is one Lord, one faith, one Spirit, one baptism and one loaf. We take the supper in a worthy way when we take it in solemn union with each member of Christ's body who has been baptized into his saving and sanctifying grace.

MISCONCEPTIONS

In some ways, we have already been dealing with some of the common misconceptions about the Lord's Supper. One is the misconception that the supper is mainly a personal ordinance. We have seen how the corporate element is essential. Another misconception deals with how we can take the supper in an unworthy manner. We must be careful how we handle the 1 Corinthians 11 passage because, in one sense, no one ever takes the supper in a worthy manner—none of us is worthy of the supper based on our own good works. Paul was telling the Corinthian church they were taking the supper in a way that belittled the gospel. So while personal reflection is good, we never want to give the impression that some people take the supper because they are worthy of it, while others are excluded because they aren't worthy of it. *Everyone baptized into Christ has been made worthy.* We must strive to administer the ordinance in a way that honours it and, more importantly, honours Christ.

There are a few more misconceptions that need our attention. One is what we might call the *real absence* misconception. In an attempt to deny the physical body and blood of Jesus in the bread and the cup, the church has sometimes gone too far in removing Christ from his ordinances. Some churches have come to so undervalue the supper they only administer it once or twice a year, and they so over-emphasize the memorial aspect, they miss out on the promise of Jesus to be present with his people. While it is true your Bible isn't physically the man Jesus Christ, it is true you meet with Jesus when you read your Bible. The same is true of the ordinances. The bread and the cup aren't literally the physical man Jesus Christ, but by faith we do feast on Christ as we partake of the supper. It is participating in the body and blood, spiritually, in a way Jesus himself is present with us. We may not want to affirm real presence, but we dare not affirm real absence. Jesus is with us, and he is especially with us when his Word is preached and when his ordinances are administered. To deny his special presence with us is to neglect his gracious promise, "and lo, I am with you always, even to the end of the age."[8] Jesus moves toward his people in love as they approach him in love through communion.

Another misconception has to do with *how often* the church enjoys the Lord's Supper. While the Bible doesn't prescribe an exact amount, it seems like the church in the New Testament gathers regularly for preaching, praying, singing and administering the ordinances. There is definitely openness to how often communion is observed. But the misconception comes with a certain line of reasoning that believes taking the Lord's Supper too often would cause it to lose significance. Granted, there may be those who buy into this misconception because their church seems to take it every week in a way that is flat, ritualistic and mundane. For them, it begins to feel like a religious ritual rather than a loving embrace. But even with this in mind, the real problem here is *the way* it is carried out. If frequently partaking of the supper means it loses its significance, one must ask if they are tired of hearing the gospel. Christians need to be *daily* reminded of Christ's death and resurrection on their behalf. Christians need to walk with God in daily confession and repentance of sin. Christians need to renew their hearts toward Christ and toward his body daily. If Christians need these daily reminders, then it doesn't make sense why they wouldn't benefit from a weekly solemn reminder in the form of Christ's instituted ordinance of the Lord's Supper. If taking it too often would cause

---

8 Matthew 28:20.

it to lose its significance, that might say something more about us than about the supper. Our hearts are hard, our sins create callousness and our worldliness is a barrier. Taking the supper frequently doesn't cause it to lose its significance, but feeling the weight of our sin too little, and thinking too few thoughts of Jesus, may cause the supper to lose its significance. It is true the Bible is vague about how often a church should take the supper, but our subjective roller-coaster approach to the gospel should never keep us from seeing the Word and tasting the gospel afresh.

A final misconception is the idea that practicing *close communion* is legalism. Obedience, law and discipline don't always fit in the context of legalism. In fact, the New Covenant, which is the most gracious covenant in the history of the world, promises to give believers the Holy Spirit so they can keep the law. Believers are made holy so they can grow in holiness. Many times in life, boundaries, laws and rules are for our good. Setting the Lord's Supper within the context of a believing and baptized community is for the good of those people who are excluded. To offer a false sense of inclusion could give someone a false sense of assurance of salvation. Each church needs to practice wisdom and grace in knowing how to best administer the Lord's Supper, but emphasizing baptism as a prerequisite to participation in the supper is a healthy boundary and the God-ordained order of the ordinances. Baptism happens once in the life of a believer and is the initiation into the covenant community. The Lord's Supper is the ongoing nourishment and regular opportunity for renewal and repentance in the life of the church. In the long run, it is more loving to non-believers to ask them to wait for participation in the Lord's Supper until they have placed their faith in Christ. It is more loving to believers walking in disobedience as non-baptized believers, to encourage them to humble themselves under the waters before receiving the body and blood of Jesus in the bread and the cup.

APPLICATION
<hr>

Article XVI: The Lord's Supper

> The Lord's Supper is an ordinance of Jesus Christ, to be administered with the elements of bread and fruit of the vine, and to be observed by his churches till the end of the world. It is in no sense a sacrifice, but is designed to commemorate his death, to confirm the faith and other graces of Christians, and to be a bond, pledge and renewal of their communion with him, and of their church fellowship.

___

1. We should elevate the significance of the Lord's Supper.

The Lord's Supper is an integral part of the life and health of the local church. Many churches treat the supper as an occasional garnish in the practice of the church. Far from it, the Lord's Supper is one of the regular ways God reminds his people of the gospel, and of their communion with him and with one another.

2. We should encourage families to explain to their children why the Lord's Supper is for baptized believers.

In the Lord's Supper, families have an opportunity to help their kids understand we are all born into sin and in need of a Saviour. Their kids get a tangible picture of the fact they aren't automatically saved just because their parents might be. As a child observes their parents taking the supper, it presents an opportunity for them to ask why they do it. Parents are given regular opportunities to talk with their children about the gospel until their children profess faith and are baptized.

3. The Lord's Supper should encourage us to examine the body of Christ and our own hearts.

The Lord's Supper has significance for the gospel and for our relationship with God and one another. When we take communion, we are given the opportunity to examine the life of our church, to ask if there are any divisions or impurities. When churches find such things, they should engage in corporate repentance before taking the supper. And when we take communion, we should examine our own hearts. The supper is meant to both humble and encourage us. Sin should not keep us from the table, but unrepentance should give us pause. When we examine ourselves, we aren't searching for reasons not to come to the table, we are searching for those sins and idols which we should lay down at the table.

4. The Lord's Supper should give us the opportunity to explain its fullness.

When we take the Lord's Supper, we should avoid drowning out its significance by dragging people through the same explanation again and again. In one sense, the supper always means what it means, but there is a depth and richness to its significance in the Scriptures. When Paul used the Lord's Supper to appeal for church unity in 1 Corinthians, he showed us how we can see the supper as a picture of the gospel and its implications—and there are endless ways the explanation of the Lord's Supper can remain fresh and its application sharp. Jesus was not afraid of being misunderstood when he challenged the crowed to drink his blood and eat his flesh, and we should not be afraid to be misunderstood either. When we call people to the table, we are not calling them to a sanitized and sentimental version of our modern god of love. We are calling people to feast by faith on the body and blood of our Lord Jesus Christ.

XVII

The Lord's Day

The Lord's Day is a Christian institution for regular observance, and should be employed in exercises of worship and spiritual devotion, both public and private.

The Lord's Day

INTRO + OVERVIEW

O ver the last few articles on the church, baptism and the Lord's Supper, we have seen how there were important Old Testament types which—after finding their termination in Christ—are reflected forward in the life of the church. These types are never one-to-one correlations, but they do help us see how the unity of the Bible is held together by a powerful thread: Jesus Christ. For example, Israel is not the church, but Israel pointed forward to the church. And, circumcision is not baptism, but circumcision pointed forward to baptism. The Passover is not the Lord's Supper, but the Passover pointed forward to the Lord's Supper. We must remember, however, there is also an important organic *link* between them, Christ himself. It is Jesus who is the real fulfilment of these types. Jesus is the true Israel, Jesus is the true circumcision and Jesus is the true Passover. And it is through fulfilment in Jesus Christ, and the formal establishment of the New Covenant community, that these types relate to the institutions and ordinances of the church.

This pattern is continued in another important area. Under the Old Covenant, Israel was to set apart a day as holy to the Lord. This day was to be a day of rest and refreshment, and for pondering God's providence and rejoicing in God's faithfulness. This special day was called the *Sabbath*. Just like Israel, circumcision and the Passover, the Sabbath found its ultimate fulfilment in Jesus Christ. He is himself the rest of God, and the future and final fulfilment of rest for the people of God. When the Sabbath is reflected into the New Covenant church through Christ, there are some aspects which continue while other aspects change.[1]

---

1   It is important to note that the Sabbath is slightly different in nature than Old Testament Israel, circumcision and the Passover. The particular Old Covenant expression of the Sabbath has been done away with, just as circumcision has been done away

What stays the same

A few of the things which remain the same are weekly corporate gatherings for worship, acts of generosity and service to the Lord, and time to rest, reflect and rejoice in God's faithfulness. Christians of the New Covenant community trust in and worship the same God who called Israel to be his people under the Old Covenant. So they continue to preach the same Scriptures, pray the same prayers and sing the same songs, with a new emphasis on Jesus of Nazareth as the long-awaited Messiah who has come to rescue his people. Since Jesus fulfiled all the types and shadows of the Old Covenant, he became the focal point under the New.

What changes

The most notable change is that rather than setting apart the *last day* of the week to worship, rest and reflect, the New Covenant community set apart the *first day* of the week to gather, worship and celebrate the life, death and resurrection of Jesus. So we must ask, why the change? With Jesus as the new focal point, gathering to worship on the first day of the week is a constant reminder of the resurrection of Jesus. Jesus conquered death and rose on the first day of the week to signify the dawn of a new creation. This shows both the importance of the life, death and resurrection of Jesus for the church and the importance of regular rhythms and patterns of worship. The Sabbath on the last day of the week reminded the Israelites of creation, the Exodus and the law. While Christians do not want to do away with these important truths and aspects of our identity, it is entirely appropriate to move the "set apart" day from the last day of the week to the first. In doing this, the New Testament church was highlighting our new creation in Christ with the backdrop of the first creation, our entrance into the eternal promised land (heaven) with the backdrop of the Exodus and our vindication by the work of Jesus on the cross with the backdrop of

---

with, but because the Sabbath *preceded* the Old Covenant and is embodied in the moral law, it should be approached differently than the neutral command of circumcision. There is debate about how the Sabbath command may be fulfilled in the New Covenant, but at bare minimum we can say God has always desired his people to set aside a day for rest, reflection and refreshment in him. The Lord's Day is not synonymous with the Sabbath, but the Sabbath command may well be fulfilled by appropriate rest and rejoicing in Christ on the Lord's Day.

the law. The first day of the week does not completely do away with what was celebrated and remembered on the last, but it does draw our attention to fuller, deeper and greater New Covenant realities. On the first day of the week, Jesus was raised for our justification, he was raised as the last Adam of the new creation and he was raised as the first artifact from the eternal promised land—the real rest which is entered only by faith in him.

As exciting as this new emphasis on the first day of the week is, it is important to remember that each week of our lives has a first day of the week. This is an inescapable rhythm in the life of the church. Every year, fifty-two days of the year are set apart to celebrate the resurrection of Jesus Christ from the dead. This weekly rhythm exists to shape us, change us and sanctify us. As we gather on the Lord's Day and celebrate the One who is himself the true Sabbath, we become conformed to his image as we learn to walk in the newness of resurrection life.

SCRIPTURAL FOUNDATIONS

Genesis 1:14-19; 2:1-3

Then God said, "Let there be lights in the expanse of the heavens to separate the day from the night, and they shall serve as signs and for seasons, and for days and years; and they shall serve as lights in the expanse of the heavens to give light on the earth"; and it was so. God made the two great lights, the greater light to govern the day, and the lesser light to govern the night; He made the stars also. God placed them in the expanse of the heavens to give light on the earth, and to govern the day and the night, and to separate the light from the darkness; and God saw that it was good. And there was evening and there was morning, a fourth day....

And so the heavens and the earth were completed, and all their heavenly lights. By the seventh day God completed His work which He had done, and He rested on the seventh day from all His work which He had done. Then God blessed the seventh day and sanctified it, because on it He rested from all His work which God had created and made.

From these first important chapters of the Bible, we learn something important about days. God has specific plans and designs for the movements of times and seasons. When God set different lights in the sky, he intentionally made these lights to be signs. It was important to God for us to have seasons, days and years. Days aren't supposed to all run together. There is supposed to be a way to tell the difference between day and day. And before we leave the creation narrative, we see God interacting with different days in this way. The seventh day, the last day of the week which was known by the lights God put in the sky, was set apart by God. This seventh day was unique, special and holy to God. God himself worked six days and then rested on the seventh. This would provide the framework for human beings to set aside a day as holy unto God. All days are God's days, but this day belonged to him in a unique way. This day was blessed by God.

Matthew 28:1–10

Now after the Sabbath, as it began to dawn toward the first *day* of the week, Mary Magdalene and the other Mary came to look at the tomb. And behold, a severe earthquake had occurred, for an angel of the Lord descended from heaven and came and rolled away the stone, and sat upon it. And his appearance was like lightning, and his clothing as white as snow. The guards shook from fear of him and became like dead men. And the angel said to the women, "Do not be afraid; for I know that you are looking for Jesus who has been cruci-fied. He is not here, for He has risen, just as He said. Come, see the place where He was lying. And go quickly and tell His disciples that He has risen from the dead; and behold, He is going ahead of you to Galilee. There you will see Him; behold, I have told you."

And they left the tomb quickly with fear and great joy, and ran to report to His disciples. And behold, Jesus met them and said, "Rejoice!" And they came up and took hold of His feet, and worshiped Him. Then Jesus *said to them, "Do not be afraid; go, bring word to My brothers to leave for Galilee, and there they will see Me."

He is risen! Jesus conquered death. He was dead, and yet he lives forevermore. And he was raised on the first day of the week. Matthew tells us it was "after the Sabbath." While all Israel rested on the Sabbath which was the type, Jesus finished his work which was the fulfilment of the Sabbath. When he rose on the first day of the week, there was now a new, more blessed day than the last day of the week. A new order—a new creation—dawned on that first day of the week, as Christ rose from the grave.

Acts 20:7-12

> On the first day of the week, when we were gathered together to break bread, Paul *began* talking to them, intending to leave the next day, and he prolonged his message until midnight. There were many lamps in the upstairs room where we were gathered together. And there was a young man named Eutychus sitting on the window sill, sinking into a deep sleep; and as Paul kept on talking, *Eutychus* was overcome by sleep and fell down from the third floor, and was picked up dead. But Paul went down and fell upon him, and after embracing him, he said, "Do not be troubled, for he is still alive." When *Paul* had gone *back* up and had broken the bread and eaten, he talked with them a long while until daybreak, and then left. They took away the boy alive, and were greatly comforted.

As a book, Acts is not always *prescriptive*, instead it is *descriptive*. In other words, it isn't always telling us what to do, but it is telling us what the Spirit of God was doing in and through the life of the church. Acts is our opportunity to witness the early church in action. Jesus had promised to empower the church through his Spirit to be his witnesses to the ends of the earth, and the book of Acts shows us what the empowered church looked like. Here, in Acts 20, we see one instance of the church gathering on the Lord's Day, the first day of the week. Apparently their gathering included breaking bread and preaching. Paul's sermon went long, and a young man was overcome by sleep and fell to his death. Remarkably, on the same day Jesus was raised from the dead, the gathered church got to witness a resurrection. The boy who had died went away alive. This was a Lord's Day miracle.

1 Corinthians 16:1-2

Now concerning the collection for the saints, as I directed the churches of Galatia, so you are to do as well. On the first day of every week, each of you is to put aside and save as he may prosper, so that no collections *need* to be made when I come.

Unlike the book of Acts, 1 Corinthians is *prescriptive*. We aren't just being told what happened, we are joined together with the church of all ages and told what to do. And there are two things we learn in this chapter. First, we see that just as the Sabbath was for doing good and giving life, the Lord's Day is for doing good and giving life. For that reason, it is entirely appropriate for an offering to be taken on the Lord's Day. Along with reading and preaching the Scriptures, praying, singing and participating in the ordinances, the Lord's Day is for acts of mercy and generosity. Second, we notice Paul clearly sets apart the first day of the week. There was something unique and special about this day. The first day of the week is special because it is the Lord's Day, the day when Christ was raised and the day when the church gathers.

Revelation 1:10-16

I was in the Spirit on the Lord's day, and I heard behind me a loud voice like *the sound* of a trumpet, saying, "Write on a scroll what you see, and send *it* to the seven churches: to Ephesus, Smyrna, Pergamum, Thyatira, Sardis, Philadelphia, and Laodicea."

Then I turned to see the voice that was speaking with me. And after turning I saw seven golden lampstands; and in the middle of the lampstands *I saw* one like a son of man, clothed in a robe reaching to the feet, and wrapped around the chest with a golden sash. His head and His hair were white like white wool, like snow; and His eyes were like a flame of fire. His feet were like burnished bronze when it has been heated to a glow in a furnace, and His voice was like the sound of many waters. In His right hand He held seven stars, and out of His mouth came a sharp two-edged sword; and His face was like the sun shining in its strength.

Again, while this passage in Revelation is not prescriptive, it is important because we learn that before the death of the last apostle, John, there was a day set aside as the Lord's Day. The apostle John had been exiled to the Island of Patmos, and still, he was doing all he could to celebrate and worship the resurrected Christ. Even without the company of other brothers and sisters in Christ, he set out to worship. To our amazement, while he was all alone on the Lord's Day, the Lord himself came and met him. Jesus, in all of his resurrected glory, came to visit his dear friend, John. If the Lord's Day was important for John, even when he had no access to the New Covenant community, it should be clear to us that this was the norm for practice and spiritual health in the early church.

EXPLANATION

"The Lord's Day is a Christian institution for regular observance..."

By *Lord*, we mean the Lord Jesus Christ. The first day of the week, when Jesus rose from the dead, is a day set apart to him. It is a blessed day! All food belongs to the Lord, but not all food is the Lord's Supper. In the same way, all days belong to the Lord, but in a special and unique way, the first day of the week is the Lord's Day. It is special because we do different things and engage with God's people in unique ways. As we gather, we experience Christ's presence in and through the preaching of the Word, in the commingling of believers and in participating in his ordinances. We are not at liberty to observe the Lord's Day on our own terms. While we may experience difficult seasons where we are kept from gathering with God's people by God's providence, even then we can observe the Lord's Day. And when we are not kept from gathering, we should make every effort to honour the day and to honour the Lord of the day, by gathering with the Lord's people to rest, reflect and rejoice in him.

"and should be employed in exercises of worship and spiritual devotion..."

This day has been set aside to exalt Christ and for us to be shaped and sanctified by Christ. On the first day of the week, we begin afresh by lifting Jesus high. On the first day of the week, we humbly confess our sins, quietly receive the Word and jubilantly sing praises to the God of our salvation. Breaking bread with God's people, prayer, Bible reading, singing, reflecting on God's goodness and seeing the gospel in the ordinances should stir our hearts to devotion and love for Christ.

"both public and private."

The Lord's Day is a day set aside for God. This will include unique and special worship with the gathered saints, but it will also include unique and special private worship. The Lord's Day is an opportunity to read the Bible a little longer, pray a little deeper, sing a little louder and love a little harder. The Lord loves us through his day, and we love him in return.

MISCONCEPTIONS

When it comes to misconceptions about the Lord's Day, most of them come down to how people live out their Christian lives. For example, the first misconception we will consider is, "I can worship God on my terms." We may be tempted to think all this conversation about days is too stuffy and cramps our lifestyle. However, the Lord's Day is really an exercise in trust. It is trusting God with our lives—God understands how the world works—and it is trusting God knows how he is best worshipped. God is God, and he gets to tell us how to love him. God gets to tell us how to celebrate him. If gathering on the first day of the week to worship and celebrate Jesus is what God wants us to do, then it means there is blessing in doing it.

Another misconception about the Lord's Day is that meeting with God's people is unimportant. We can start to believe our personal worship is enough. But the Lord's Day is for gathering with the Lord's people to hear the Word of the Lord and to take part in the Lord's Supper. As the Lord's Day, it is not our day. We best experience the Lord when we are together with his people under the preaching of his Word. Even if, in our subjective experience, we feel like things are better for us on our own, we know that our own hearts can deceive us.[2] Gathering on the Lord's Day is the best thing we can do on that day, and it is the best thing we can do on the best day of the week.

A final misconception about the Lord's Day has to do with how we view days, as opposed to how the Bible views days. We tend to count days from sunup to sundown, but the Bible is the opposite. The Bible records days beginning with evening and ending with morning. With that being said, we should be thoughtful about how we observe the Lord's Day. There are many who treat sunup to sundown on Sunday as though it is equivalent to the Old Covenant Sabbath. This not only misses the joy of seeing the Sabbath as organically connected to Christ, but it also misses the all important step of careful Bible reading. If someone really wanted to be rigid about the Lord's Day, then biblically they would observe the day beginning Saturday evening and running through Sunday evening. With this in mind, we ought to observe the Lord's Day with grace and generosity. We can call each other to a high level of accountability in setting the first day of the week apart for worship and rest, but we should be careful not to allow the preciousness of the Lord's Day to become a point of bitterness, judgment and unnecessary division.

---

2   See James 1:26.

APPLICATION

Article XVII: The Lord's Day

The Lord's Day is a Christian institution for regular observance, and should be employed in exercises of worship and spiritual devotion, both public and private.

---

1. *We must consider why it is important for Christians to gather together and worship on the Lord's Day.*

There are at least three different reasons for the Lord's Day. First, my personal spiritual life is dependent on gathering with God's people on the Lord's Day. If I am to grow as a Christian, then I am called to not neglect gathering together with God's people.[3] I need to hear the Word read, preached, sung, prayed and made visible in the ordinances.

Second, if this is true personally, then it is also true corporately. My fellow believers need me to gather together with them on the Lord's Day for worship. If everyone decided not to show up, then there would be no gathering, no singing, no encouragement and no celebration of the Lord. I go for myself, but I also go for my brothers and sisters. It is so they will hear my voice singing, when they don't feel they can sing. It is so I can pray for my brother or sister when they don't know what to pray. And it is so I can speak a word of encouragement to my brother or sister, when they don't see any hope in their life.

Third, it isn't just personal and corporate reasons calling us to gather—it is also for the sake of the lost world. The gathering of God's people is an opportunity for an outsider to peer into the kingdom of God. On the Lord's Day, as God's people gather under the authority and ministry of God's Word, an outsider sees the closest picture of God's kingdom as can be found on this earth. Our gatherings aren't for the lost, so to speak, but they do speak prophetically to the lost.

---

3   See Hebrews 10:25.

When we gather on the Lord's Day, we bear witness to the resurrected Lord and to his ongoing reign in and over our lives.

2. When it comes to our approach to the Lord's Day, we have a lot to learn from the Old Testament Sabbath.

The Sabbath was God's gift to men and women at creation. It was the grace of rest which allowed God's people to thrive. In the same way, the Lord's Day should be approached as a gift and not a task, as a grace and not a duty. For those who take the Lord's Day seriously, they will not regret it. Their lives will be marked by regular, joyous celebrations in the Lord Jesus Christ. There is no way a Christian will get to the end of their life and be dissatisfied for having set apart one day a week for devotion to Jesus. How helpful to wake up at least one day a week, and think, "This day isn't about me—it is about the Lord!"

XVIII

Liberty of Conscience

God alone is Lord of the conscience; and he has left it free from the doctrines and commandments of men— those that are contrary to his Word, or not contained in it. Government authorities are established by God, so it is good for us to obey the laws commanded by them as long as they do not contradict God's Word.

Liberty of Conscience

INTRO + OVERVIEW

The first amendment to the United States Constitution reads,

> Congress shall make no law respecting an establishment of religion, or prohibiting the free exercise thereof; or abridging the freedom of speech, or of the press; or the right of the people peaceably to assemble, and to petition the Government for a redress of grievances.[1]

What's so wrong with the state establishing a religion? What's the problem with legislating worship? A quick glance at history teaches us that people have regularly been treated harshly, spoken of with slander and even been killed for *what they believe*. In fact, at the dawn of the newly constituted United States of America, there was religious persecution which carried with it a haunting inconsistency[2] to both the Declaration of Independence and the Constitution itself. This religious persecution didn't come from the outside. Rather, it was from those who claimed to hold faith in Christ who persecuted other believers over matters of conscience.[3]

This brings up some important questions about conscience. Conscience is one of those things most people feel like they understand, but when an attempt is made to articulate what it is and what it does, it is more difficult than we expect. So what is the conscience?

---

1   See https://constitution.congress.gov/constitution/amendment-1/.

2   As is also the case with slavery.

3   Baptists, Quakers and other other nonconformists experienced persecution in colonial America in the form of imprisonment, false accusations and beatings, especially in Virginia. They agitated for religious liberty and the full separation of church and state. The Bill for Establishing Religious Liberty in 1786 was the precedent for some of the language in the first ammendment of the Constitution regarding religious liberties.

What role does it play in our lives? How does conscience relate to matters of faith and religion? And how do these factors relate to the forming of a society?

What is the conscience?

Conscience comes from God, and it is an integral aspect of the human nature. It works together with the human mind, will and affections to allow people to relate to God and to live in God's world appropriately. Like the will, the conscience is an immaterial and inner aspect of humanity. While the conscience is always influenced and shaped by a person's environment, it cannot be reduced to a person's shaping influences. The conscience whether clean or defiled, seared or sensitive, cannot be removed but can be redeemed.

Conscience is *our internal witness and judge which accuses and condemns us according to some particular standard of morality*. Conscience comes into play after a standard is broken, and then works together with memory to produce future behaviour according to that standard.[4] We are to think of conscience as that aspect of our human nature which *produces conviction*. Conscience is not conviction, but conscience produces conviction. When conscience speaks, that is conviction. A person's convictions, then, become a person's law. So, when they live below their convictions, their conscience convicts them. Memory of past guilt steers a person according to their convictions.

How can a conscience become bound or seared?

Now before thinking about how conscience relates to religion and society, we need to consider how a conscience can be bound on the one hand or seared on the other. If conscience is that thing God has given us to establish conviction, and conscience can be influenced and shaped, then a *bound conscience* is a conscience which feels guilty for things about which it should not. A bound conscience convicts itself of things that God's law would not convict. When the pressures of intentional coercion or unintentional leadership bind a conscience, then some other law is put in the place of God's law.

---

4 I have been greatly helped with some of this nuance by John Y. Clagett, *The Christian Conscience* (Arlington Heights: Regular Baptist Press, 1984).

Conscience can also be defiled in another way. A conscience becomes *seared* when, while a person feels guilty for things for which they ought to feel guilty, they suppress the guilt and neglect the conviction of conscience. If, time after time they suppress this guilt, the conscience is quieted, but not because it is clean. Rather, the mind, will and affections become numb to the voice of the conscience so it no longer produces its God-ordained effects. Both the binding of the conscience and the searing of the conscience negate the principle of liberty of conscience. God wants the conscience to be free—not of him—of the laws of men and the laws of self. When man's law or the law of self take the place of God's law, the conscience is defiled.

Conscience and matters of faith

With that in mind, we turn to matters of faith. Because we will all answer to God at his judgment throne, we are called to leave judgment to him.[5] This does not mean we do not proclaim the truth of God and attempt to shape the conscience according to his law. An awakened conscience is an important beginning to faith in Christ and repentance toward God. But it does mean no one is to be forced or coerced into religious form. While it is not a binding of conscience, for example, to preach the exclusivity of salvation in Jesus alone, it would be a binding of conscience to force someone to attend a Christian church against their will. This also means, within the household of God, while there are some things which are explicitly stated in the Scriptures as matters of obedience, there are many other things which are to be understood as matters of wisdom. When matters of wisdom are treated as matters of the law, the conscience is bound and defiled. At the same time, when matters of the law are treated as matters of wisdom, the conscience is seared and defiled.

Conscience and matters of government and society

This finally brings us to matters of government and society. On the one hand, it is not wrong for a society to legislate morality. In fact, it has the responsibility, for the good of all of its citizens, to do so. But there is a difference between legislating morality and binding the conscience. For a government to enforce a particular *kind* of religious

---

5 Ecclesiastes 3:17.

worship contradicts God's own purposes for the conscience. A society should legislate morality in such a way that it protects the health, life and liberty of its citizens. Liberty of conscience is not total and unbridled freedom, but it is freedom from the imposition of the laws of man on the one hand, and it is freedom to live and worship within the limits of a person's ideal of wisdom. In other words, liberty of conscience means no state should enforce religious duty beyond what is conducive to health, life and liberty for all its citizens—and, it means any person is free to live before the face of God instead of in submission to the laws of the land when they contradict the law of God. Healthy societies will be those who seek to legislate for health, life, and liberty, while leaving religious worship to the convictions of men and women. Healthy churches will be those who proclaim the reality of God's law with clarity and consequence, while leaving matters of wisdom to the convictions of men and women.

SCRIPTURAL FOUNDATIONS

Matthew 15:1–9

Then some Pharisees and scribes came to Jesus from Jerusalem and said, "Why do Your disciples break the tradition of the elders? For they do not wash their hands when they eat bread." And He answered and said to them, "Why do you yourselves also break the commandment of God for the sake of your tradition? For God said, 'HONOR YOUR FATHER AND MOTHER,' and, 'THE ONE WHO SPEAKS EVIL OF FATHER OR MOTHER IS TO BE PUT TO DEATH.' But you say, 'Whoever says to his father or mother, "Whatever I have that would help you has been given to God," he is not to honor his father or mother.' And by this you have invalidated the word of God for the sake of your tradition. You hypocrites, rightly did Isaiah prophesy about you, by saying:

'THIS PEOPLE HONORS ME WITH THEIR LIPS,
BUT THEIR HEART IS FAR AWAY FROM ME.
AND IN VAIN DO THEY WORSHIP ME,
TEACHING AS DOCTRINES THE COMMANDMENTS OF MEN.'"

Binding the conscience is a serious offense in the eyes of God. In Matthew 15, Jesus confronted the Pharisees and scribes for binding the consciences of their fellow Israelites. Jesus appeals to God's law as a legitimate standard before which we will all one day give an account. However, he cries out against setting standards within the religious community based on the commandments of men. He goes so far as to say, when we treat matters of wisdom as matters of the law, we not only defile the conscience, we actually defile the very Word of God. When commandments of men are mixed with the commandments of God, the commandments of God are "invalidated."

Acts 5:27-42

When they had brought them, they had them stand before the Council. The high priest interrogated them, saying, "We gave you strict orders not to continue teaching in this name, and yet, you have filled Jerusalem with your teaching and intend to bring this Man's blood upon us." But Peter and the apostles answered, "We must obey God rather than men. The God of our fathers raised up Jesus, whom you put to death by hanging Him on a cross. He is the one whom God exalted to His right hand as a Prince and a Savior, to grant repentance to Israel, and forgiveness of sins. And we are witnesses of these things; and *so is* the Holy Spirit, whom God has given to those who obey Him."

But when they heard *this*, they became infuriated and *nearly* decided to execute them. But a Pharisee named Gamaliel, a teacher of the Law, respected by all the people, stood up in the Council and gave orders to put the men outside for a short time. And he said to them, "Men of Israel, be careful as to what you are about to do with these men. For, some time ago Theudas appeared, claiming to be somebody, and a group of about four hundred men joined him. But he was killed, and all who followed him were dispersed and came to nothing. After this man, Judas of Galilee appeared in the days of the census and drew away *some* people after him; he also perished, and all those who followed him were scattered. And so in the present case, I say to you, stay away from these men and leave them alone, for if the source of this plan or movement is men, it will be overthrown; but if the source is God, you will not be able to overthrow them; or else you may even be found fighting against God."

They followed his advice; and after calling the apostles in, they flogged them and ordered them not to speak in the name of Jesus, and *then* released them. So they went on their way from the presence of the Council, rejoicing that they had been considered worthy to suffer shame for *His* name. And every day, in the temple and from house to house, they did not stop teaching and preaching the good news of Jesus *as* the Christ.

While liberty of conscience does emphasize the importance of not binding people's consciences on matters of religious freedom, it also provides the framework for faithful and courageous living for the sake of Christ. As we see in this account in Acts, Peter and the apostles were told not to speak the truth of the gospel. They were threatened and ordered not to be faithful to Jesus. So what would they do? How would liberty of conscience come in to play? Peter's response expresses the true freedom of liberty of conscience when he says, "We must obey God rather than men." So in this sense, while liberty of conscience teaches us how we ought to treat others, it also teaches us how to live before the face of God. Ultimately, while the conscience is free from the commandments of men, all humans will give an account to God. That is why Peter and the apostles rejoiced in being counted worthy to suffer dishonour for Jesus name—their confidence was in obedience to God rather than obedience to man. Liberty of conscience frees Christians to proclaim Christ no matter the consequences.

Romans 2:12-16

For all who have sinned without the Law will also perish without the Law, and all who have sinned under the Law will be judged by the Law; for *it is* not the hearers of the Law *who* are righteous before God, but the doers of the Law *who* will be justified. For when Gentiles who do not have the Law instinctively perform the *requirements* of the Law, these, though not having the Law, are a law to themselves, in that they show the work of the Law written in their hearts, their conscience testifying and their thoughts alternately accusing or else defending them, on the day when, according to my gospel, God will judge the secrets of mankind through Christ Jesus.

Here in Romans 2, Paul really explains for us what the conscience is and how it works in everyday life. The conscience is an internal witness. With our minds, we either receive the conviction of our conscience or we suppress the conviction of our conscience. This is one convincing reality of being created and formed by God. Even those who do not worship God still respond to his law with their consciences. While their minds work to accuse and excuse the guilt they feel, this experience is a proof we live in God's world and will all be judged by God's law. So part of the journey of coming to faith in Christ is being convinced and convicted of true guilt according to God's law.

Romans 13:1-7

> Every person is to be subject to the governing authorities. For there is no authority except from God, and those which exist are established by God. Therefore whoever resists authority has opposed the ordinance of God; and they who have opposed will receive condemnation upon themselves. For rulers are not a cause of fear for good behavior, but for evil. Do you want to have no fear of authority? Do what is good and you will have praise from the same; for it is a servant of God to you for good. But if you do what is evil, be afraid; for it does not bear the sword for nothing; for it is a servant of God, an avenger who brings wrath on the one who practices evil. Therefore it is necessary to be in subjection, not only because of wrath, but also for the sake of conscience. For because of this you also pay taxes, for *rulers* are servants of God, devoting themselves to this very thing. Pay to all what is due them: tax to whom tax *is due*; custom to whom custom; respect to whom respect; honor to whom honor.

The Bible explicitly spells out how the church should relate to governing authorities. Liberty of conscience exists both to free a person to submit to governing authorities without defiling the conscience and to submit to God when faithfulness to God and the gospel are at stake. So things like paying taxes, respecting authorities and honouring laws are, in a sense, matters of obedience *to God*, since God himself has sovereign control over all the nations of the world. To avoid paying taxes, respecting authority or honouring people, for the sake of personal gain or selfish ambition, does not honour Christ and sears the conscience.

Christians live before the face of God, which most of the time means submitting to the authority of the government—rendering to Ceasar what is Ceasar's and to God what is God's.[6]

Romans 14:1-23

Now accept the one who is weak in faith, *but* not to have quarrels over opinions. One person has faith that he may eat all things, but the one who is weak eats *only* vegetables. The one who eats is not to regard with contempt the one who does not eat, and the one who does not eat is not to judge the one who eats, for God has accepted him. Who are you to judge the servant of another? To his own master he stands or falls; and he will stand, for the Lord is able to make him stand.

One *person* values one day over another, another values every day *the same*. Each person must be fully convinced in his own mind. The one who observes the day, observes it for the Lord, and the one who eats, does so with regard to the Lord, for he gives thanks to God; and the one who does not eat, *it is* for the Lord *that* he does not eat, and he gives thanks to God. For not one of us lives for himself, and not one dies for himself; for if we live, we live for the Lord, or if we die, we die for the Lord; therefore whether we live or die, we are the Lord's. For to this *end* Christ died and lived *again*, that He might be Lord both of the dead and of the living.

But *as for* you, why do you judge your brother *or sister*? Or you as well, why do you regard your brother *or sister* with contempt? For we will all appear before the judgment seat of God. For it is written:

"AS I LIVE, SAYS THE LORD, TO ME EVERY KNEE WILL BOW,
AND EVERY TONGUE WILL GIVE PRAISE TO GOD."

So then each one of us will give an account of himself to God.

Therefore let's not judge one another anymore, but rather determine this: not to put an obstacle or a stumbling block in a brother's *or sister's* way. I know and am convinced in the Lord Jesus that nothing is unclean in itself; but to the one who thinks something is unclean, to that *person it is* unclean. For if because of food your

---

6 See Mark 12:17.

brother *or sister* is hurt, you are no longer walking in accordance with love. Do not destroy with your *choice* of food that *person* for whom Christ died. Therefore do not let what is for you a good thing be spoken of as evil; for the kingdom of God is not eating and drinking, but righteousness and peace and joy in the Holy Spirit. For the one who serves Christ in this *way* is acceptable to God and approved by *other* people. So then we pursue the things which make for peace and the building up of one another. Do not tear down the work of God for the sake of food. All things indeed are clean, but they are evil for the person who eats and causes offense. It is good not to eat meat or to drink wine, or *to do anything* by which your brother *or sister* stumbles. The faith which you have, have as your own conviction before God. Happy is the one who does not condemn himself in what he approves. But the one who doubts is condemned if he eats, because *his eating* is not from faith; and whatever is not from faith is sin.

While Romans 13 deals mainly with liberty of conscience as it relates to society, Romans 14 deals with liberty of conscience within the household of faith. Romans 14 is our model for appropriately categorizing issues of law and issues of wisdom. Notice how Paul calls us not to pass judgment on the servant of another. In other words, because we all will give an account to God, we are not to serve as another person's conscience. When it comes to matters of wisdom, we must not force our convictions on another member of the body of Christ. The key, though, is not to use liberty of conscience *as an excuse to sin* but rather to use liberty of conscience as *an opportunity to live for Christ*. God will not be mocked. If we use liberty of conscience as an excuse to sin, we must remember we will one day stand before the true Judge, who knows the thoughts, intentions and motives of our hearts. Paul calls us to see the bounds of Christian freedom not in terms of what we can get away with, but in terms of what we can learn to live without, for the sake of loving our brother or sister. We must even engage with matters of wisdom with wisdom! Just because something isn't law, doesn't necessarily mean it is profitable. And yet, we must guard ourselves from determining for another servant of Christ what is profitable and what is not. The burden of liberty of conscience is on the stronger believer, not the weaker one. The whole idea is that Christians are *free to love and serve* because they live before the face of God, rather than the law of man or the law of self. It is a great blessing to embrace liberty of conscience in a way that builds others up, and engenders courageous and faithful living for the sake of the gospel.

1 Timothy 2:1–4

First of all, then, I urge that requests, prayers, intercession, *and* thanksgiving be made in behalf of all people, for kings and all who are in authority, so that we may lead a tranquil and quiet life in all godliness and dignity. This is good and acceptable in the sight of God our Savior, who wants all people to be saved and to come to the knowledge of the truth.

Liberty of conscience encourages Christians to be prayerfully involved in the affairs of their society. Because Christians understand the importance of health, life and liberty for *all* people, they should pray for whatever leaders God has placed them under. And if Christians are called to pray and intercede for their government officials, it stands to reason, if they themselves so desire, they should seek out those political positions when appropriate. As Christians work for and pray toward creating a peaceful and safe society, they can put their hope in God, the true and eternal Saviour of their souls.

EXPLANATION

"God alone is Lord of the conscience..."

All people will one day stand before God to give an account for their lives. It will be *his* law that will finally convict or confirm how we lived before him. Knowing God alone is Lord of the conscience sets people free to live their lives for his honour and glory, no matter the circumstances. It also reminds us that it is in fearing God that we begin to see life correctly and know how to walk in wisdom before him.

**"and he has left it free from the doctrines and command-
ments of men—those that are contrary to his Word, or
not contained in it...."**

God has been very clear in his Word about many things he commands
us to do. However, there are many other things he has not been clear
about or left to a person's discretion or wisdom. There are areas of
Christian life where the lines of conviction will fall in different places
for different believers. This is expected, and in some sense provides
opportunities for brothers and sisters to love one another in unique
ways. When we love people who hold different convictions than we
do, it shows that our unity is *in Christ* and not in ourselves. This truth
also means that when a command of man comes up against a command of God, we are obligated to obey God rather than man.

"Government authorities are established by God..."

The Bible teaches that God's sovereignty and providence extends to
every area of life. This includes the power and authority of nations and
kingdoms. God, in all wisdom and understanding, places governments
and kings into place. This does not make him responsible for their
sinful actions, just like his providence does not make him the author
of sin in any way. However, we can assume, in all times and at all
places, God has us exactly where he wants us. Knowing this, forces us
to take a different posture toward the authorities in our lives. God used
evil and tyrannical government authorities to bring salvation to the
world. The nations raged against God's anointed King, Jesus Christ,
condemning and crucifying him unjustly. And yet, every moment, God
was sovereignly orchestrating his plan in the world.[7]

"so it is good for us to obey the laws commanded by them
as long as they do not contradict God's Word."

There will be times when for the sake of God's glory and the gospel we
will need to disobey the laws established by government authorities.
However, in most times and places, submitting to local authorities will
further gospel witness rather than hinder it. In maintaining a good
reputation in the eyes of outsiders[8] and in praying and working to

---

7   See Acts 4:23–28.
8   1 Timothy 3:7.

establish a peaceable society, Christians can seek first the kingdom of God and his righteousness, while living as humble, faithful citizens of whatever nation they belong to. When the laws of the land specifically contradict the Word of God, Christians are free to obey God rather than man. God alone is Lord of the conscience, both in the church and in the world.

MISCONCEPTIONS

When it comes to misconceptions related to conscience there are some in the church and some in society at large. One of the biggest misconceptions in society at large is the origins and meaning of separation of church and state. With the first amendment to the Constitution, the United States became one of the first nations to be founded on principles which included religious freedom. The reason religious liberty was needed was not actually to keep *faith* out of the state, it was instead to keep the *state* out of faith. It was the imposition of religion by the government which gave rise to the need for the separation of church and state. Both the state as an institution and the church as an institution function best as separate entities. This does not mean the church and state should be enemies or they should not work together for the common good of society. However, it does mean keeping clear lines of distinction to protect the principle of liberty of conscience in important ways. As long as the state is friendly to religious liberty and the church encourages political participation, as both should, then there will be some organic connections between church and state. The key is maintaining the free exercise of worship without the imposition by government in the church.

As we turn to a few of the misconceptions regularly appearing in the church, we begin with the false notion that religious freedom only applies to Christians. Many Christians love the idea of religious freedom *in theory*, but what they really mean is religious freedom for Christians. Christians should seek to establish liberty of conscience for both Christians and non-Christians. Whatever freedoms and opportunities afforded to Christians by a government, should be afforded to all peaceful religions in society. No person has ever been won to Christ by coercion. And, by maintaining charity toward people of other religions or no religion at all, Christians can attempt to secure that same kind of charity in return. It is hypocritical to operate otherwise.

Another misconception is that liberty of conscience means freedom to sin. Those who claim to follow Jesus are never encouraged to use freedom in Christ as an excuse to sin. In fact, this kind of thinking is explicitly condemned.[9] Over and over, believers are challenged to use their freedom in the love and service of others. Above all, Christians are constantly reminded God is Lord of their conscience—they are commanded to do everything they do to the glory of God.[10]

Because liberty of conscience encourages freedom in areas of wisdom, it may be easy to misunderstand church discipline. Some people think liberty of conscience means any kind of church discipline is a violation of conscience. Church discipline occurs when a member of a local church continues in unrepentant sin and particular sanctions are brought about in the life of that member—with the hope of softening their heart and drawing them back to Christ. Church discipline does not violate liberty of conscience for two reasons. First, because as a member of the church, the believer has agreed they believe in a particular standard and will live by it. It was their voluntary decision to align themselves with the church and to submit to its leadership and the accountability of the congregation. Second, church discipline does not pertain to areas of wisdom but to areas of command, and some commands in Scripture are not up for debate. They are clear and straightforward. So, when a church member sins without repentance in matters of straightforward obedience, then liberty of conscience is in no way violated when sanctions are brought into their lives. Church discipline, when practiced biblically,[11] is nothing but the authority of God himself being exercised in the life of a church member.

Finally, the most common misconception about liberty of conscience is the idea that the Holy Spirit is the conscience. Many people believe that if they feel an internal sense, nudge or conviction, it automatically means the Holy Spirit is convicting them. Christians, at

---

9 Romans 6:1.
10 1 Corinthians 10:31.
11 Matthew 18:15–17.

times, feel guilty about things they should not, and they do not feel guilty for things they should. We must remember our conscience, like our mind, will and affections, will be sanctified by the Holy Spirit in a progressive way. We can sear our conscience and grieve the Holy Spirit, and our conscience can be cleansed by faith in the blood of Jesus. While the Spirit of God does cleanse, shape and sanctify our conscience, he is not synonymous with our conscience.

APPLICATION

Article XVIII: Liberty of Conscience

God alone is Lord of the conscience; and he has left it free from
the doctrines and commandments of men—those that are
contrary to his Word, or not contained in it. Government
authorities are established by God, so it is good for us to obey
the laws commanded by them as long as they do not contradict
God's Word.

---

1. Christians should respect other religions while proclaiming Christ alone for salvation.

Respecting another's religion does not mean we are neglecting the
truths of God. Liberty of conscience means we must respect other
people's beliefs. Proclaiming Christ does not cross the line of disre-
spect, but sadly Christians have at times crossed those lines. We
must seek to be charitable to all and prayerful for all.

2. Christians should live before the face of God and not under the judgments of man.

The ultimate authority to whom we must give an account is God himself. This means we are free to obey God no matter the consequences.
When our obedience to God means disobedience to the world or
enduring mockery, we can assuredly live before God's face trusting
his ultimate authority.

3. Christians should always let the Bible be our guide.

The Bible speaks clearly to many issues and many situations. There
are other things the Bible speaks to by implication. We should trust
the Bible's sufficiency to guide us throughout all our days. Even in
situations where wisdom and discernment are needed, we have been
trained by the wisdom of the Bible in how to approach different life
situations. Liberty of conscience should never be used as an excuse
to sin. It should also be acknowledged that anything not done in

faith is sin.[12] Christians ought to listen carefully to the Word, both its commands and its wisdom, and then live wholeheartedly to the glory of God in all things.

4. Christians should always be cautious not to bind or sear another person's conscience.

When we treat things as of little importance that God really cares about, we run the risk of searing someone's conscience. And when we make confident assertions about which the Bible is silent, we run the risk of binding someone's conscience. The Bible has not spoken clearly about every single issue in a way that carries the weight of obedience or disobedience, so we can leave to God to judge the motives and intentions of all people's hearts. We all have responsibility for ourselves before the Lord, but we will also bear responsibility for the ways in which we shaped and guided others. Let us commit to do our best never to sear or bind any person's conscience, but to allow God alone to be Lord of the conscience.

---

12 Romans 14:23.

The Resurrection

INTRO - OVERVIEW

ARTICLE

XIX

The Resurrection

The bodies of men after death return to dust, but their spirits return immediately to God—the righteous to rest with him; the wicked, to be reserved under darkness to the judgment. At the last day, the bodies of all the dead, both just and unjust, will be raised.

The Resurrection

INTRO + OVERVIEW

I n chapter 3, we talked about *dualism* as it relates to God. This dualism pitted God the Father against God the Son, as if they had their own individual wills, attributes and plans, opposed to each other. We talked about the dangers of dualism as it relates to our conception of God. However, there is another kind of dualism the church has dealt with over the centuries: dualism between the material world and the immaterial world, between body and soul.

Throughout church history, there have been a number of instances of this kind of dualism.[1] The idea is that the material in the world is bad but the spiritual is good. So, when we talk about human beings, the body is bad and the soul is good. The problem with this view is God made *both* the material and the immaterial, *both* the body and the soul—and he declared it all good.[2]

This dualism places moral value judgments where God has not. This is problematic, in and of itself, but it becomes most harmful as it relates to the person and work of Jesus Christ. This kind of dualism forces a reinterpretation of the story of the gospel—and what it leaves behind is nothing short of tragic.

This kind of dualism approaches Jesus in a dehumanizing way. If the body is bad, how do we deal with the incarnation of the eternal Son of God? If the body is bad, then why was Jesus raised—bodily— from the dead? When those committed to a dualism between an evil body and a good soul are met with the historical fact of Jesus' resurrection, they deny its reality and diminish its necessity.

The irony is, before the closing of the canon of Scripture, the apostle Paul had *already* dealt with the implications of those who deny or diminish the resurrection—not just the resurrection of Jesus but the

---

1   Docestism, Gnosticism and higher criticism.
2   See Genesis 1.

resurrection of all flesh. Look at how strongly Paul emphasizes the *reality* and *necessity* of the resurrection of the body,

> For if the dead are not raised, then not even Christ has been raised; and if Christ has not been raised, your faith is worthless; you are still in your sins. Then also those who have fallen asleep in Christ have perished. If we have hoped in Christ only in this life, we are of all people most to be pitied (1 Corinthians 15:16-19).

The entire Christian faith hinges on the resurrection—again, not just the resurrection of Jesus but the resurrection of all flesh. The good news of the gospel is not good news unless the bodily resurrection is affirmed. This is what makes Christianity more than an intellectually satisfying theory, a therapeutic balm or an excuse to detach from the pains of life. The message of Christianity is one of concrete existence and legitimate hope.

Let's consider some reasons why the bodily resurrection must be affirmed.

The resurrection proves the goodness of God's creation

When God made everything, he made it good. God intends for human beings to have bodies—that is an integral aspect of being human. If God didn't want human beings to exist in an embodied state, he wouldn't have declared them good in their embodied state. There, in the Garden of Eden, Adam and Eve were *complete*—just as God wanted them to be. They were the total package of God's idea of a blessed humanity, a perfect composite of body and soul.

The resurrection gives life meaning

If this world and this life were all there was, what would be the point of living? A world without the resurrection of the dead invokes a life of aimlessness, purposelessness and hopelessness. If this is all there is— we are dead and then we evaporate—what are we all so worried about? If the resurrection is not true, certainly our brains have tricked us into succumbing to feelings of nostalgia and longings for significance.

The resurrection is the hope of the gospel

The gospel is an announcement of "good news"—it is what God has done for us in Christ. But if what God has done for us in Christ only has value in this life (i.e., an intellectually satisfying theory, a therapeutic balm or an excuse to detach from the pains of life), then "we are of all people most to be pitied," as Paul says. The gospel provides real and concrete hope because it is the announcement that Jesus has conquered the enemy, *death*, he has secured a purposeful and meaningful existence for us and he has redeemed our bodies in which we will live forever. If there is no resurrection of the dead, then there is no hope of the gospel, because this miserable, sin-riddled existence is all we have to look forward to—forever.

Typically, when Christians consider the resurrection, they mainly think about Jesus' resurrection from the dead. And rightly so! The resurrection of Jesus Christ is debatably the single most important event in the history of the universe. But, the resurrection of Jesus is presented in the Bible as *firstfruits*.[3] His resurrection is the promise of a *new* creation. The resurrection of Jesus from the dead was proof there will be a general resurrection, in which *all* humanity will be raised up again. This resurrection will mark the end of time as we know it—but it will be the dawn of eternity. This resurrection will be permanent, and it will usher all people into either eternal communion with God or into the eternal judgment of God. Let us join with the Apostles' Creed and the church of all generations as we declare, "I believe in the Holy Spirit; the holy catholic church; the communion of saints; the forgiveness of sins; the resurrection of the body; and the life everlasting. Amen."

SCRIPTURAL FOUNDATIONS

Daniel 12:1–3

"Now at that time Michael, the great prince who stands *guard* over the sons of your people, will arise. And there will be a time of distress such as never occurred since there was a nation until that time; and

---

3   1 Corinthians 15:20.

at that time your people, everyone who is found written in the book, will be rescued. And many of those who sleep in the dust of the ground will awake, these to everlasting life, but the others to disgrace *and* everlasting contempt. And those who have insight will shine like the glow of the expanse of heaven, and those who lead the many to righteousness, like the stars forever and ever.

As one reads the New Testament, it becomes clear that the concept of the resurrection from the dead had already been embedded in Israelite theology. There was dispute about this, as is seen especially between the Pharisees and the Sadducees—two leading groups with a fair amount of disagreement.[4] But it is passages like this one in Daniel that form the Old Testament witness to the resurrection. Like with most prophetic and eschatological literature in the Bible, it is not easy to pin down the meaning of each particular detail in this passage. But, what is clear is this speaks to a time when a cataclysmic event occurs. This event would be the destruction of everyone, if it weren't for God's deliverance. And then, more to the point of this article, the Scripture tells us there will be those who come awake out of the dust. Throughout the Bible, the term *sleep* is used to describe those who have died and are awaiting resurrection. So, to "sleep in the dust of the ground" is to die and be buried. This Scripture clearly teaches it is not just those whose names are written in God's book who are raised. Some are raised to shine like stars forever, while others whose names were not written in God's book are raised to experience shame and contempt for all eternity.

Matthew 22:23-33

On that day *some* Sadducees (who say there is no resurrection) came to Jesus and questioned Him, saying, "Teacher, Moses said, 'If a man dies having no children, his brother as next of kin shall marry his wife, and raise up children for his brother.' Now there were seven brothers among us; and the first married and died, and having no children, he left his wife to his brother. *It was* the same also *with* the second *brother*, and the third, down to the seventh. Last of all, the woman

---

4   See Matthew 22:23–46.

died. In the resurrection, therefore, whose wife of the seven will she be? For they all had her *in marriage*."

But Jesus answered and said to them, "You are mistaken, since you do not understand the Scriptures nor the power of God. For in the resurrection they neither marry nor are given in marriage, but are like angels in heaven. But regarding the resurrection of the dead, have you not read what was spoken to you by God: 'I AM THE GOD OF ABRAHAM, THE GOD OF ISAAC, AND THE GOD OF JACOB'? He is not the God of the dead, but of the living." When the crowds heard *this*, they were astonished at His teaching.

Here in Matthew's Gospel we are introduced to the theology of the Sadducees. They were a group of Israelites who did not believe in the resurrection. They apparently came to Jesus to test him. And it is in his response to the Sadducees, where we clearly see Jesus himself believed in the the general resurrection. They ask Jesus a detailed and tricky question about marriage and the resurrection. Jesus immediately puts them in their place, by both answering their question and confounding their objection. He answers their question by teaching that the institution of marriage will not carry over after the resurrection. But seeing past their question, Jesus goes on to affirm the doctrine itself. Rather than dealing with philosophy or using trickery to argue his point, Jesus goes to the Scriptures themselves. He reminds them that if there was no bodily resurrection and people cease to exist after death, then for God to identify himself with those who were dead would be foolish. Since God identifies himself with those who had died, it is proof that death is not the end for them. Even after death, God continues to be the God of Abraham, Isaac and Jacob. Jesus explicitly taught the resurrection of the dead—not just his own, but the resurrection of all of humanity.

1 Corinthians 15:12-58

Now if Christ is preached, that He has been raised from the dead, how do some among you say that there is no resurrection of the dead? But if there is no resurrection of the dead, then not even Christ has been raised; and if Christ has not been raised, then our preaching is in vain, your faith also is in vain. Moreover, we are even found *to be* false witnesses of God, because we testified against God that He raised Christ, whom He did not raise, if in fact the dead are not raised. For if the dead are not raised, then not even Christ has been raised; and if Christ has not been raised, your faith is worthless; you are still in your sins. Then also those who have fallen asleep in Christ have perished. If we have hoped in Christ only in this life, we are of all people most to be pitied.

We now come back to 1 Corinthians 15 and, because it is so rich and so important to our understanding of the bodily resurrection, we will break it up into sections. Apparently, while Paul was still serving in ministry, just a few decades after Jesus had ascended bodily to the right hand of the Father, there were already those who were questioning the bodily resurrection. Notice how Paul moves in a direction we might not initially consider. Rather than moving from the resurrection of Jesus to prove the general resurrection, Paul argues the other way around. He starts with the general resurrection of all flesh first, and then moves toward the resurrection of Jesus. He is arguing that if there is no general bodily resurrection, then what is the point of the resurrection of Jesus? The only reason the resurrection of Jesus matters is, in his resurrection, he secured the resurrection of *all* flesh. The logic of Paul here is so severe that he says the entire Christian faith rests on belief in Jesus resurrection from the dead, and the entire meaning of hope in the resurrection of Jesus is that God is going to raise everyone bodily, just as he raised Christ. To proclaim the resurrection of Jesus but not to believe in the general resurrection is a logical contradiction, in Paul's mind, and worse it makes liars of those who are witnesses to the resurrection. The doctrine of Christ's resurrection and the doctrine of the general resurrection go together, as a unified witness to God's salvation. Genuine faith, gospel hope and forgiveness of sins rest on the foundation of the resurrection of the dead.

But the fact is, Christ has been raised from the dead, the first fruits of those who are asleep. For since by a man death *came*, by a man also came the resurrection of the dead. For as in Adam all die, so also in Christ all will be made alive. But each in his own order: Christ the first fruits, after that those who are Christ's at His coming, then *comes* the end, when He hands over the kingdom to *our* God and Father, when He has abolished all rule and all authority and power. For He must reign until He has put all His enemies under His feet. The last enemy that will be abolished is death. For He has put all things in subjection under His feet. But when He says, "All things are put in subjection," it is clear that this excludes the *Father* who put all things in subjection to Him. When all things are subjected to Him, then the Son Himself will also be subjected to the One who subjected all things to Him, so that God may be all in all.

For otherwise, what will those do who are baptized for the dead? If the dead are not raised at all, why then are they baptized for them? Why are we also in danger every hour? I affirm, brothers *and sisters*, by the boasting in you which I have in Christ Jesus our Lord, that I die daily. If from human motives I fought with wild beasts at Ephesus, what good is it to me? If the dead are not raised, LET'S EAT AND DRINK, FOR TOMORROW WE DIE. Do not be deceived: "Bad company corrupts good morals." Sober up morally and stop sinning, for some have no knowledge of God. I say *this* to your shame.

As Paul moves through his argument for why the bodily resurrection is essential to the Christian faith, he uses the illustration of *firstfruits.* The idea of firstfruits would have been commonly understood by both Jews and Greeks alike. The firstfruits was the first part taken from a harvest. Whatever it was, it was a representation of the rest. The first-fruits was like a miniature image of the rest of the crop. In this sense, Jesus is the first image of what all humanity will be. He was reaped first, but the whole of humanity will one day be called up from the dust of the earth, just as Christ was called out of the tomb. This image works for two humans who have lived on the earth: Adam and Christ. Both Adam and Christ stand as representative figures for humanity. Adam was the firstfruits of the first creation and Jesus is the firstfruits of the new creation. The difference between Adam and Jesus is that Adam *brought death* to all humanity, and Jesus will give life to all humanity. Through Adam, all men and women return to dust, but through Jesus all men and women will be raised from the dust.

Paul is set on convincing us of the bodily resurrection, so he moves from the theological and biblical argument to the *practical* argument. Apparently, there was some sort of ritual the church practiced in hon-our of the dead, which would make no sense if there wasn't a bodily resurrection. Paul appeals to our own traditions and practices with regard to those who go to sleep in the dust, to prove we should believe in a resurrection from the dead. But it isn't just a practical argument he makes, it also has a practical *implication*. In Paul's mind, if there is no resurrection from the dead, then what are we living for? What do Christians suffer for? What do Christians die for? The purpose is stripped out of life if there is no bodily resurrection. And, in almost sarcastic fashion, Paul basically says, "Hey, if there is no resurrection, let's just live it up and dive head first into the frivolity of this world because that is all there is to live for." This is the implication of a world with no belief in the bodily resurrection of the dead, and it deserves to be rebuked.

But someone will say, "How are the dead raised? And with what kind of body do they come?" You fool! That which you sow does not come to life unless it dies; and that which you sow, you do not sow the body which is to be, but a bare grain, perhaps of wheat or of something else. But God gives it a body just as He wished, and to each of the seeds a body of its own. All flesh is not the same flesh, but there is one *flesh* of mankind, another flesh of animals, another flesh of birds, and another of fish. There are also heavenly bodies and earthly bodies, but the glory of the heavenly is one, and the *glory* of the earthly is another. There is one glory of the sun, another glory of the moon, and another glory of the stars; for star differs from star in glory.

So also is the resurrection of the dead. It is sown a perishable *body*, it is raised an imperishable *body*; it is sown in dishonor, it is raised in glory; it is sown in weakness, it is raised in power; it is sown a natural body, it is raised a spiritual body. If there is a natural body, there is also a spiritual body. So also it is written: "The first MAN, Adam, BECAME A LIVING PERSON." The last Adam *was* a life-giving spirit. However, the spiritual is not first, but the natural; then the spiritual. The first man is from the earth, earthy; the second man is from heaven. As is the earthy one, so also are those who are earthy; and as is the heavenly one, so also are those who are heavenly. Just as we have borne the image of the earthy, we will also bear the image of the heavenly.

Now I say this, brothers *and sisters*, that flesh and blood cannot inherit the kingdom of God; nor does the perishable inherit the imperishable.

Now Paul moves to address some objections. These objections sound similar to those of the Sadducees who questioned Jesus. After calling the one asking, "You fool!" Paul proceeds to teach an invaluable lesson about the nature of resurrection bodies. Resurrected bodies really are just that, they are bodies which have been raised up. However, while they really are the same bodies—organically connected and related to the old bodies which died—they are glorified, powerful, spiritual and imperishable. Just like there is an organic connection between a kernel and the head of grain, there is an organic connection between the dead body and the resurrected body. But, just like the kernel and the head of grain have significant differences, the dead body and the resurrected body will have significant differences. Think of how, after he was raised from the dead, Jesus both ate and passed through walls. If Jesus can eat fish, then he must really be an earthly human. At the same time, if he can ascend to the right hand of the Father in heaven, then he must really be a heavenly human.[5]

> Behold, I am telling you a mystery; we will not all sleep, but we will all be changed, in a moment, in the twinkling of an eye, at the last trumpet; for the trumpet will sound, and the dead will be raised imperishable, and we will be changed. For this perishable must put on the imperishable, and this mortal *must* put on immortality. But when this perishable puts on the imperishable, and this mortal puts on immortality, then will come about the saying that is written: "DEATH HAS BEEN SWALLOWED UP in victory. WHERE, O DEATH, IS YOUR VICTORY? WHERE, O DEATH, IS YOUR STING?" The sting of death is sin, and the power of sin is the Law; but thanks be to God, who gives us the victory through our Lord Jesus Christ.
>
> Therefore, my beloved brothers *and sisters*, be firm, immovable, always excelling in the work of the Lord, knowing that your labor is not *in vain* in the Lord.

In this final section of 1 Corinthians 15, Paul points to a mystery. In the Bible, a mystery is not something sneaky or concealed, rather it is something God reveals only by his sovereign revelation. The mystery God has revealed is that even those who don't die and "go to sleep"

---

5   See Luke 24:42–43.

before Christ returns, will still experience the change of the resurrection. A change will occur and the new eternal bodies of *all* human beings will be imperishable. The immortality God intended for all humanity will in fact become a reality through Christ. To those found in Christ, this immortality will be their eternal glory, and to those found in Adam, this immortality will be their eternal shame. Jesus Christ is the firstborn from the dead, but there will be a final cataclysmic event by which, in an instant, all flesh will be raised up and changed. This will be the end—creation will be redeemed and human beings will be raised.

1 Thessalonians 4:13–18

> But we do not want you to be uninformed, brothers *and sisters*, about those who are asleep, so that you will not grieve as indeed the rest *of mankind* do, who have no hope. For if we believe that Jesus died and rose *from the dead*, so also God will bring with Him those who have fallen asleep through Jesus. For we say this to you by the word of the Lord, that we who are alive and remain until the coming of the Lord will not precede those who have fallen asleep. For the Lord Himself will descend from heaven with a shout, with the voice of *the* archangel and with the trumpet of God, and the dead in Christ will rise first. Then we who are alive, who remain, will be caught up together with them in the clouds to meet the Lord in the air, and so we will always be with the Lord. Therefore, comfort one another with these words.

As we look at this final Scripture in 1 Thessalonians, notice how Paul does not want us to be uninformed. The doctrine of the resurrection has important practical implications for our lives. One implication relates to how we grieve. Paul does not say we shouldn't grieve, but he argues our grief should be infused with hope, since we know those who have died are merely asleep until the resurrection. Another implication is the comfort of knowing that those who are in Christ will live out their eternal existence with Jesus, bodily. We aren't going to be separated from the bodily Jesus, and we aren't going to be separated from our bodies. In the same ways we give and receive comfort and affection with those we love here on earth, we will give and receive affection with Jesus forever. A final implication is these truths should serve to fuel our encouragement. We suffer well, make sacrifices, deny the flesh and glorify God in our deaths—all because we rest on the promise of the resurrection. We can offer up our bodies, knowing that even if this mortal flesh is spent and consumed, God will raise us up in an immortal and imperishable body, and we will thrive in his presence for all eternity.

EXPLANATION

"The bodies of men after death return to dust, but their spirits return immediately to God..."

God formed Adam from the dust of the ground. When we die, our bodies are returned to the dust. As God told Adam, "For you are dust, and to dust you shall return."[6] But our spirits or our souls go to God. This disembodied state is not our eternal existence. It is temporary as we await the final resurrection. Those who have died, while their future is sealed, are not where or what they will be forever.

"the righteous to rest with him..."

When a person dies who has placed faith in Christ alone for their righteousness before God, their spirit goes to be with God in rest. While they are not fully complete until the resurrection of the dead, they have entered the presence of their God and Savior Jesus Christ. This state is better than being here on this unredeemed earth, but it is not the ultimate future which all those who hope in Christ await.

"the wicked, to be reserved under darkness to the judgment...."

On the other hand, while it is also true that the spirits of those who have not placed faith in Christ return to God, they do not return to him in rest. Along with the righteous in Christ, they go to the place of the dead, but they are removed from the loving and comforting presence of God while they await the final resurrection and judgment.

---

6 Genesis 3:19.

There is a chasm which exists in the place of the dead which no man can cross.[7] There is neither opportunity for those reserved for judgment to receive mercy nor the possibility for anyone on earth to do anything on their behalf to cause them to receive mercy. Those who die without Christ await the resurrection of the dead, not in hope, but with trembling. Their future is sealed and the resurrection will only serve to add to their torment in judgment.

"At the last day, the bodies of all the dead, both just and unjust, will be raised."

The resurrection will be the bodily rising of all human beings who have ever lived. Jesus is the only human being who currently exists in the state of resurrection. All other humans must wait until that last day, when all flesh will be raised. The bodies of the raised will be their actual bodies, but they will be changed bodies. They will be immortal and imperishable. These raised bodies will serve as their eternal home, and there will be no end to their existence. What they will then be, they will be forever.

MISCONCEPTIONS

There are a number of misconceptions related to the resurrection of the dead. The first deals with the Bible's teaching on the *place of the dead*. The confusion can be seen in our English translations of the Apostles' Creed. For example, there is a line which has been translated, "He descended into hell," which refers to where Jesus went after breathing his last breath on the cross. Many times, in both the Old Testament and the New Testament, the place of the dead is a topic of conversation. This place of the dead is where all spirits go. One side is a place for those reserved for judgment, while the other side is a place for those reserved for eternal life, with an untraversable chasm between them. The place of the dead, however, is one of the sad consequences of sin for all those who die. Even for those who fly to be in God's rest, to be disembodied—the separation of body and soul—is a

---

7   Luke 16:19–31.

consequence of sin and death. Jesus did not descend to "hell" as many of us imagine hell. Jesus did, though, go to the place of the dead where all disembodied spirits go when they die. The confusion exists because the words *Sheol* and *Hades* in the Bible, sometimes refer to the place of the dead *in general* and sometimes refer to the *side* of the place of the dead reserved for those under judgement. The creed did not intend to teach that Jesus descended to the lake of hell's fire, but rather that Jesus' soul went to the *place of the dead,* where all those who die go.

This brings up another related but different misconception: the idea that those who have died have already gone to be where they will be forever. It is believed by many that those who have died in Christ are now running up and down the streets of gold. This belief takes the images of the consummated new creation and applies them to the current disembodied state of those who have died in the Lord. While it is true the Scriptures teach that to be absent from the body is to be present with the Lord,[8] it is not true that believers who die have entered the new creation or already possess their resurrected bodies. Likewise, it is also true that those who have died without the Lord are not currently where they will be forever. They are not burning in the lake of fire—they are not in hell, as we conceive of it. All those who die go to the place of the dead while they await the final resurrection and the final judgment. Only then, with raised bodies, will all men and women be led to their eternal homes, whether the lake of fire or the new creation.

The question might be asked: Does this place of the dead give people the opportunity to repent or to be saved after they die? This leads us to the misconception or belief in purgatory. Purgatory is a teaching that those who die must go and suffer and "burn off" their remaining sin, in order to get into heaven. The Christian teaching of the place of the dead is in no way synonymous with purgatory. Those who go to the place of the dead have their future sealed. For those who have been made righteous in Christ, they wait in the rest and peace of God until they are resurrected into eternal life. For those without Christ, they wait in darkness for the day of judgment. It is not a time to have dross consumed or gold refined; it is not a place where one can repent. After earthly death, there is no further opportunity for salvation.

---

8   2 Corinthians 5:8.

One of the saddest misconceptions is the idea that we live in a disembodied state in our eternal heaven. God intends human beings to have bodies. He plans to raise those bodies, so if we have bodies, we will be in an environment conducive to *physical* bodies. With seriousness and sadness, we must realize that for those who die without Christ, the resurrection means experiencing an eternal lake of fire both physically and spiritually. However, in utmost joy and jubilation, we must celebrate and wait with eager expectation for the bodily resurrection of the righteous, by which the new heavens and the new earth will be enjoyed forever. For believers in Jesus, the vision of God himself will pass from faith to sight. The resurrection is the hope of a concrete future of love, justice, peace and rest for all those who have put their hope in Jesus.

A final misconception is the idea that the resurrection is overly theoretical and impractical. Nothing could be further from the truth. What we believe about our future, always immediately affects our present reality. The resurrection of the dead has serious and radical implications for all of life. To neglect the practical implications of the resurrection of the dead would be to deny the *hope* of the gospel. Like Paul said, "If we have hoped in Christ only in this life, we are of all people most to be pitied."[9] His whole point is *the hope of the resurrection has everything to do with how we live and die in this life.* That is why Paul ends his great chapter on the resurrection by saying,

> Therefore, my beloved brothers *and sisters*, be firm, immovable, always excelling in the work of the Lord, knowing that your labor is not *in vain* in the Lord.[10]

---

9   1 Corinthians 15:19.
10   1 Corinthians 15:58.

APPLICATION

Article XIX: The Resurrection

> **The bodies of men after death return to dust, but their spirits return immediately to God—the righteous to rest with him; the wicked, to be reserved under darkness to the judgment. At the last day, the bodies of all the dead, both just and unjust, will be raised.**

---

1. ***We should live with immense hope.***
   Hope is faith rooted in a future promise. The promises of God are certain, and the specific promise of the resurrection is proven in Jesus Christ. We can know for certain that death is defeated, and our existence is not meaningless, because Jesus rose from the dead. And there would be no reason for Jesus to rise from the dead if we were not to rise also. In all things, we have an extremely bright future ahead of us.

2. ***Resurrection hope is the basis for legitimate joy.***
   The Christian life comes with many sorrows, but yet it is always rejoicing.[11] There is always reason for joy because we know what is coming. Jesus Christ has risen and therefore we will rise. Even in the face of death, we can have joy. As we face the enemy of death, we can do so with rejoicing knowing it has already been conquered.

3. ***The resurrection teaches us how to approach the material world and our bodies.***
   Clearly, if the material world and our bodies were evil, then Jesus would not have been resurrected bodily. While it is true this world and everything in it awaits redemption, it is also true God made it all good. The marring of sin has not rendered the physical creation or our bodies evil. God has designed humans to live in a material

------

11 2 Corinthians 6:10.

world and to inhabit an embodied existence. We should treat our bodies and/or the bodies of others with dignity and care, and we should give thanks to God for the ways he blesses us through his good creation.

4. The resurrection reminds us to spend our whole lives for the glory of God.

We can give everything we have to the mission of Christ, even to the point of death, because we know we have a resurrection awaiting us. Hold nothing back, keep nothing hidden and reserve no energy. When it is all said and done, God has promised to make all things new—including our bodies. O, to end our lives where Paul ends the great passage on the resurrection, "Therefore, my beloved brothers *and sisters*, be firm, immovable, always excelling in the work of the Lord, knowing that your labor is not *in vain* in the Lord."[12]

---

12 1 Corinthians 15:58.

The Judgment

INTRO + OVERVIEW

ARTICLE

XX

The Judgment

God hath appointed a day, wherein he will judge the
world by Jesus Christ, when every one shall receive
according to his deeds; the wicked shall go into
everlasting punishment; the righteous, into
everlasting life.

The Judgment

INTRO + OVERVIEW

I n many ways, these last two articles on the resurrection and the judgment go hand in hand. We live in the body and so we will be judged in the body. What we said with our tongues, thought with our minds and did with our hands, will all be brought to light at Christ's judgment. But beyond being connected to the previous article on the resurrection, this article is connected to almost all the articles we have considered. In particular, notice how the last phrase in this article plays a central role in the one on election: "Election is God's eternal choice of some persons unto everlasting life."[1] God's eternal plan for creation and redemption culminates in this: a people for his own possession who share in his life, as they glorify him and enjoy him forever.

However, the great drama of history is that those created for everlasting life with God—men and women—fell into sin. And God, "having in and of himself, all perfections, and being infinite in them all,"[2] is required by the righteousness and justice of his nature to condemn sin. God could not approve or overlook sin. To do so would be to contradict his being. So if human beings have, "a nature corrupt and wholly opposed to God and his law, [and] are under condemnation,"[3] how can they be restored to their original purpose?

According to God's infinite wisdom and purpose, he had chosen some persons unto everlasting life, to be saved by grace. Still, sin must be dealt with and God must judge. In love, God sent forth his Son, "having taken upon himself human nature, yet without sin, he perfectly fulfilled the law; suffered and died upon the cross for the salvation of sinners. He was buried, and rose again the third day, and ascended

---

1 Article V.
2 Article II.
3 Article VI.

to his Father, at whose right hand he ever lives to make intercession for his people."[4] God poured out his wrath toward sinners on Jesus, justifying them through faith in him, and thus the drama of reconciliation—the drama of history—came to its climax. Everlasting life, then, while it will endure forever, is more a *kind* of life than a *length* of life. Everlasting life is life lived in reconciled communion with God through Jesus Christ. With the drama resolved, someone may be tempted to ask: What is the point of living life on this earth before the day of the resurrection? This question shows the importance of understanding the judgment.

Pitfalls about judgment

There are a number of different pitfalls about judgment we must avoid. One pitfall is to believe God does not judge sin. Similar to the doctrine of the resurrection, were this the case, it would render our existence meaningless. A world without justice is a purposeless world. When there is no right and wrong, good and bad, we remove the boundaries which mark out all that is true, good and beautiful. Without justice, life becomes one big mush of bland meaninglessness.

But, assuming God does judge sin and he has sent Christ into the world, there are still two other pitfalls we can fall into about the last judgment. One is to treat the cross of Jesus Christ as a formality, while still preaching a works-based judgment unto salvation. As we will see, the Bible clearly teaches we will be judged *according to our works*. But we get in trouble if we believe those passages somehow negate the *necessity of the cross* for salvation. While we will all be *judged* by our works, no one will be *saved* by their works. This article on the judgment is not somehow undoing all we said in Article XI, which so clearly teaches, "Justification is God's gracious and full acquittal of sinners, who believe in Christ, from all sin, through the satisfaction that Christ has made." The reality of the final judgment does not somehow put the burden of justification back on the shoulders of believers.

Another pitfall we must carefully guard against is to treat the cross of Christ as though it removes the *necessity* of a final judgment. When we look at the cross this way, at least two things happen. First, we are left feeling the need to cross out major portions of the Scriptures. Even

---

4   Article VII.

those writings which came chronologically after the historical death and resurrection of Jesus have much to say about the final judgment and its implications for our lives. Further, to use the doctrine of justification to negate the doctrine of the final judgment would be to render our lives on this earth pointless, from now until Christ returns. Justification deals with our *ultimate standing* before God, and it relates to our new identity in Christ, that of family and friend of God. This does not, however, render *what we do* meaningless. Even those justified by faith in Christ will still give have to give an account of their lives to God. No one will be saved by works, but we will all be judged according to what we had done. Rather than seeing the cross as the *end* of God's justice, we should see it as the *proof* of God's justice. He will not be fooled and he will not be mocked. Rather than using the cross to render life meaningless, we should be empowered by the vision of God we see at the cross to make every effort to walk forward in the good works God has prepared for us to carry out in the name of Jesus.[5]

Judgment is real

Our hope that God will make all things right, and our motivation to live in fear before the face of God all the days of our lives, rests on the reality of God's righteous judgment. While the fear of the Lord may incorporate more than the reality of future judgment, it is certainly not less. And we know that as, "The fear of the Lord is the beginning of wisdom,"[6] then to live in light of the final judgment should not make us see God as hard, but rather make us more wise with how we spend the life we have been given.[7] "But the wisdom from above is first pure, then peace-loving, gentle, reasonable, full of mercy and good fruits, impartial, free of hypocrisy,"[8] and we know that, "against such things there is no law."[9]

---

5   Ephesians 2:10.
6   Proverbs 9:10.
7   Luke 19:11–27.
8   James 3:17.
9   Galatians 5:23.

SCRIPTURAL FOUNDATIONS

Psalm 7:6-17

Arise, LORD, in Your anger;
Raise Yourself against the rage of my enemies,
And stir Yourself for me; You have ordered judgment.
Let the assembly of the peoples encompass You,
And return on high over it.
The LORD judges the peoples;
Vindicate me, LORD, according to my righteousness and my integrity
    that is in me.
Please let the evil of the wicked come to an end, but establish
    the righteous;
For the righteous God puts hearts and minds to the test.
My shield is with God,
Who saves the upright in heart.
God is a righteous judge,
And a God who shows indignation every day.

If one does not repent, He will sharpen His sword;
He has bent His bow and taken aim.
He has also prepared deadly weapons for Himself;
He makes His arrows fiery *shafts*.
Behold, *an evil* person is pregnant with injustice,
And he conceives harm and gives birth to lies.
He has dug a pit and hollowed it out,
And has fallen into the hole which he made.
His harm will return on his own head,
And his violence will descend on the top of his own head.

I will give thanks to the LORD according to His righteousness
And will sing praise to the name of the LORD Most High.

The Old Testament, and especially the Psalms, is filled with the reality of God's judgment. The Psalms use the truth of the judgment both to warn those who are unrepentant and to comfort those who are victims of injustice because of their faithfulness to God. Here in Psalm 7, David is appealing to God as his refuge, and he is expressing the safety that comes from knowing God will finally judge the earth. David is eager for God to come and act on his anger toward sin and injustice. He knows God has appointed a day of judgment, and in his desperation, David is ready for that day. But in his cry for justice, David does not leave out himself. He wants the wicked to be judged, but he also asks God to judge him. David understands what will happen on the final judgment day—the wicked will come to an end and the righteous will be established. Ultimately, the perfection of God which David celebrates as he longs for the judgment day of God, is God's righteousness. Because God is righteous, we can expect him to make all things right in the end.

Matthew 25:31–46

[Jesus speaking] "But when the Son of Man comes in His glory, and all the angels with Him, then He will sit on His glorious throne. And all the nations will be gathered before Him; and He will separate them from one another, just as the shepherd separates the sheep from the goats; and He will put the sheep on His right, but the goats on the left.

"Then the King will say to those on His right, 'Come, you who are blessed of My Father, inherit the kingdom prepared for you from the foundation of the world. For I was hungry, and you gave Me *something* to eat; I was thirsty, and you gave Me *something* to drink; I was a stranger, and you invited Me in; naked, and you clothed Me; I was sick, and you visited Me; I was in prison, and you came to Me.' Then the righteous will answer Him, 'Lord, when did we see You hungry, and feed You, or thirsty, and give You *something* to drink? And when did we see You as a stranger, and invite You in, or naked, and clothe You? And when did we see You sick, or in prison, and come to You?' And the King will answer and say to them, 'Truly I say to you, to the extent that you did *it* for one of the least of these brothers *or sisters* of Mine, you did *it* for Me.'

"Then He will also say to those on His left, 'Depart from Me, you accursed people, into the eternal fire which has been prepared for the devil and his angels; for I was hungry, and you gave Me nothing to eat; I was thirsty, and you gave Me nothing to drink; I was a stranger, and you did not invite Me in; naked, and you did not clothe Me; sick, and in prison, and you did not visit Me.' Then they themselves also will answer, 'Lord, when did we see You hungry, or thirsty, or as a stranger, or naked, or sick, or in prison, and did not take care of You?' Then He will answer them, 'Truly I say to you, to the extent that you did not do *it* for one of the least of these, you did not do *it* for Me, either.' These will go away into eternal punishment, but the righteous into eternal life."

In Matthew 25, Jesus makes use of a simile, not a parable. This is not a fictional story. The story Jesus describes will actually happen at the end of history. He uses the comparison of a shepherd who separates his herd into two groups: sheep and goats. The sheep are likened to the righteous. These are those who have been declared righteous by faith in Jesus Christ. The goats are likened to the wicked. These are those who are dead in their trespasses and sins. That is what separates the two groups. But even still, God will judge the two groups. And what he will find in those who are righteous are good works done in Jesus name. What he will find in those who are dead in sins will be a neglect of any good works done in Jesus name. The end of the wicked, Jesus tells us, is eternal punishment, but the end of the righteous is eternal life.

John 5:22–30

"For not even the Father judges anyone, but He has given all judgment to the Son, so that all will honor the Son just as they honor the Father. The one who does not honor the Son does not honor the Father who sent Him.

"Truly, truly, I say to you, the one who hears My word, and believes Him who sent Me, has eternal life, and does not come into judgment, but has passed out of death into life.

"Truly, truly, I say to you, a time is coming and even now has arrived, when the dead will hear the voice of the Son of God, and those who hear will live. For just as the Father has life in Himself, so He gave to the Son also to have life in Himself; and He gave Him authority to execute judgment, because He is *the* Son of Man. Do not

> be amazed at this; for a time is coming when all who are in the tombs
> will hear His voice, and will come out: those who did the good *deeds*
> to a resurrection of life, those who committed the bad *deeds* to a
> resurrection of judgment.
>
> "I can do nothing on My own. As I hear, I judge; and My judgment
> is righteous, because I do not seek My own will but the will of Him
> who sent Me."

In John 5, the tension of the narrative is turned up. John informs us,
"For this reason therefore the Jews were seeking all the more to kill
Him, because He not only was breaking the Sabbath, but also was
calling God His own Father, making Himself equal with God."[10] If this
wasn't enough, Jesus went on to make his co-eternality and co-author-
ity with the Father even more explicit. Jesus claimed the final judgment by which God judges every person will actually be *his*
responsibility. Jesus set himself up as both a watershed and a measuring stick. In one sense, the judgment will be all about Jesus because
the difference between being judged unto death and judged unto life
will be whether a person believed in Jesus.

Lest we think Jesus is somehow preaching a works-based salvation,
in the next chapter Jesus clearly says, "This is the work of God, that
you *believe* in Him whom He has sent."[11] Jesus Christ is the watershed
of history.

At the same time, Jesus emphasizes the importance of what we
do—not for salvation, but for the final judgment. Those who are judged
unto life will have done good works in Jesus name. Those who are
judged unto death will be found to have done evil deeds. Jesus Christ
is the *measure* of judgment, since he is the embodiment of the law of
God as one who kept the law perfectly. Every person will have to deal
with Jesus Christ on the last and final day of judgment.

Romans 2:1-11

> Therefore you have no excuse, you *foolish* person, everyone *of you*
> who passes judgment; for in that matter *in which* you judge someone

---

10 John 5:18.

11 John 6:29. Emphasis added.

else, you condemn yourself; for you who judge practice the same things. And we know that the judgment of God rightly falls upon those who practice such things. But do you suppose this, you *foolish* person who passes judgment on those who practice such things, and *yet* does them *as well*, that you will escape the judgment of God? Or do you think lightly of the riches of His kindness and restraint and patience, not knowing that the kindness of God leads you to repentance? But because of your stubbornness and unrepentant heart you are storing up wrath for yourself on the day of wrath and revelation of the righteous judgment of God, who WILL REPAY EACH PERSON ACCORDING TO HIS DEEDS: to those who by perseverance in doing good seek glory, honor, and immortality, *He will give* eternal life; but to those who are self-serving and do not obey the truth, but obey unrighteousness, *He will give* wrath and indignation. *There will be* tribulation and distress for every soul of mankind who does evil, for the Jew first and also for the Greek, but glory, honor, and peace to everyone who does what is good, to the Jew first and also to the Greek. For there is no partiality with God.

The apostle Paul, a champion of salvation by grace through faith in Christ, is clearly stressing the truth of the final judgment. Here in Romans 2, he is challenging us to be careful how we judge others because it is God who ultimately will judge us. Paul explains there is a day of wrath when "the righteous judgment of God" will be revealed. Some people who feel they are living unnoticed and unaccountable, are actually storing up wrath for themselves. This final judgment day will be a day when *all people* appear before God and receive something or another. This judgment will be a works judgment—again, not for salvation, but for rewards. Those who sowed to the Spirit will reap the life of the Spirit and those who sowed to the flesh will reap the death of the flesh.[12] God is totally impartial. There will be no favours, no winks, no coupons and no bribes at the final judgment. The God who sees all and knows all will reveal all.

---

12 See Galatians 6:8.

2 Thessalonians 1:5-12

> *This is* a plain indication of God's righteous judgment so that you will be considered worthy of the kingdom of God, for which you indeed are suffering. For after all it is *only* right for God to repay with affliction those who afflict you, and *to give* relief to you who are afflicted, *along* with us, when the Lord Jesus will be revealed from heaven with His mighty angels in flaming fire, dealing out retribution to those who do not know God, and to those who do not obey the gospel of our Lord Jesus. These people will pay the penalty of eternal destruction, away from the presence of the Lord and from the glory of His power, when He comes to be glorified among His saints on that day, and to be marveled at among all who have believed—because our testimony to you was believed. To this end also we pray for you always, that our God will consider you worthy of your calling, and fulfill every desire for goodness and the work of faith with power, so that the name of our Lord Jesus will be glorified in you, and you in Him, in accordance with the grace of our God and *the* Lord Jesus Christ.

Lest we think the grace and kindness of Jesus negate his righteousness and justice, the Bible has given us passages like this one to give us the full and real picture of who Jesus is. It is true Jesus is gracious and he loves sinners, but it is also true he will judge the earth. The end of the world will be one big payday. For thousands of years, payment has been delayed, but when Jesus is revealed at his second coming, God's righteous repayment will be retroactive. The payments will be eternal, they will mean either life in God's presence or life away from God's presence, and the payments will be given out based on our response to Jesus Christ. In God's justice, he will repay afflictions to those who were instruments of affliction and he will repay comfort to those who were afflicted for the sake of Jesus. In light of the seriousness of this truth, Paul earnestly prays God would make the church at Thessalonica worthy of his calling. The doctrine of the final judgment sobers us all, and calls us to fulfil every good resolve no matter the cost, trusting God will repay in due time.

2 Peter 3:5–14

For when they maintain this, it escapes their notice that by the word of God *the* heavens existed long ago and *the* earth was formed out of water and by water, through which the world at that time was destroyed by being flooded with water. But by His word the present heavens and earth are being reserved for fire, kept for the day of judgment and destruction of ungodly people.

But do not let this one *fact* escape your notice, beloved, that with the Lord one day is like a thousand years, and a thousand years like one day. The Lord is not slow about His promise, as some count slowness, but is patient toward you, not willing for any to perish, but for all to come to repentance.

But the day of the Lord will come like a thief, in which the heavens will pass away with a roar and the elements will be destroyed with intense heat, and the earth and its works will be discovered.

Since all these things are to be destroyed in this way, what sort of people ought you to be in holy conduct and godliness, looking for and hastening the coming of the day of God, because of which the heavens will be destroyed by burning, and the elements will melt with intense heat! But according to His promise we are looking for new heavens and a new earth, in which righteousness dwells.

Therefore, beloved, since you look for these things, be diligent to be found spotless and blameless by Him, at peace

Paul was not the only apostle who saw the severity and the value of holding fast to the truth of the final judgment. Peter proclaimed the truth of the final judgment in Acts[13] and he wrote about it in his letters. Here, Peter reminds us of how foolish it is to overlook the final judgment day. He calls believers not to be foolish, but rather to live wise lives in view of God's coming judgment. But if someone were to ask, *If God is going to judge the earth, what is he waiting for?* Peter appeals to God's *patience* in our lives. God's patience is our salvation.

We must not forget that this final day of judgment is going to sneak up on us. No one will know when it is coming and no one will be alerted. The Lord will come when we least expect it. Peter, addressing

---

13 Acts 10:42.

Christians, asks this pointed question, "What sort of people ought you to be in holy conduct and godliness, looking for and hastening the coming of the day of God?" It is believers who know the truth of the final judgment who should be moved to live repentant lives. Those who fear the Lord realize this world and our bodies are passing away and awaiting redemption.[14] As we await better and brighter realities, we ought to be fueled toward diligence and genuineness in our walk before the face of God.

Revelation 20:11-15

> Then I saw a great white throne and Him who sat upon it, from whose presence earth and heaven fled, and no place was found for them. And I saw the dead, the great and the small, standing before the throne, and books were opened; and another book was opened, which is *the book* of life; and the dead were judged from the things which were written in the books, according to their deeds. And the sea gave up the dead who were in it, and Death and Hades gave up the dead who were in them; and they were judged, each one *of them* according to their deeds. Then Death and Hades were thrown into the lake of fire. This is the second death, the lake of fire. And if anyone's name was not found written in the book of life, he was thrown into the lake of fire.

Through the apostle John, God has given us a prophetic vision of what this final judgment day will be like. Over and over we have seen, in both the Old and New Testament, all humanity will be judged by their deeds. God has seen and kept record of every word, every thought and every intention of the heart. There, before we all enter our eternal place, he will reveal everything before the eyes of all—and he will be perfectly just. This passage also gives us a vision for what the future eternal hell will really be like, a lake of fire. With real and resurrected bodies, those judged apart from Christ will be thrown into the fire to burn forever. This sobering thought is intended to startle and alarm us like nothing else could! It is intended to display for us how serious it is to sin against God. The infinitely holy, pure, loving, righteous and

---

14 See Romans 8:18–25.

wonderful Lord of history will not be unjust. His glory will shine forth on the last day, and all that is hidden will be revealed and all that was wrong will be made right. On that day—finally—he will be the ultimate focal point of all things at all times. All other rival worldly glories will be silenced before him for eternity.

EXPLANATION

"God hath appointed a day, wherein he will judge the world by Jesus Christ..."

History has a beginning and it has an end. God is working out his purposes, through his providence, and nothing will stop him. God already knows when this final day will be, and it will surely come. When it comes, everything will be exposed, and the standard by which we will be judged will be Jesus Christ himself. Jesus is the eternal Son, who came into the world and lived a life of perfect obedience to God's law. Jesus is God in the flesh, and to him has been given authority to judge and reign over the earth.

"when every one shall receive according to his deeds..."

The final judgment day will be a deeds-based judgment. Our whole lives will be exposed before all intellectual and moral beings, and God will give what is due in the sight of all. God is a perfect and righteous judge, and he will not be impartial. What we have sowed, we will reap.

"the wicked shall go into everlasting punishment..."

Once this judgment has taken place, God will cast those outside of Christ into everlasting punishment. This will be terrible. It will be unending, but it will be deserved. No one will receive one ounce more or less than what is owed. The punishment will correspond with the crime, for such is the perfect justice of God.

"the righteous, into everlasting life."

Once this judgment has taken place, then Jesus will established his eternal reign in the new heavens and the new earth. All those who placed their faith in him and received his gift righteousness through

Christ will have good works to show for it. Because all those who are justified are also sanctified, the Spirit of God will have worked *genuine and real holiness* into the lives of believers. Their real righteousness, worked out in them by the Spirit of God, will prove on the last day that they truly were saved by the sufficient sacrifice of Jesus Christ alone. After being saved through the final judgment, God's people will be thrust into bodily life with Jesus for ever and ever. It will always get better, there will be no opportunity to fall, and there will be no hindrance to the most pure reflection and communion with the God of all glory.

MISCONCEPTIONS

There are a number of misconceptions related to the final judgment. A first misconception is the judgment makes God unloving. Many people ask how a loving God could judge people and punish them forever. Two things are important to remember. First, there was a time not long ago when the predominant question was the exact opposite: *How could a holy God love people and send his Son to save them?* We must be careful not to impose our cultural sensitivities onto the Bible. Second, the Bible never pits love and righteousness against one another. In fact, it is just the opposite. As the famous love chapter reminds us, love, "does not rejoice in unrighteousness, but rejoices with the truth."[15] Like all God's perfections, love and righteousness go hand in hand.

A second misconception is that to preach the judgment is to contradict grace. Think about how foolish this is. If there were no judgment, then there would be no grace. Grace is receiving what we do not deserve. Built into the very definition of grace is the reality of merit. If God did not judge, then he could not show grace. In a similar way to love, the proclamation of judgment and the announcement of grace fit together in the Scriptures.

A third misconception is that the Bible doesn't say much about the judgment. Really, the only way we could come to this conclusion is in

---

15 1 Corinthians 13:6.

not having read the Bible. It isn't just the Old Testament that speaks about the final judgment. Rather, we get our clearest statements about the judgment from the New Testament. Almost every book of the New Testament, directly or indirectly, teaches the reality of the final judgment.

A fourth misconception is that we can interpret God's judgments in this life. Just as there are many who hold to a "prosperity gospel" where they pull the promises of the future consummated kingdom of God down into the present, there are also those who pull the future judgment of God down into the present. Many do this, not because they have been theologically convinced, but because when bad things happen to us, we assume God is angry with us. In many ways, this is the major problem tackled in the long and winding book of Job. Job's friends can't imagine such a tragedy could have occurred in his life unless it was the judgment of God. However, the Bible is clear: Job was not suffering because he was being judged, it was the exact opposite! He was suffering because he was so righteous. It is true, God does discipline his children and he does execute his wrath at times before the final day of judgment. But we must be extremely cautious in how we discern God's sovereign hand, for who has known the mind of the Lord?[16]

A finally misconception is that hell is just a metaphor. The Bible presents hell as a *real* and *terrifying* place. We may think it is loving to remain quiet about hell, but nothing could be further from the truth. The fear of hell is legitimate. We must bow down to the authority of God's Word and humbly submit to the righteousness of God. None of us is fit to judge and none of us is fit to decide what kind of punishment suits the crime of offending a infinitely holy God. Hell is not something to flaunt and find delight in, but neither is it something to minimize or deny. We must take hell seriously because the Bible takes it seriously.

---

16 Romans 11:33–35.

APPLICATION

___

Article XX: The Judgment

God hath appointed a day, wherein he will judge the world by Jesus Christ, when every one shall receive according to his deeds; the wicked shall go into everlasting punishment; the righteous, into everlasting life.

---

1. The judgment proves life is not meaningless.

What we do matters. How we choose to live will matter. The sacrifices we make, the priorities we set and the people in whom we choose to invest, all have eternal consequences. While on the one hand, life is not a harsh, works-based system because God is a God of grace, life is also not a free-for-all because God is a God of justice. We can celebrate God's grace and celebrate life's meaning with equal force, knowing that grace and justice are not in competition in God.

2. We should live our lives in holy fear.

Every thought, every word and every motive of our hearts will one day be exposed before the whole world. This ought to sober us. It is wrong to be afraid of God, but it is right to fear God. We do not need to live in terror of our loving Father, but we do grow in wisdom as we consider his vast glory and unscrutable judgment.

3. We should consistently repent.

God is so patient with us and he desires we repent of our sins against him. His patience is our opportunity to turn back to him from idols and sins in our lives. Knowing the reality of the future judgment should be a catalyst in our lives for ongoing repentance.

4. We should find great comfort in knowing God is going to judge the whole world by Jesus Christ.

When we are taken advantage of, wounded, abused or mocked, we can feel helpless. But knowing God is going to level the scales and make all things right, gives great hope to his people. One day, God will vindicate all those who are in Christ.

5. *We should praise God for his justice!*

What an amazing God we have, one who is perfectly righteous and just! His righteousness is the ground of his faithfulness. His righteousness is the purity of his love. His righteousness is the boundary of his wisdom. His righteousness is the perfection of his judgments. His righteousness is the glory of his grace. That is why the final prayer found in the Bible is a prayer for Christ's return, "He who testifies to these things says, "Yes, I am coming quickly." Amen. Come, Lord Jesus."[17] We praise God for his justice with the same heart we pray for Christ's return. The God of justice, who gives meaning and order to our existence and who has promised to come again to make all things right, *he alone* is worthy of glory and honour and dominion and power and praise forever and ever. Amen!

---

17 Revelation 22:20.

Deo Optimo et Maximo Gloria
To God, best and greatest, be glory

hesedandemet.com

CPSIA information can be obtained
at www.ICGtesting.com
Printed in the USA
FSHW011628090222
88188FS